The Creative Curriculum® for Family Child Care, Third Edition

Volume 1: The Foundation

Diane Trister Dodge; Sherrie Rudick;
and Laura J. Colker, EdD

TeachingStrategies® · Bethesda, MD

Illustrations: Anthony LeTourneau

Teaching Strategies, LLC
Bethesda, MD 20814

www.TeachingStrategies.com

Library of Congress Control Number: 2017935429

978-1-60617-875-1

Printed and bound in the United States of America.
2021 2020 2019 2018 2017
10 9 8 7 6 5 4 3 2 1

Table of Contents

Volume 1: The Foundation

Introduction

There are approximately 1 million paid providers caring for children in a home-based setting (National Survey of Early Care & Education, 2015). As a member of this profession, you offer children and families a crucial service. You open your home, offering a safe environment where children feel comfortable and learn to build relationships with people other than the members of their immediate families. You work with children during the period of life when the greatest amount of development and learning occurs. You plan activities each day that support children's progress, helping them build a strong foundation for their success in school and in life. The partnerships you build with families and the knowledge that their children are in capable, loving hands enable them to attend to their work.

Many families choose family child care because they recognize and appreciate its important benefits. Family child care homes are often conveniently located in the communities where families live, and families are more likely to find providers who speak the families' home languages. Family child care providers often offer care for children of all ages and will accommodate siblings. Finding care for infants and toddlers is especially challenging, and families like the smaller, homey environment. Group sizes are small, so providers are able to give children more individual attention and maintain a calmer atmosphere. Perhaps the most important reason why families prefer family child care is that they can depend on reliable, loving, and responsive care from a knowledgeable person: you! You have chosen a very important profession.

The Role of a Family Child Care Provider

Child care is a profession that requires many different skills. In your work with children and families, you serve as an educator, a caregiver, a child development specialist, and often as a nutritionist and social worker. To care for children well, you must be knowledgeable about child development, how children learn, what children should be learning at each stage, and how to partner with families. Being a provider requires ongoing learning and a commitment to providing the very best service possible.

Most states have licensing requirements that apply to opening and operating a family child care program. The requirements vary considerably from state to state. These requirements usually address health and safety issues, but they rarely set standards for the educational program. However, providers strive to achieve high standards of quality care beyond simply meeting licensing requirements. Those standards are set by the National Association for Family Child Care (NAFCC), a membership organization dedicated to promoting high-quality family child care by setting standards, supporting providers in meeting the standards through an accreditation process, and helping families understand the value of placing their children in an accredited family child care program. When you meet or exceed the standards set by your profession, you are someone who knows how to provide a high-quality program and supportive environment for the children and families you serve.

Many family child care providers join professional organizations such as NAFCC and the National Association for the Education of Young Children (NAEYC). Membership gives them access to the latest information about current issues in the field. Local child care resource and referral agencies offer community-based training and opportunities to network with other providers. Find out what providers are doing in your area and develop relationships with those who are also striving to achieve program excellence.

Why Quality Matters

High-quality care during the early years of life makes a profound and lasting difference. More brain development takes place in the first 3 years of life than during any other period. Every interaction and every bit of information a child receives by seeing, tasting, touching, smelling, and hearing affects the child's brain development. Furthermore, the trusting relationship you build with each child is central to healthy development and all learning.

High-quality care for preschool children prepares them to enter school ready to learn and succeed. A major study of child care programs conducted by researchers at four universities found that children from all backgrounds who attended high-quality child care programs at ages 3 and 4 were better prepared for school than children in low-quality programs. They had stronger math, language, and social skills through second grade. The study also found that children who formed close relationships with their teachers had better social skills through elementary school. They had better thinking skills, were more able to attend to tasks, were more able to make friends, and had fewer behavioral problems (Peisner-Feinberg, et al., 1999). Relationships matter, as do appropriate and engaging experiences in preschool. In 2013, the Society for Research in Child Development and the Foundation for Child Development reported that "interactions that help children acquire new knowledge and skills provide input to children, elicit verbal responses and reactions from them, and foster engagement in and enjoyment of learning" (Hirokazu, Weiland, Brooks-Gunn, et al., 2013). Their research also pointed to how the "effective use of curricula focused on such specific aspects of learning as language and literacy, math, or socio-emotional development provide a substantial boost to children's learning."

The expectations for what preschool children should know and be able to do before entering kindergarten are more clearly defined today than in the past. Every state has developed early learning standards for 4-year-olds. Such standards provide guidance for planning learning experiences in early childhood programs. In addition to identifying knowledge and skills in content areas (literacy, mathematics, science, technology, social studies, and the arts), most state standards include objectives related to social–emotional skills, approaches to learning, and physical development. An increasing number of states are also developing standards for infants and toddlers. If you provide a prekindergarten program, it is important to become familiar with your state's early learning standards and to see how *The Creative Curriculum® for Family Child Care* addresses those standards.

School-age children benefit from high-quality care as well. They need to be in safe places when they are not in school. They also need caring adults who provide structure and interesting activities. The family child care program should complement school and enable school-age children to relax, socialize with peers and an adult, work on special projects, and become involved in the community beyond home and school.

Excellent care makes a difference for children of every age. The care children receive and their experiences in your program have a powerful influence on how they view the world, how they relate to others, and their ability to succeed as learners. Next to their families, you are probably the most important person in the lives of the children in your care. What you do every day is critical, so it cannot be left to chance. Providers who want to be thoughtful and intentional about the care they offer use a comprehensive curriculum and ongoing assessment to guide their work.

The Role of Curriculum in Family Child Care

A curriculum is like a road map because it helps you get where you want to go. A comprehensive, developmentally appropriate curriculum specifies objectives for children's development and learning. Objectives define what you want children to know and be able to do. The curriculum also tells you how to get there—how to help children achieve the objectives.

The Creative Curriculum® for Family Child Care explains how to offer a high-quality program that meets the standards established by NAFCC. It also helps you address the early learning standards that states have developed for children under age 5 and for children entering kindergarten. It describes the "what, why, how, when, and where" of providing care and education for children from birth to age 12. It explains all aspects of a developmentally appropriate program and leads you through the processes of planning and implementing every aspect of caring for children and partnering with their families.

Just as a road map gives you choices about what routes to take, *The Creative Curriculum®* offers choices and encourages flexibility. Caring for children is enjoyable and satisfying because of your ability to appreciate the everyday discoveries that delight a child: the bells that jingle in a pull toy, the amazing accomplishment of a first step, finally fitting a puzzle piece into place, learning to write, and finding the answers to interesting questions. *The Creative Curriculum®* shows how everyday routines and experiences are opportunities to build relationships and promote learning. It helps you choose materials and plan experiences intentionally while still having flexibility to respond to the ever-changing interests and abilities of young children.

Family child care providers are educators as well as business owners. A curriculum addresses the first role, so you will find educational guidance in *The Creative Curriculum® for Family Child Care.* Other resources are available to help you set up and manage the business aspects of caring for children in your home.

The Role of Curricular Objectives

The Creative Curriculum® defines 36 objectives for the development and learning of all children (birth through third grade) and two more objectives for dual-language learners. The objectives that relate to children's social–emotional, physical, language, and cognitive development are explained in Chapter 1, "Knowing How Children Develop and Learn." The objectives for content learning—literacy, mathematics, science and technology, social studies, and the arts—are listed in Chapter 3, "What Children Are Learning." *Volume 3: Objectives for Development & Learning, Birth Through Third Grade* lists the 38 objectives to help you better understand how children typically develop and learn so you can individualize activities to meet their needs.

Objectives serve several purposes. Because they define the development and learning you usually expect of children from birth through third grade, they enable you to follow children's progress and celebrate their skills. By keeping the objectives in mind as you observe children every day, you find out what each child can do and what each child is ready to learn. Objectives also help you intentionally plan meaningful experiences for children of various ages. For example, when you involve children in making molding dough, you can focus on the math skill of measuring ingredients, the literacy skill of following a picture recipe, and the motor skills used to mix and mold the dough. Your emphasis might be different for each child, and your focus guides the way you interact with children during a particular experience. Throughout *The Creative Curriculum®,* we show how one or more objectives can be addressed simultaneously through your interactions with children and the experiences you provide.

Fundamental Beliefs

A number of fundamental beliefs underlie *The Creative Curriculum® for Family Child Care.* You probably already consider them central to your work.

- Responsive, individualized care is based on what you learn about each child.
- Ensuring children's safety and health is a critical program component.
- Care and learning environments must support and encourage play and exploration.
- Family child care providers and the children's families support children's development and learning by forming partnerships that respect cultural, family, and individual differences.
- Children's social–emotional development is a primary goal of the program.
- Dual-language learners must be supported as they learn more than one language.
- Children with disabilities must be included in all aspects of the program.

How the Curriculum Is Organized

The graphic below shows how the components of *The Creative Curriculum®* fit together. Like the frame of a puzzle with many pieces, it offers a way to organize all aspects of the curriculum. *The Creative Curriculum®* rests on a solid foundation of theory and research.

Here is an overview of what you will find:

Volume 1 is "The Foundation." It begins with a section examining the theory and research on which *The Creative Curriculum®* is based, and it includes chapters 1–5.

The section "Applying Theory and Research to Practice" explains the curriculum's focus on providing a safe and healthy environment, why relationships are the foundation for all learning, how children learn through play and interactions with people and their environment, the importance of individualizing learning, and why partnerships with families are essential. When you know the theory and research behind *The Creative Curriculum®* approach, you can make and explain deliberate decisions about what you do.

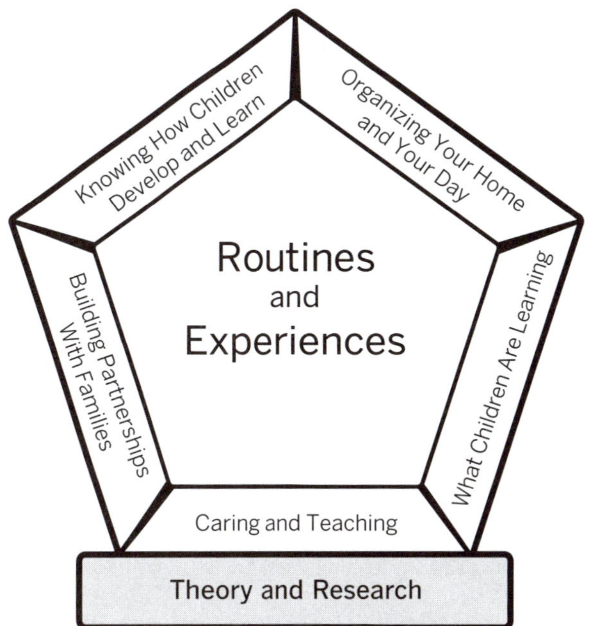

Chapter 1, "Knowing How Children Develop and Learn," describes the social–emotional, physical, language, and cognitive development of children from birth through the elementary years. It outlines the characteristics and experiences that make each child unique, including gender, temperament, interests, learning styles, life experiences, and special needs.

Chapter 2, "Organizing Your Home and Your Day," offers guidance about organizing your space and materials and whether to use your entire home or only part of it for child care. It shows how to create a daily schedule and make weekly plans in ways that give you direction but allow flexibility.

Chapter 3, "What Children Are Learning," shows how to foster learning through the positive relationship you form with each child, the interactions you have every day, and the materials and experiences you offer. What children should be learning and how they learn at each developmental stage are also discussed. That information is organized according to the content areas: language and literacy, mathematics, science and technology, social studies, and the arts.

Chapter 4, "Caring and Teaching," offers strategies for building positive relationships, helping children develop self-regulation, and responding to challenging behaviors. It describes how to guide children's learning during daily routines and during experiences. Finally, it explains the role of ongoing assessment in learning about each child, following children's progress, and planning.

Chapter 5, "Building Partnerships With Families," explores the benefits of working with families as partners in the care of their children. It explains how partnerships are built from the first time you meet families and enroll their children. It discusses daily exchanges of information, communicating in respectful ways, and working through differences in ways that sustain the partnership and benefit the child.

Volume 2 has two parts.

Part A, "Routines," includes chapters 1–5. They discuss the five routines that make up an important part of the day: hellos and good-byes, mealtimes, diapering and toileting, sleeping and resting, and getting dressed. Each chapter begins by asking you to think about your personal views about the routine. It then explains the importance of the routine and how you can set up your home to make the day go smoothly. Guidance is given for involving children in routines and for partnering with families.

Part B, "Experiences," includes chapters 6–16. They address the wide range of experiences you can offer children: blocks, dramatic play, art, toys and games, stories and books, sand and water, discovery, music and movement, cooking, technology, and outdoor play. Each chapter describes the selection and display of materials and ways to interact with children of different ages as they play with the materials you provide. Each chapter also includes a letter to families explaining what children learn from the experience and what families can do at home.

LearningGames®

A set of 200 *LearningGames*® activities is offered as part of *The Creative Curriculum® for Family Child Care*. The activities are a resource to share with families and use in your own work with children. Four or five *LearningGames*® activities are described at the end of the chapters on routines and experiences along with ways to share them with families. In most, one activity is included for each age-group from birth to age 5. Each *LearningGames*® activity shows how everyday interactions with children lead to positive relationships and important learning. Each game sheet includes information about what the child is experiencing, how she or he may react to the game, and an explanation of why the activity is important for the child's development. Each game is illustrated, includes clear directions, offers ideas for extending the activity, and lists a children's is related to the game. At the end of each chapter in *Volume 2: Routines and Experiences*, we recommend related *LearningGames*® activities to share with families. These activities reinforce what children are learning in your care and strengthen your connection with families.

LearningGames® have been validated by 21 years of research showing positive gains for children that last through the school-age period and into early adulthood (Campbell et al., 2002). Careful research conducted in eight states found that children who participate in many of these games in child care and at home have better measured development than those who do not play them or who play only a few (Sparling et al., 1991). More recent research has even found that these experiences in early childhood affect physical health in adulthood including better cardiovascular measures and disease prevention (Campbell et al., 2014). In light of these findings, we have made them an important part of *The Creative Curriculum® for Family Child Care.* Many of the teaching strategies we describe in Chapter 4, "Caring and Teaching," are used in these *LearningGames*® activities. These include acknowledging and describing, coaching, extending, demonstrating, and giving information. By using the activities and sharing them with families, you contribute to a true partnership for supporting their children's learning at home and in your program.

A Typical Day in Family Child Care

Consider the following scenario, which describes what might be a typical day for a family child care provider serving children of different ages. As you read, notice how the scenario compares to your own experience.

Preparation and Family Responsibilities

Well before the children arrive, you begin to prepare for the day. First you make a quart of fresh bleach solution so that you'll be ready to clean toys and surfaces throughout the day. Then you check the paint supplies to make sure the children will have enough. Remembering that Nathan was very excited yesterday about the train ride he took last weekend with his family, you decide to build on this new interest. In the closet, you find a train set and books about trains. The children have not seen them before, so you set them on a table. You look up the Spanish word for *train* so you can use it as you introduce the materials to Jorge and Rosa. Then you look at your menu and begin to prepare breakfast for the children. You make one last check before their arrival, glancing in the bathroom to be sure that soap, paper towels, toilet paper, and a step stool are in place. Then you wake your daughter, Keisha (4 1/2 years), point out two outfits, and ask her to choose one. You accompany her to the bathroom and talk with her as she brushes her teeth, washes her hands and face, and gets dressed. While brushing her hair, you ask Keisha if she wants to have breakfast right away or wait until some of her friends arrive. She decides to wait. When you both go to the living room, Keisha takes out the collage materials and continues to work on a project she started several days ago.

Arrival

Tamika (19 months) and Tyrone (8 years) arrive first. You greet each child and their mother by name, offer a big smile, hug the children, and ask their mother how the evening went yesterday. As you converse, you check quickly to be sure that the children do not seem sick, as you check every arriving child. When their mother leaves, Tyrone, Tamika, and you wave good-bye to her. You ask Tyrone if he is ready for school and invite him and Tamika to look at books or play with puzzles. Noticing that Tyrone is eyeing the train on the table, you show the train set to them and talk about train travel. Both children are interested in the set, and Tyrone enthusiastically helps Tamika connect the pieces of track. When the track is finished, Tyrone loses interest and asks whether he may use the computer. You help him get started on the computer while Tamika starts exploring the train cars and Keisha continues working on her collage.

Jeremy (8 months) is next to arrive. You greet him and his mother warmly. You talk with Jeremy's mother about his schedule at home and how he ate and slept. Jeremy's mother hands you an insulated bag that contains several bottles of breast milk that she expressed. She tells you that the milk is fresh and the bottles are dated. She explains that Jeremy is getting hungry but she is running too late to feed him as she does most mornings when they arrive. She asks you to feed him as soon as possible. After you thank her for the bottles and information, you and Jeremy say good-bye. As his mother walks away, Jeremy begins to cry. You give him a hug and say, "I know you'll miss your mommy. She'll be back later to pick you up. Are you hungry? Let's go warm your bottle." You carry Jeremy to the kitchen, where you place one of the bottles in a container of hot water and put the remaining bottles in the refrigerator. Jeremy nestles into your arms.

When the milk is warm, you sit down at the table next to Tamika, who is still playing with the train. You hold Jeremy in your arms, positioning him so that you can make eye contact with him while he drinks. Keisha brings her collage over to show you and then asks you to hold her. You hug her, saying, "Okay, my little sunshine. I will hold you as soon as Jeremy finishes his bottle. In the meantime, will you please put the collage materials away and wash your hands? Let's also find a good place to hang your collage. I'm glad that you signed your artwork."

Rosa (4 years) and Nathan (3 years) arrive next. You hold Jeremy as you greet their families. Rosa reaches up to pat Jeremy. You smile at Rosa and say, "*¡Buenos dias, Rosa! ¿Como esta*"?

Rosa replies, "*Bien*".

You say, "I'm glad you're well today!" Then you turn to Nathan. "Good morning, Nathan. How are you today?"

Nathan replies, "*¡Bien*"!

This delights you because you know that Nathan has trouble speaking and *bien* is a new word for him. You say, "Nathan, you are learning Spanish by talking with Rosa! I'm glad you're feeling well, too." You remind Nathan's father that the children are finishing their study of trees, and you ask him if he will be able to participate in the final celebration next Friday. Rosa's mother tells you she will be picking Rosa up early that afternoon for a doctor's appointment, so neither she nor Rosa will be able to be part of the celebration. You ask her and Nathan's father about alternative dates and say you'll let them know which day will be best for most of the families.

Breakfast

Tamika interrupts you, tugging on your pants and insisting, "Eat, eat!" Jeremy squirms to get down, so you place him on the living room rug where you can still see him from the kitchen. He pulls some of his favorite toys off the low shelf and begins to play with them. Realizing that it is time to feed the children breakfast, you locate *Mighty Minutes* 87, "Let's Go!" You turn to Keisha, Tamika, and Tyrone and say, "Let's clean up and get ready for breakfast. Let's wash our hands so we can eat." You help Tamika turn on the water and wash her hands, singing, "Let's go wash your hands, let's go wash your hands....," and you use a paper towel to turn off the water together when finished. Then you wash your own hands, and the other children wash and dry theirs.

Tyrone passes out the plates while Nathan puts out the napkins and Rosa places the silverware. Meanwhile, you put Tamika in her high chair. You pick Jeremy up, wash his hands, and then place him in another high chair. You pull the two high chairs up to the table and place the food on the table so the children can help themselves, family style. As the children pass the food to each other, you encourage the older children to serve themselves. You ask Nathan what he is eating. As he points, you say, "You have toast today," and wait for him to repeat the word *toast*. You place a sippy cup of water, a few pieces of cereal, and some banana slices on Jeremy's tray, and he immediately puts a piece of cereal in his mouth. You sit near the high chairs so that you can talk and eat with the children and assist Tamika and Jeremy if they need help. You talk about plans for the day, noting to yourself that none of the family members alerted you to anything that might affect the children's day.

After breakfast, the older children put their plates and cups on the counter. You check Tamika's and Jeremy's diapers and find that both need to be changed. After changing Jeremy's diaper, washing Jeremy's hands, and sanitizing the changing surface, you wash your hands before changing Tamika. Meanwhile, the other children use the bathroom and wash their hands. Then you help Tamika wash her hands and remind Tyrone to get ready to leave for school. You and the children walk Tyrone to the bus stop as you talk with them about safety rules. The children and you tell Tyrone good-bye as he boards the bus.

Outdoor Time

It's a beautiful day, so you decide to change the schedule and play outdoors before doing anything else. Pointing out the large appliance boxes that the children have been playing with for several days, you suggest that they make a train out of the boxes and pretend they are taking a ride like the one Nathan's family took last weekend. Jorge (2 1/2 years) arrives as the children are arranging the boxes, and he runs to see what they are doing. You greet Jorge's mother and comment on Jorge's enthusiasm. Jorge's mother smiles, calls good-bye to Jorge, and leaves. You say, "*Buenos dias, Jorge.* Welcome aboard our train." Then you get a prop box of costumes from the shed for the children to use as they play.

Nathan says, "D'ive" and pretends to steer.

Keisha says, "Okay, Nathan, here's your hat. I'm going to be in the caboose."

"*Yo también*", Jorge chimes in.

Rosa decides she wants to play with balls. You suggest that she and Tamika roll balls back and forth, and you kick a ball to Rosa lightly. Jeremy points at a bird flying overhead, and you say, "Yes, you see a crow," imitating a crow caw for Jeremy. When it is about time to go in, you tell the children that they have 5 more minutes to play. You notice that Jeremy is rubbing his eyes.

Large Group, Read-Aloud, and Snack

The children troop inside. You check Jeremy's and Tamika's diapers and find that only Jeremy's needs changing. After changing his diaper and washing both your hands and Jeremy's, you lay him down for a nap, placing him on his back in his crib. You help the children wash their hands and ask them to sit down for your group meeting. You begin with a morning song using *Mighty Minutes* 03, "Hello Cheer," and then do *Mighty Minutes* 42, "Two Little Ducks," as a fingerplay. You go over the safety rules they have been talking about and then prompt a conversation about the train they constructed with the boxes. Next you pick up a new book, *Chugga-Chugga Choo-Choo*, by Kevin Lewis, to read to them. The children are excited to learn that the book is about an imaginary train like the one they just made. The book is filled with rhymes and predictable phrases that the children love saying with you, like "Chugga-chugga choo-choo, whistle blowing, whoooooooo! Whoooooooo!" You notice that Nathan is able to say "Whoooooooo!" clearly.

After a while, both Tamika and Jorge leave the circle to play with toys. They glance at you occasionally as you read with Nathan, Rosa, and Keisha. Jorge decides to return to the circle to listen to the train book. Tamika listens from a distance. Every time you get to the refrain, Jorge shouts, "Chugga-chugga choo-choo, whistle blowing, whoooooooo! Whoooooooo!" You smile and hug him.

A little later, Jeremy is still sleeping, and Jorge and Nathan are playing with the train. Keisha is sitting at the dining room table, rolling some molding material, while Rosa sits opposite her, drawing. You take Tamika by the hand and ask her to help you set food on the table so the children can help themselves to a morning snack. As you place word and picture signs that invite the children to take four crackers and four apple slices, you explain to Tamika what you are doing. You then tell all of the children that the snack is ready for them to get when they are hungry. You review the sign cards with them and remind them to wash their hands before they take their snack and after they finish eating. As Keisha gets her snack, you hear her say, "These crackers are squares."

You agree, "Yes, they are. How did you know that?"

Keisha responds, "'Cause they have four sides, and all the sides are the same." You ask, "Are all crackers square?" Keisha laughs, "No, some are circles, and some are fish!" As the children finish their snack, they throw their napkins away and place their cups on the counter. When all the children have had a snack, Nathan washes the snack table.

Morning Choice Time

You tell the children, "Today you may choose to paint, play with clay, draw, build with blocks, play with the train set or other toys, dress up and pretend, work at the computer, look at books, listen to music, or write. Think about what you want to do." Keisha and Rosa head toward the dramatic play area. Jorge begins painting while Nathan looks to you for guidance. You show Nathan pictures of the various choices and name each one with him. He points to the picture of the train, and you prompt, "You want to play with the train today."

Nathan smiles and says, "Train. Now."

As you change Tamika's diaper, you ask her where she would like to play. She points to Nathan. "Let's wash our hands. Then you may join Nathan." Meanwhile, Jeremy begins to whimper. You pick him up saying, "Did you have a good nap, Mr. Jeremy? We're glad you are awake now. Let's change that diaper so you are more comfortable."

After laying him gently on the changing table, you change his diaper and talk to him about his toes, which he grabs and releases with great delight. After cleaning and sanitizing the changing table and washing hands, you take him to the kitchen, place him in a high chair, and say, "I'm going to get your lunch ready now. I know you are hungry. Here is a cracker for you to eat while you wait. I'll put some fresh water in your sippy cup, too." After checking to see that the other children are happily engaged, you sit down and begin feeding Jeremy. Between spoonfuls of pureed carrots, Jeremy waves another spoon and takes a few sips from his cup. You take a bottle of his mother's expressed milk out of the refrigerator and begin warming it in a container of hot water. You pick Jeremy up from the high chair, wash his face, help him wash his hands, and then wash your own. You take Jeremy back to the kitchen, get his bottle, and then sit on the floor next to Nathan and Tamika, holding Jeremy in your arms. You sing to Jeremy softly as he drinks his bottle and watches Nathan and Tamika play with the train. When Jeremy finishes his bottle, you place him on a blanket with a couple of his favorite toys. He especially enjoys toys he can hold and bang together.

Keisha and Rosa approach you, offering plates of make-believe food. You pretend to eat the food saying, "Mmm, this is delicious. How did you make this delicious snack?" Then you ask the girls if they will write a menu for today's lunch. As the girls scurry to the writing table to make a menu, Jorge brings his picture to show you. You describe it, saying, "I see you used a lot of bright colors: red, purple, and yellow. Tell me about your painting."

Jorge tells you that it is a train that goes "Chugga-chugga choo-choo." You laugh together and ask Jorge how he would say that in Spanish. Jorge thinks for a moment and says, "Chugga-chugga choo-choo!" Laughing together, you invite Jorge to show Nathan and Tamika his painting. After the children admire Jorge's painting, you ask him to help you find a place on the refrigerator to display it. Afterward, you sit with Jeremy on your lap, talking with Nathan, Tamika, and Jorge about what they are doing as they play with the train.

Things are going well until Jorge pulls a train car out of Tamika's hand. Tamika starts to cry, and Jorge buries the car in his lap. After talking to Jorge about the importance of being kind, you hand Tamika a similar train car. You know that providing duplicates helps children avoid frustration until they are ready to learn to share.

Nathan lines the train cars up according to a pattern of red, blue, green; red, blue, green. You comment about that. You review the pattern out loud, pointing to a corresponding car as you say the name of each color. You ask the children to repeat each color name after you say it, and you wait long enough for Tamika and Nathan to say it, too. Then you lead the children in laying out the next three colors in Nathan's pattern. Delighted, you take a photo of the children as they continue the pattern with the cars.

Lunch

As choice time draws to a close, you give the children a 5-minute warning, telling them that it will soon be time to clean up the toys and get ready for lunch. You check Tamika's diaper as the children wash their hands. Then you help Tamika wash her hands and wash your own.

In the kitchen, you set Jeremy down on a blanket with some vinyl books to explore for a few minutes. You take out the sandwiches and salad that you prepared the previous evening and place them on the table. The older children set the table. You put Tamika in her high chair and serve her. The older children sit down and pass the plate of halved sandwiches and the bowl of salad. They serve themselves, family style. You pick Jeremy up and sit at the table with him in your lap. He has already eaten, but you want him to be part of the social experience. You pull Tamika's high chair close to the table, making a cozy grouping. As you and the children eat, you lead them in a lively discussion of the morning's events. Jeremy waves a small piece of bread enthusiastically. As they finish, the older children scrape their plates, put them on the counter, use the bathroom, wash their hands, brush their teeth, and prepare to nap. You put Jeremy down where you can see him while you help Tamika brush her teeth. Then you change her diaper, help her wash her hands, and wash your own hands.

Read-Aloud and Nap Time

After the cots are set up, you gather the children to read a story aloud. At Jorge's suggestion, you read *Dinosaur vs. Bedtime*, by Lane Shea. Jorge has requested this book all week. He loves the idea that the dinosaur has trouble staying awake, just as he does. As you are reading, Tamika starts nodding off, and you suggest that she listen to the rest of the story from her cot. When the story ends, Nathan, Rosa, and Keisha lie down on their cots. Holding Jeremy, you cover the children, pat each one, and tell them you will see them when they wake up. "Sleep tight," you say as you take Jeremy to the kitchen so you can clean up from lunch. Keisha plays quietly on her cot with her doll as the others fall asleep.

While you clean up the kitchen, Jeremy has tummy time on a blanket where you can watch each other. When you are finished cleaning, you sit down to play peek-a-boo and other interactive games with him. Jeremy giggles but soon starts to rub his eyes. You say, "It looks like you're getting sleepy, too, Jeremy." You change his diaper again, wash his hands and your own, and lay him on his back in his crib.

While the children are resting, you print the train photo, write a short description of what the children were doing when you took it, and add it to Nathan's portfolio. Now you have a little time to sit down and think about the day. Clearly, a number of the children are very interested in trains. Maybe this is a good time to plan a trip to the local train station with the children. You look up some fingerplays and songs about trains so you can teach them to the children. You wonder if the children are interested enough in trains for that to be a good topic for a study. You decide to explore this idea at your morning meeting tomorrow. After jotting some notes to yourself, you check to be sure the children are resting well. Then you go over some paperwork and write a shopping list. You think about the novel you started to read last week and wonder whether you have time to read a little before the children wake up. Doubting that possibility, you pour some tea and enjoy a few minutes of quiet before setting out the children's afternoon snack.

Afternoon Experiences

As the children begin to wake up, you give them each a hug and have them use the bathroom and comb their hair. Each child picks something quiet to play with until everyone is awake. Those who are hungry help themselves to orange sections, whole wheat crackers, and water that you put out for them on the table. Tamika and Jeremy wake up last. You hug them, change their diapers, and wash their hands and yours. You put some simple puzzles on a blanket for the babies, but Tamika wants to join the older girls, who are working with molding dough at the table.

At three o'clock, everyone prepares to walk to the bus stop to meet Tyrone. During the walk, the children count the cars and buses that pass. When Tyrone steps off the school bus, the children give him a hug. You talk to Tyrone about his day and his plans for the afternoon. Arriving back home, Tyrone talks with the children as he takes yogurt and a granola muffin out of the refrigerator for his snack. The children tell Tyrone excitedly about their box train in the backyard. After a while, Tyrone sits down to do his homework while the other children choose from the activities that you suggest: drawing, trains, puzzles, blocks, computer, discovery, and books. Keisha and Rosa sit down at the discovery table and take out the rock collection. They begin weighing the rocks on the balance scale and "writing" the weights in a journal. Jorge and Nathan play with blocks while you sit on the floor and read a book to Tamika and Jeremy. When Tyrone is finished with his assignments, you ask him if he'd like to play outside with the other children. When he says, "Yes," you ask him to carry some paper, crayons, and markers outside in case anyone wants to draw or write at the picnic table.

Outside Time and Departure

The children eagerly run outside to play, pulling Tyrone along with them to show him their box train. Tyrone announces that he will be the engineer. Rosa and Keisha decide to be passengers. They tell Nathan that he may be the conductor. Nathan yells, "All 'board!" and begins to collect pretend tickets. Tamika and Jeremy peek into the boxes, laughing.

Rosa's mother comes to take her home. You chat briefly about Rosa's day and remind her please to get a copy of Rosa's immunization record while they are at the doctor's office. Keisha gives Rosa a hug.

Jeremy's mother arrives next. When he sees her, Jeremy squeals and holds his arms toward her. His mother picks him up and gives him a big kiss. You tell her about Jeremy's naps, what he ate, and what else he did during the day. When his mother prompts him, Jeremy waves good-bye as they leave.

When Jorge's father arrives and joins him near the box train, Jorge tells him about it excitedly. You explain how much Jorge seems to like trains and that you would like to take the children to the local train station. Jorge leaves with his father, talking about trains in Spanish. You listen, hoping to pick up some Spanish vocabulary.

Nathan's mother comes next. You talk to her about Nathan's continued interest in trains and the possibility of doing a study about trains. Excited, you tell her about the color pattern he made with the train cars. You both share the joy of this major accomplishment. When he can hear you, you do not talk about what Nathan cannot yet do, and you know that Nathan's mother gets discouraged when people focus primarily on his needs. You do tell her how helpful it has been to work with Nathan's speech therapist and how all of the children are benefitting from the strategies she has taught you for supporting Nathan. Nathan gives you a good-bye hug.

When Tamika's and Tyrone's father arrives, you tell him about the homework Tyrone completed and how eager the younger children were to share their train with him. You report that Tamika also enjoyed playing with the new train set and squishing molding dough with the older girls. Tamika and Tyrone both give you good-bye hugs.

You take Keisha's hand, saying, "Now it's just the two of us for a little while. Come; sit on my lap. Let's talk about the day. Then you can help me straighten up a bit. I have a new song I want to sing with you if you'd like to learn it."

Getting Started

The Creative Curriculum® for Family Child Care is a comprehensive resource for planning and implementing your program. It covers all aspects of providing care and education for children and offers a range of choices. It may seem like a lot of information. Do not feel as though you have to read the entire book at once. Find the topics that are of most importance to your work and start with those chapters. If you are just setting up your program, you may be seeking guidance about organizing your home and planning your day (Chapter 2, "Organizing Your Home and Your Day"). Perhaps you want ideas about welcoming families and enrolling children (Chapter 5, "Building Partnerships With Families"). If you have been operating a program for a while, pick a routine that presents some challenges and try the suggestions in that chapter. Choose one of the experiences that particularly interests you and try some new ideas. Become familiar with the objectives for children's development and learning by posting them as a reminder of where you are heading. Remember, *The Creative Curriculum®* is your road map for getting there. We hope you enjoy the journey!

Applying Theory and Research to Practice

Applying Theory and Research to Practice

Having a high-quality family child care program means that you act in the ways that are best for children. To do that, you must understand why particular strategies and approaches are considered best practices and why the curricular objectives are important. We turn to research findings to understand how children develop and learn.

This section explains the major research and theory that guide *The Creative Curriculum® for Family Child Care.* When you are familiar with this research, you will know why it is important to respond quickly to a crying baby and talk with children during routines and experiences. You will also understand why play is absolutely necessary even though you might feel pressured to focus on academics. You can be confident that your program is based on a solid foundation.

This chapter explores four guiding principles on which *The Creative Curriculum® for Family Child Care* is based. They guide practice and help us understand the reasons for intentionally setting up and carrying out family child care programs in particular ways. These are the principles:

- Relationships are the foundation for learning.
- Children learn through play.
- Children learn by interacting with people and their environments.
- Partnerships with families are essential.

Relationships: The Foundation for Learning

Nurturing, stable relationships with adults are central to every child's development. **Attachment theory** describes the process by which babies bond with the important people in their lives. Children who develop secure attachments to one or more adults are more likely to develop positive social skills and to be emotionally secure.[1] Moreover, children who have secure attachments are more curious and engaged in school activities than children with less secure attachments.[2] Secure attachments develop when adults consistently, appropriately, and lovingly care for infants and meet their basic needs (i.e., to be fed, changed, given rest, kept safe, stimulated, and comforted). Consistent, nurturing care teaches children that they are important and helps them develop a positive sense of self.

Famous psychologist **Erik Erikson**[3] theorized that the child's first psychological task is to develop trust. Babies who receive consistent and loving care learn to trust others, themselves, and the world around them. When they feel safe, babies feel free to explore. Children learn about their world within the security of trusting relationships with caregivers. As they explore and experiment, children gain knowledge. Erikson also thought it is important for children to develop autonomy and initiative. Those terms refer to doing things independently, developing confidence in one's own abilities, taking on new tasks, and completing them.

Child psychiatrist and psychoanalyst **Stanley Greenspan**[4] views the infant's development of trusting relationships as a milestone in his or her emotional growth. By 5 months of age, some infants eagerly seek social interaction. They return your smiles, watch your face with great interest, and relax when held. Others are more hesitant. These infants need you and their parents to continue to reach out to them, even when they ignore or reject some of your attempts to engage them. All children need to develop secure attachments. Mastery of this milestone means that a baby has learned that relationships can be joyful and that warmth and love are possible.

We now know that relationships do not just provide a context for learning, they actually affect the way the brain develops.[5] The absence of warm, secure relationships can be devastating to children. A lack of caring, reliable relationships in a young child's life has lifelong implications related to learning abilities, behavior, and health.[6] Nurturing and positive interactions release chemicals that promote brain development. Without the support and comfort of a close personal relationship, children cannot cope with stress.

Your Teaching Practice

Provide responsive, loving care. Keep each child safe and healthy, offer comfort and affection, and share the joy of everyday experiences by interacting with each child.

Use routines, such as hellos and good-byes, diapering and toileting, mealtimes, and sleeping and resting, to develop a trusting relationship with each child.

Talk to all children one-on-one as well as in groups. Let children know that you care about what they think and how they feel. Give children nonverbal cues to tell them that they are valued. Reach out to every child, including those who are hesitant.

Use relationships to guide children's learning and encourage their continuing efforts. Instead of expecting children always to follow an adult's lead, often let them initiate activities among themselves and with you.

Comfort and otherwise respond intentionally to children, especially those who are under stress.

Learning Through Play

Children learn about themselves, other people, and the world by playing. Play takes many forms. For example, a baby drops a wooden bead into a container again and again, a toddler bangs the keys of a piano, a preschool child sinks objects in a tub of water, and a school-age child flies a kite. As they play, children acquire language, learn to solve problems, learn to control their behavior and feelings, and explore social roles.

One of the first persons to recognize the importance of play was **Jean Piaget,**[7] a Swiss philosopher, scientist, and developmental theorist. According to Piaget, play serves many purposes and provides an excellent vehicle for learning. By handling many different materials, children learn to observe, compare, sort, and sequence them. Their knowledge grows as they experiment, make discoveries, and modify their current thinking to incorporate new insights.

Building on Piaget's theory about how play helps children learn, Russian psychologist **Lev Vygotsky**[8] argued that children think in complex ways as they play. They make rules, use symbols, and create narratives. Vygotsky thought that adults and competent peers enhance a child's ability to learn through play. He used the term *zone of proximal development* (ZPD) to explain how learning takes place during play. The lower limit of the zone is what a child can learn by playing independently. The upper limit of the zone is what a child can learn by watching and talking to peers and adults. With the guidance and support of a teacher or provider, children build new knowledge by fitting new information and experiences with what they already know. Vygotsky found that in sociodramatic play, which is characterized by high levels of pretending, children to talk to themselves and each other about what they are playing and how they are going to play. He thought that such talk enhances self-regulation, the ability to control one's emotions and behavior and to resist impulses. More recent research has confirmed the validity of Vygotsky's theories. **Laura Berk's** studies of children's play explored the relationship between pretend play and self-regulation. These studies found that pretend play "strengthens a wide variety of mental abilities, including sustained attention, memory, logical reasoning, language and literacy, imagination, creativity, understanding of emotions, and the ability to reflect on one's own thinking and take another's perspective.[9] Similarly, play researcher **Sara Smilansky** found that children who engaged in high levels of sociodramatic play in preschool performed better academically in fourth grade than peers whose preschool play was less mature.[10] The research findings are strong: Pretend play is related strongly to self-regulation and academic achievement.

Your Teaching Practice

Provide all children with opportunities to play, including school-age children. Children of all ages need to play.

Provide at least an hour of free, unstructured play daily so children have opportunities to make choices and decisions, solve problems, pursue their interests, build language and literacy skills, discover mathematical relationships, be scientists, and see themselves as competent.

Observe children's interests and build on them. Ask probing questions that will stretch children's thinking: "How else might you…?" "In what ways is this similar to…?" "How can you solve that problem?" Play with children one-on-one and encourage small-group work with peers.

Encourage children to engage in make-believe play with at least two other children. Invite children to make up scenarios. Encourage children to remind themselves and each other of what they decided to do and say as they play.

Provide long periods of unstructured, imaginative play. Realistic props are good for very young children, but encourage preschool and older children to use more abstract props.

Learning by Interacting With People and the Environment

Piaget found that children learn through the direct manipulation of objects and by using all of their senses. As described by Piaget, learning is a dynamic process with a number of stages. He explained that children must engage in tasks actively in order to develop and learn. Children seek and process new information on the basis of what they already know. They also modify their thinking in order to make sense of new information and experiences.

Vygotsky found that children need to be able to talk about problems in order to solve them and talk about concepts in order to understand and apply them. In his theory, thought and language are intertwined. As a child discusses a problem or task with an adult, the adult supplies language to assist the child in solving or doing it. The child gradually internalizes the language and more mature thought processes. Eventually, responsibility for the task is shifted from the adult to the child. The instructional technique in which an adult helps the child gradually develop higher level skills has become known as *scaffolding*.

Over the past 20 years, scientists have been able to study neurological aspects of how children learn. We call their work ***brain research***. Studies have confirmed that a safe and predictable physical environment and the quality and continuity of day-to-day care contribute significantly to healthy brain development and learning.[11]

Brain research also shows that children's cognitive, emotional, and social capabilities are intertwined. Academic learning cannot be separated from social–emotional growth. Children's physical and emotional well-being are closely linked to their ability to think and learn effectively. For children to excel in school, educators need to address all aspects of their development.[12]

We have also learned more about how the brain functions. Early experiences and interactions directly affect the physical structure of the brain. For a brain connection to become permanent, it must be used repeatedly. Connections that are not used eventually disappear.[13]

Brain research has shown us that, even though the brain continues to change in response to experiences throughout life, there are sensitive periods for certain kinds of learning (including emotional control, social attachment, and language).[14] These are times when children are most receptive to what the environment has to offer. Most of these optimal times for learning are during the early childhood years. However, questions about the brain areas involved in various kinds of learning are still being explored. Although particular kinds of learning are easier at certain times, learning continues throughout life unless circumstances are extreme. It appears as though the brain remains open, so appropriate experiences are important.

Your Teaching Practice

Teach the whole child. Remember that social–emotional, physical, cognitive, and language development are intertwined.

Give children many choices and chances to investigate how things work. Allow children time to explore and experiment with books, art materials, music, dramatic play, sand and water, blocks, toys and games, cooking, technology, and the outdoors.

Encourage children to solve problems and take appropriate risks.

Model self-talk that supports children's cognitive development (thinking). Offer ideas about how to approach tasks.

Surround children with language. Sing and read with them and have back-and-forth vocal exchanges with them even before children can speak. If you have dual-language learners, support them as they learn more than one language.

Offer opportunities for children to work together.

Essential Partnerships With Families

When children receive consistent messages and support from both their families and their care providers, everyone benefits. Family participation involves both formal and informal connections between parents and their children's educational programs. Your regular communication with the children's families is critical to the children's development and learning.

Four decades of research confirm the importance of strong partnerships between families and early childhood programs. Bonds between homes and programs enhance children's problem-solving skills and social competency, and they can reduce aggression at home and at the educational program.[15] Indeed, a successful home–program relationship can help overcome the effects of poverty. Moreover, these benefits are sustained over time.[16]

Research also underscores the need to reach out to fathers and other extended family members. Paternal participation is linked with both school readiness and children's emotional self-regulation.[17]

Your Teaching Practice

Develop positive relationships with families, both formally and informally.

Communicate with families regularly. Hold family conferences, share information in person and by phone, and send newsletters, texts, and email messages.

Encourage children's families to volunteer in your program. Invite them to join field trips and eat meals with the children.

Reach out to all family members. Everyone who is special to a young child has an important role.

Summary

Our understanding of best practice in early childhood education is shaped by the researchers and theorists who laid the groundwork for our thinking about how children develop and learn. Their work is the foundation for defining high-quality early childhood education and care.

The research described in this chapter validates and expands our knowledge. As a family child care provider, you translate research and theory into practice every day. The ways you set up your program, plan your day, interact with children and families, and follow learning objectives for children are informed by this research. Being familiar with the research makes you a knowledgeable professional.

[1] Siegel, D. J. (2015). *The developing mind: Toward a science of neurobiology of interpersonal experience.* (2nd ed.). New York: Guilford Press.

[2] Williford, A. P., & Wolcott, C. S. (2015). SEL and Student-Teacher Relationships. In J. A. Durlak, C. E. Domitrovich, R. P. Weissberg, & T. P. Gullotta (Eds.). *Handbook of Social and Emotional Learning* (pp. 229–243). New York: Guilford Press.

[3] Erikson, E. H. (1950). *Childhood and society.* New York: Norton.

[4] Greenspan, S. I. (with Greenspan, N. T.). (1985). *First feelings: Milestones in the emotional development of your infant and child from birth to age 4.* New York: Viking Press.

[5] Bernier, A., Calkins, S. D. and Bell, M. A. (2016), Longitudinal Associations Between the Quality of Mother–Infant Interactions and Brain Development Across Infancy. *Child Development, 87,* 1159–1174.

[6] Center on the Developing Child at Harvard University (2016). *From Best Practices to Breakthrough Impacts: A Science-Based Approach to Building a More Promising Future for Young Children and Families* http:/www.developingchild.harvard.edu

[7] Piaget, J. (1972). *Play, dreams, and imitation in childhood.* London: Routledge and Kegan Paul. (Original work published in 1945)

[8] Vygotsky, L. S. (1978). *Mind in society: The development of higher psychological processes.* Cambridge, MA: Harvard University Press. (Original work published in 1934)

[9] Berk, L. (2013). *Child development* (9th ed.). Boston, MA: Pearson Education, Inc.

Elias, C. L., & Berk, L. E. (2002). Self-regulation in young children: Is there a role for sociodramatic play? *Early Childhood Research Quarterly, 17*(1), 6–238.

[10] Smilansky, S., & Shefatya, L. (1990). *Facilitating play: A medium for promoting cognitive, socio-emotional and academic development in young children.* Gaithersburg, MD: Psychosocial and Educational Publications.

[11] Thompson, R. A. (2016). What More Has Been Learned? The Science of Early Childhood Development 15 Years After Neurons to Neighborhoods. *Connecting Science, Policy, and Practice,* 18.

Shonkoff, J. P., & Phillips, D. A. (Eds.). (2000). *From neurons to neighborhoods: The science of early childhood development.* Washington, DC: National Academies Press.

National Association of Social Workers. (2008). *Early childhood development current trends.* Retrieved October 22, 2008, from http://wwww.helpstartshere.org/Default.aspx?PageID=383

National Scientific Council on the Developing Child. (2004). *Young children develop in an environment of relationships* (Working paper no. 1). Cambridge, MA: Author.

Oberklaid, F. (2006). *Early brain development: Implications for work with young children and their families.* Melbourne, Australia: Centre for Community Child Health.

[12] Sabol, T. J., & Pianta, R. C. (2017). The state of young children in the United States: School readiness. *Handbook of Early Childhood Development Programs, Practices, and Policies*, 3.

[13] Berk, L. (2013). *Child development* (9th ed.). Boston, MA: Pearson Education, Inc.

[14] Music, G. (2017). *Nurturing Natures: Attachment and Children's Emotional, Sociocultural and Brain Development.* New York: Psychology Press.

[15] Ou, S. (2005). Pathways of long-term effects of an early intervention program on educational attainment: Findings from the Chicago longitudinal study. *Applied Developmental Psychology, 37*(4), 379–402.

[16] Harvard Family Research Project. (Spring 2006). *Family involvement in early childhood education* (No. 1). Retrieved October 22, 2008, from http://www.hfrp.org/publications-resources/browse-our-publications/family-involvement-in-early-childhood-education

[17] McBride, B. A., Dyer, W. J., & Rane, T. R. (2008). Family partnerships in early childhood programs: Don't forget fathers/men. In M. M. Cornish (Ed.), *Promising practices for partnering with families in the early years: A volume in family-school-community partnerships*, (pp. 41-58). Charlotte, NC: Information Age Publishing.

Downer, J. T., & Mendez, J. L. (2005). African American father involvement and preschool children's school readiness. *Early Education and Development, 16*(3), 317–40.

1 Knowing How Children Develop and Learn

Knowing How Children Develop and Learn

The Creative Curriculum® for Family Child Care is based on theory and research about child development. This enables you to build a program that meets the needs, interests, and abilities of all the children in your care, no matter what their ages. When you know what to expect of children at each stage of development, you can create a responsive environment and plan appropriate experiences for the children in your family child care program. Being responsive to children's developmental strengths and needs is the best way to support their development and learning.

In addition to knowing how children typically develop and learn, it is also important to recognize that children develop at their own rates and learn in their own ways. This chapter will provide you with information you need to meet children's developmental and individual needs. It highlights some of the ways you can create a responsive program.

This chapter includes three sections:

What Children Are Generally Like shows you how to use your knowledge of how children typically develop and learn. Four areas of development are discussed: social–emotional, cognitive, language, and physical. In this section, we also introduce you to the children who are cared for in our example of *The Creative Curriculum®* family child care home—yours!

Areas of Development presents 14 objectives for social–emotional development, physical development, language development, and cognitive development and two objectives for English language acquisition. (Twenty-two additional objectives for content area learning are addressed in Chapter 3, "What Children Are Learning.")

Individual Differences discusses the variations in gender, temperament, interests, learning styles, life experiences, culture, language learning, and special needs.

What Children Are Generally Like

Your knowledge of typical child development is the starting point for offering a responsive program. Every stage of development is an exciting period of growth and learning. Think about a 2-year-old in your program. She loves opening and closing cupboard doors and insists that you read *Goodnight Moon* to her a dozen times in a row. The 4-year-old in your program enjoys using paper, markers, and crayons. Knowing that these are typical behaviors enables you to respond in meaningful and appropriate ways.

Developmental Characteristics of Age-Groups

When you begin to think about each of the four developmental areas (social–emotional, physical, language, and cognitive), it is also useful to consider examples of how infants, toddlers, preschool, and school-age children typically behave and develop. When teaching and caring for a group of children from various age groups, it can be difficult to know all of the specific characteristics of each age. It is important to get to know individual children so you can meet their needs and plan meaningful experiences that supports them in all developmental areas. In the paragraphs below, we have created some hypothetical children and scenarios that illustrate the ideas and strategies you can use to support children at different developmental levels.

Infants (Birth–18 Months)

Jeremy is 8 months old now and has been in family child care since he was 6 weeks old. He has just learned to crawl and is beginning to pull himself up to a standing position. He loves playing peek-a-boo and laughs heartily whenever you uncover your face. He babbles constantly, saying, "Da-da-ba-ba," and experimenting with other strings of sounds and with various intonations.

Babies must have their basic needs met by adults they can trust. Once their basic needs are met, they become eager explorers who use all of their senses to examine objects within reach. They are fascinated by people and soon learn to smile and interact with them. As babies learn about others and explore and manipulate things in their environment, they begin to acquire new skills.

Learning about and observing infants in your care will allow you to meet their individual needs and nurture their development and learning. The chart below lists some of the major aspects of infant development and indicates how this knowledge supports you in planning a responsive program.

Aspects of Infants' Development	What Providers Can Do
Socially and emotionally, infants...	*As a provider, you...*
depend on adults to meet their basic needs (to be fed, changed when soiled or wet, comforted to sleep, and loved).	respond to each child individually, building the child's trust and sense of security. Once babies trust you, they feel safe to explore the environment.
form strong attachments to the important people in their lives.	offer consistent, responsive care for all infants. Children who are cared for and nurtured consistently are more likely to feel confident and become independent.
like to watch other children and be included in activities.	talk about what other children are doing: "Tamika is beating the drum. We can do that, too." Include infants in activities, such as finger painting while other children are painting with brushes.
Physically, infants...	*As a provider you...*
explore and move by rolling over, sitting, creeping, crawling, pulling themselves up, cruising, and walking.	arrange floor space with soft mats or floor coverings so that there is a large space for babies to move about freely and safely. Provide sturdy furniture and railings so they can pull themselves up.
are developing small-muscle skills such as touching, grasping, patting, and grabbing.	provide opportunities for infants to develop a pincer grasp (holding objects with the thumb and index finger) and other small-muscle skills. Include a variety of age appropriate materials for them to explore.
In terms of language, infants...	*As a provider you...*
understand many words long before they can speak.	talk to babies, sing with them, and read to them throughout the day. Their brains are already learning language, so talk and encourage their attempts to imitate speech.
communicate first by babbling and through gestures and facial expressions and then by speaking.	respond to babies' gestures, smiles, and coos. Start a "conversation" with them, even if they only respond with a smile or a coo.
begin to learn the names of objects in their environment.	encourage children to repeat speech sounds and words as you converse.
Cognitively, infants...	*As a provider you...*
use their five senses to explore the world.	make sure that the infant toys and objects in your home are safe to be mouthed, squeezed, shaken, and tossed. Provide a variety of sensory and tactile activities for infants to explore.

Aspects of Infants' Development	What Providers Can Do
hold and manipulate objects, discovering the effects of their actions.	encourage infants to explore and experiment with toys and materials. Comment on what you see and hear: "Jacob, when you picked up that basket, all of the toys fell out of it."
begin to understand that objects and people exist even when they are out of sight.	play games such as peek-a-boo to help infants learn that people and objects are still somewhere, even when they are not visible. This concept is known as "object permanence." Understanding it is a developmental milestone.

Toddlers and Twos (18–36 Months)

Tamika, who is 19 months old, is a sociable toddler. Two of her favorite activities are water play and digging in sand. Tamika is just starting to talk and speaks in two-word phrases. Her favorite expressions are "My turn!" and "No." She picks up books to look at on her own, but she especially enjoys being read to and turning the pages, herself. Her older brother is Tyrone, who is 8 years old.

Jorge is a determined 2 ½-year-old. He is in constant motion, running to do everything. Jorge is a dual-language learner. He is learning Spanish at home and English in family child care. He often mixes the two languages, for example, saying, "*Mas* milk," or "*Quiero* ball." Some days he speaks mostly Spanish, but he understands more and more English every day.

Children of this age are very active from the moment they awaken. Toddlers walk, run, hop, throw balls, and even pedal tricycles. They know how to put large pegs in a pegboard, snap beads into a chain, and pour water from a child-sized pitcher into a cup. Twos make purposeful marks on paper, pound and poke molding dough, and repeatedly build towers to knock down. The world is an exciting place for toddlers and twos, but it can also be overwhelming. Sometimes they want the impossible: to be big and to stay little at the same time. The same child who says, "My turn!" when you try to help him wash his hands may want you to cuddle him like a baby 5 minutes later. Toddlers and twos want and need to practice their new skills, make their own decisions, and do things themselves, even though those things do not always work out the way they would like them to.

Aspects of Toddlers' and Twos' Development	What Providers Can Do
Socially and emotionally, toddlers and twos...	*As a provider, you...*
assert themselves and want to do things independently.	provide a safe way for them to practice self-help skills (for example, handwashing, nose blowing, and toothbrushing) as independently as they can. Offer simple puzzles, foam blocks, sturdy books, and water-based markers that children can use successfully on their own.
are beginning to learn about taking turns and waiting, but sharing is still difficult for them.	provide opportunities for children to learn to take turns. Provide duplicates of favorite toys so children can play with them at the same time.
are starting to use caring behaviors to help and comfort others.	model caring behaviors and acknowledge children's behavior whenever you see them caring for others.
are learning how to express, identify, and name feelings that they or others have.	talk with children about how they feel throughout the day. Provide books that talk about feelings and include emotion cards for children to look at.
Physically, toddlers and twos...	*As a provider, you...*
can push themselves around on wheeled toys, walk easily, run, jump, and hop.	create an environment with safe spaces for children to run and ride wheeled toys freely. Allow inside and outside time for large muscle activities where children can practice running, jumping, and climbing. Plan music and movement activities every day to promote children's physical development.
gain small-muscle skills such as turning pages, drawing with crayons, opening containers, and popping beads together and apart.	give children lots of opportunities to play with toys, puzzles, and other manipulatives. Keep your program stocked with art and writing materials that encourage small-muscle development.

Aspects of Toddlers' and Twos' Development	What Providers Can Do
In terms of language, toddlers and twos…	*As a provider, you…*
are increasing their listening and speaking vocabularies rapidly.	introduce new vocabulary by naming objects, actions, and feelings and by using descriptive words. Speak in complete sentences and in a clear, even voice.
communicate in short, two- or three- word sentences (for example, "Dat mine" or "Mommy go now.").	engage children in many conversations. This will give them opportunities to learn to express their thoughts and feelings.
enjoy books with rhymes, predictable words and phrases, and colorful illustrations.	provide unhurried time to read books with one or two children at a time. Encourage them to point to and name pictures. Ask questions and relate the stories to the children's lives.
like to sing along and repeat nursery rhymes and simple songs learned from others.	sing songs to children throughout the day. Have the children dance while they sing or use motions and gestures that go with each song.
Cognitively, toddlers and twos…	*As a provider, you…*
like to practice new skills by using them again and again.	provide opportunities for children to participate in familiar experiences as often as they would like.
enjoy imitating and pretending.	provide dramatic play clothing, props, and furnishings that encourage children to explore familiar roles and to play together. Offer children opportunities to do adult-like things, such as cooking, sorting laundry, and cleaning up after themselves.
are beginning to understand basic concepts about sequence and the order of daily events.	use a daily schedule to help children learn that there is a predictable order to the day. This helps children feel safe and learn about sequencing.

Preschool Children (3–5 Years)

Nathan, age 3, is an outgoing child who is often frustrated by his inability to communicate. He uses a variety of language sounds and uses a few single words, but he rarely strings them together in phrases or sentences. Nathan has been diagnosed as having a language delay. As part of his therapy, a speech therapist visits him while he is at your family child care program.

Rosa, age 4, was born in Mexico and recently moved to the United States with her family. She speaks Spanish and is just beginning to understand and speak English. She was quiet at first, but she has developed a friendship with Keisha and now seems much more comfortable in the program. She offers to help the younger children, volunteering to help feed Jeremy and look at books with Tamika and Jorge.

Keisha is 4 ½ years old. In our imaginary family child care home, she is your daughter. When you first started your program, Keisha was 8 months old. She is now very accustomed to having other children in her home. She is an eager learner, can read the names of all of the children in your program, and knows how to write her own name. She loves dressing up in grown-up clothes to play house, and she enjoys making colorful collages. She especially loves to look at books and have them read to her.

Think of preschool children as scientists who are interested in understanding and mastering the world around them. They are curious about everything, theorizing about how things work, making predictions, and trying their ideas. They develop valuable social skills, including cooperation, empathy, responsibility, and a desire to resolve social conflicts. Their large-motor skills have progressed and become more complex. By the end of the preschool years, most children speak their home languages fluently and are developing early reading and writing skills.

Aspects of Preschool Children's Development	What Providers Can Do
Socially and emotionally, preschool children...	*As a provider, you...*
are learning to solve social problems through negotiation and compromise.	engage children in a social problem-solving process. Guide and support them through this process by naming solutions that they can choose from.
like to play with other children and often have one or two best friends.	provide opportunities for children to play together. Encourage children to help each other, to cooperate on tasks, and to comfort other children. Support children as they learn to make friends.
are able to recognize, name, and express their feelings and those of others.	encourage children to label and talk about their emotions. Relate the feelings of storybook characters to the children's own lives. Emphasize the importance of respecting both their own and others' feelings.
Physically, preschool children...	*As a provider, you...*
are refining large-muscle skills by running, jumping, kicking, hopping, galloping, pedaling, climbing, throwing, and catching.	plan movement experiences and obstacle courses indoors. Outdoors, make sure the space and equipment are adequate for running, jumping, climbing, constructing, playing games with balls and hoops, riding a trike, pulling a wagon, or using a scooter. Be sure to provide helmets so that children can play safely.
increase their fine motor skills and eye–hand coordination.	offer children materials to support fine-motor development. Provide experiences such as stringing beads, working with clay and molding dough, measuring cooking ingredients, and using the computer keyboard and mouse.

Aspects of Preschool Children's Development	What Providers Can Do
In terms of language, preschool children...	*As a provider, you...*
can speak in complete sentences.	engage children in conversations and model grammatically correct language. Pose open-ended questions that require more than a *yes* or *no* answer.
begin to write letters and words.	provide children with many opportunities to write (for example, on sign-up sheets, on artwork, in thank-you letters, and in dramatic play.) Provide writing materials where children can sit at a table while they explore writing.
enjoy a variety of books (stories and nonfiction) and may have favorites.	encourage families and children to bring their favorite books. Make trips to your public library, enroll the children in a book club, or get a subscription to a children's magazine. Build your library through yard sales and donations.
Cognitively, preschool children...	*As a provider, you...*
are curious about how things work and what they can do.	help children conduct in-depth investigations of meaningful topics that they want to learn more about. Ask children about their observations and predictions, posing questions to extend their thinking.
are able to match, sort, classify, compare, use numbers, and make patterns.	give children many opportunities to count objects, develop an understanding of one-to-one correspondence, sort and classify objects, compare, and measure.
connect new experiences and ideas with what they already know.	point out connections and encourage children to make these links. For example, ask, "What other plants have we grown that we were able to eat?"

School-Age Children (6–12 Years)

Tyrone, age 8, is a school-age child who has been in the program since you started offering care. He views this as his second home, especially because his younger sister, Tamika, began coming to your program. Tyrone is doing well in school and likes to do his homework when he arrives. He usually still has time to play with the other children.

School-age children have many experiences away from their homes and your program. When they are at your program, they want a supportive place where they can relax, communicate with a caring adult, perhaps work on a project of interest, and do their homework. School-age children are beginning to think and reason logically and to approach problems with greater flexibility and efficiency. Despite their growing sense of independence, it is important to remember that they are still children who need supervision without overprotection. Your family child care home can provide a safe and welcoming place for children before and after school and during school holidays, vacations, and family emergencies.

Aspects of School-Age Children's Development	What Providers Can Do
Socially and emotionally, school-age children...	*As a provider, you...*
are eager to be independent from adults.	give children opportunities to play on their own, study, and be with peers. Let them help themselves to nutritious snacks and tell them when they need to check in with you. Encourage them to help younger children.
are concerned about being accepted by peers, and they often conform to peer expectations.	create an environment where all children feel as though they are part of the group and where their unique abilities and interests are promoted. Make each child feel special. At the same time, give children opportunities to share experiences with their peers that are acceptable to you and their families.
are looking for ways to impress or receive approval from adults they interact with and care about.	be encouraging and supportive when children create things and share them with you. Tell them what you like about their work and give them ideas for what they could work on next.

Aspects of School-Age Children's Development	What Providers Can Do
enjoy cooperative games and games with rules, but they may have difficulty with losing.	offer physical activities through which school-age children can refine their motor skills. When children feel discouraged, invite them to talk about their feelings and plan ways to strengthen their skills.
are looking for ways to impress or receive approval from adults they interact with, and care about.	be encouraging and supportive when children create things and share them with you. Tell them what you like about their work and give ideas of what they could work on next.
Physically, school-age children...	*As a provider, you...*
enjoy participating in activities such as swimming, skating, riding bikes, doing gymnastics, jumping rope, and playing games of their own design, but they are not always as coordinated as they would like to be.	provide children with space, time, and the appropriate equipment so they can refine their large-muscle skills. Enhance activities by encouraging children to play with their peers.
able to use fine-motor skills to complete complex tasks.	provide many opportunities to draw, paint, weave, sculpt, play musical instruments, complete puzzles, and work on woodworking or other craft projects.
In terms of language, school-age children...	*As a provider, you...*
are fluent in their home languages and able to express their ideas and feelings verbally.	encourage children to write, read, and perform their plays for the other children. Converse with children, asking open-ended questions to encourage them to talk about their ideas and feelings in detail. Provide additional opportunities for children to talk and share ideas with peers.
enjoy learning new words and like to describe things in intricate detail.	provide lots of books with interesting vocabulary. Introduce and use new words with children when engaged in an activity or in daily conversations. Converse with children and challenge them to elaborate on their descriptions.
are increasingly skilled and interested in reading, speaking, and writing.	provide opportunities for children to make books, use the computer or tablet for reading and writing, and read stories, including reading aloud to younger children. Give opportunities for them to retell the story or their favorite part using words or pictures. Stock your family child care home with books and magazines of interest to school-age children.

Aspects of School-Age Children's Development	What Providers Can Do
Cognitively, school-age children...	*As a provider, you...*
enjoy working on long-term projects and like to make finished products.	work with children to conduct long-term studies that interest them. Encourage children to identify and verbalize their questions, do research, experiment, and represent their ideas.
like to use their imaginations.	provide lots of materials and ideas to encourage children to be creative. They can do art or woodworking projects, write plays for the other children to perform, make something special in the kitchen, or write their own stories. Remember that everything they do is an expression of their imaginations. There are no right or wrong ways for children to use their imaginations.

Areas of Development

To provide a high-quality program in your family child care home, you need to know how children develop and what you want them to learn. Child development is divided into four areas: social–emotional, physical, language, and cognitive. While the division is necessary and useful, areas of development are interrelated and overlapping. This often requires you to pay attention to every area as you plan and support children's learning.

The four areas of development and the 14 objectives that address them are explained below. There are also two additional objectives for English language acquisition included. The purpose of these descriptions is to help you focus on specific areas while keeping the whole child and the interplay of development in mind.

Social–Emotional

Social–emotional development involves the way children feel about themselves, their understanding of feelings, their ability to regulate emotions and express them appropriately, and their capacity for building relationships with others. This area of development flourishes when children have close and trusting relationships with adults. When adults are responsive, celebrate children's accomplishments and discoveries, and create an environment where children can participate in daily routines and experiences, they show children that they are important, interesting, and competent. Through frequent positive interactions, children learn about themselves and how to relate to others.

There are three objectives for social–emotional development and learning:

Objective 1. Regulates own emotions and behaviors

a. Manages own feelings
b. Follows limits and expectations
c. Takes care of own needs appropriately

Objective 2. Establishes and sustains positive relationships

a. Forms relationships with adults
b. Responds to emotional cues
c. Interacts with peers
d. Makes friends

Objective 3. Participates cooperatively and constructively in group situations

a. Balances needs and rights of self and others
b. Solves social problems

How Culture May Influence Social–Emotional Development

Young children learn by observing the important people in their lives. Their families' home cultures greatly influence their understanding of which emotions to express and how and when to express them. Some cultures value the group's well-being over the individual's (collectivism). In these cultures, it is often more important not to express strong emotions in order to maintain the harmony of the group. Cultures that value the individual's well-being over the group's (individualism) tend to appreciate the expression of an individual's feelings, such as by smiling broadly, laughing loudly, crying mightily, or scowling deeply.

Culture may also determine whether children are encouraged to express pride about individual accomplishments or whether to feel shame or embarrassment at being recognized individually in front of a group. Families who value individualism often encourage children to express pride and happiness about personal accomplishments, whereas families who value collectivism might feel shame or embarrassment if someone calls attention to an individual's success in front of a group.

Physical

Physical development includes children's gross (large muscle) and fine (small muscle) motor skills. Gross-motor skills allow children to do a variety of things, such as rolling over, sitting, crawling, walking, running, and throwing or catching a ball. Fine-motor skills, such as holding, pinching, flexing, and pointing fingers, help children do things like drawing, writing, eating with a utensil, and cutting with scissors. The physical skills that they develop allow young children to make other new and more challenging discoveries. As they explore, they begin to make sense of their surroundings. Although some skills develop at different rates, infants learn to control and move their bodies in a similar progression. Control starts from the head down and from the center of their bodies out through their arms and legs to their fingers and toes. You will notice this general pattern as you observe a child learn to lift his head and then sit, crawl, walk, and run.

There are four objectives for physical development and learning:

Objective 4. Demonstrates traveling skills

Objective 5. Demonstrates balancing skills

Objective 6. Demonstrates gross-motor manipulative skills

Objective 7. Demonstrates fine-motor strength and coordination

a. Uses fingers and hands
b. Uses writing and drawing tools

How Culture May Influence Physical Development

A family's cultural practices can influence the rate at which children develop motor skills. If a child's home culture believes strongly in independence, then a child may be encouraged to move in order to do things on her own at an earlier age. If a child's home culture values relationships with others more than personal independence, she may be discouraged from doing things independently at a young age.

Language

Language development includes children's ability to listen, understand, and express thoughts, needs, and ideas. This area is where children grow significantly in the first three years of life. They start from communicating their needs through facial expressions, gestures, body movements, and crying to using verbal or sign language. Children acquire a vocabulary with thousands of words along with the rules for using them by being around, and interacting with adults who talk with them, encourage their efforts in using language, and guide their exploration and learning. Learning to talk takes practice, so encourage children to talk instead of correcting simple mistakes. By sharing your enthusiasm and communicating with children even before they can understand, you can help children build on their desire to communicate with others.

There are three objectives for language development and learning:

Objective 8. Listens to and understands increasingly complex language

a. Comprehends language
b. Follows directions

Objective 9. Uses language to express thoughts and needs

a. Uses an expanding expressive vocabulary
b. Speaks clearly
c. Uses conventional grammar
d. Tells about another time or place

Objective 10. Uses appropriate conversational and other communication skills

a. Engages in conversations
b. Uses social rules of language

There are two additional objectives for English language acquisition:

Objective 37. Demonstrates progress in listening to and understanding English

Objective 38. Demonstrates progress in speaking English

How Culture May Influence Language Development

As in all other aspects of development, young children's use of speech varies. Some say their first words at 8 months, while others hardly speak at all until they are almost 2 years old. Many factors influence how and when language develops. Some are individual differences present from birth. Others depend on a child's experiences with language and whether a child is learning two languages at once. Dual-language learning is discussed in the next section.

A child's home culture can influence when a child speaks and the way in which he uses verbal language, facial expressions, gestures, and silence to communicate. Some families rely heavily on verbal language and direct speech. Others rely more on the facial expressions of the speaker and on indirect communication strategies. Children reared by families who value direct communication and who use many words to explain a situation or to express thoughts and feelings will probably use speech in the same way.

A child whose family culture values indirect communication is generally physically closer to his parents (being carried, sitting on a lap, or touching a family member). That physical closeness allows the adult to read the child's body signals—a change in position, a tensing of the muscles, a subtle change in expression—and respond to them. This encourages the child to continue to communicate nonverbally rather than relying on words. Understanding these different styles will help you to recognize each child's communication attempts and better support the language development of the children in your care.

Cognitive

Cognitive development involves the way children think, approach learning, develop understandings about the world, and use what they learn to solve problems. Young children interact with others and use all areas of development to actively construct their own understandings about the people and objects in their environment. Children are learning when they roll over, crawl over and around everything in their paths, run, jump, knock things over, and pick things up. They are using learned skills and abilities as they grasp a rattle, pound play dough, and smell the grilled cheese sandwiches you made for lunch. They learn through play and as they live their everyday lives in the care of providers and their families. As they eat, get dressed, have their diapers changed, or move a chair around the room, they collect information about how things work.

Objective 11. Demonstrates positive approaches to learning

a. Attends and engages
b. Persists
c. Solves problems
d. Shows curiosity and motivation
e. Shows flexibility and inventiveness in thinking

Objective 12. Remembers and connects experiences

a. Recognizes and recalls
b. Makes connections

Objective 13. Uses classification skills

Objective 14. Uses symbols and images to represent something not present

a. Thinks symbolically
b. Engages in sociodramatic play

How Culture May Influence Cognitive Development

A child's home culture can influence the way he learns and processes new information. Cultures encourage children to explore their environments in different ways. In some cultures, experimenting with toys, manipulating objects, and solving problems by using materials are highly valued as the way children learn best. Other cultures value observation more than handling materials. In some communities, children learn by observing their environments, watching others interact, and focusing on people rather than materials.

Individual Differences

An important aspect of getting to know the children in your care is finding out what makes each child unique. It does not matter how much or how often children seem to resemble each other in their general patterns of development, each child brings personal interests, different experiences, and a learning style to your home. Children have different temperaments, past experiences, and life circumstances. Some might be learning English while still learning their home language (dual-language learners). Some children have been identified and formally diagnosed as having special needs.

Think about the children currently in your care. Perhaps you have an infant who loves to explore her environment and who opens every cabinet, drawer, and box she can find. She is very active even during nap and quiet time. Perhaps you have a preschool child who is shy and hides behind his mother's legs and needs frequent encouragement and support to interact with others.

Your understanding of every child's differences helps you build a trusting relationship that makes each child feel comfortable in your care. As a family child care provider, you are in a unique position to get to know each child in your program very well. Understanding your children means appreciating their unique ways of interacting with their world and the people in it. Providers need a variety of strategies to help all children develop and learn. Your understanding of individual differences will help you plan and respond to each child while supporting their growth and development.

Gender

Gender biases are not helpful, even when it seems easy to support them with one's own limited observations and past experiences. For example, many people assume that boys like playing with trucks and building with blocks while girls enjoy playing with dolls and dressing up. Many also say that girls are more likely to be more advanced in their drawing and writing skills at an earlier age than boys. However, these kinds of anecdotal observations obscure children's individual needs. It's important to support each child based on your own observations of their individual needs and abilities regardless of gender.

Your beliefs and expectations about gender can influence how you care for and interact with children. As Sonja Tansey (2009) noted,

> Research suggests that from an early age, children's understanding of gender is influenced by their experiences with their family, culture, and lifestyle, as well as by the broader community, child care environments, and the media. Boys and girls often experience responses and expectations from those around them due to their gender, and gender role stereotypes often influence the way boys and girls begin to experience life and how they play (p. 14).

Providers should make sure that children receive positive messages about gender and focus on what individuals are capable of doing. You need to be aware of your own personal beliefs and assumptions that can influence the way you teach. Think about your own experiences with gender roles growing up. What messages did you receive from others about how boys and girls were expected to behave? Do you expect boys' play to be "rough-and-tumble" and expect girls to be gentle? Do you want to pass these beliefs and attitudes along to the children you care for? You may hear children tell their peers, "Girls can't build with blocks" or "Boys don't dress up." They are repeating things that they have heard others say.

Children explore new ideas when they are provided with a welcoming and safe environment. When children engage in play, they learn to use these experiences to make comparisons between their ideas and other children's ideas. Encourage children to examine and reflect upon their ideas about gender as they play and be more flexible about what girls and boys may and may not do.

You can help children begin to challenge their own and others' expectations of gender-related roles. You can organize and create an environment that allows children to explore these roles while feeling comfortable and safe. Think about the displays in your home and the books you read throughout the day. Are there strong female role models? Are men presented in nurturing roles? Your program's environment, along with your own expectations, influences how children learn and explore gender.

Temperament

Temperament refers to our basic way of responding to the environment. For example, some children have a positive approach to new experiences and are generally cheerful and friendly. Other children tend to withdraw. They approach new situations cautiously and often adapt slowly. Some children protest new situations by crying, becoming fearful, or acting out.

Research suggests that children are biologically disposed toward particular behavioral styles (Chess & Thomas, 1996; Rothbart, Ahadi, & Evans, 2000). This is important for you to understand. For example, knowing that Carlos is easily distracted, you can offer him a quiet place to look at books, and you can turn off the music when he is trying to concentrate. Similarly, realizing that Setsuko tends to be shy, you can invite her to enter a dramatic play episode by asking her to join you and another child at the table for "tea."

While research has shown that temperament is inborn, providing suitable support for children can promote their development and learning. An active child can calm down, and a child who is easily distracted can learn to focus his attention. No matter with what temperament children are born, you can help them be more socially and academically successful.

While people have a tendency to maintain the same temperament throughout their lives, environment and experience do have an impact. You should not be surprised if a child's temperament at home seems different from her temperament in your care. Similarly, a child who likes to play actively with his peers might become quiet around adults.

Note each child's behavior in a variety of settings and at various times of day. Doing so will help you make appropriate decisions. Understanding how children are likely to react to people and events helps you be a more responsive and effective teacher and caregiver.

1. **Activity level**—How active is the child? Does he kick vigorously or is he often still? Does he squirm while having his diaper changed? Does he prefer to explore the world by watching and listening or by crawling and climbing?

2. **Biological rhythms**—How predictable are the child's sleeping and eating habits?

3. **Tendency to approach or withdraw**—Does the child respond positively to (approach) something new or does she pull away (withdraw) from it? When something new happens, does she fuss, do nothing, or seem to like it? For example, does she reach for a new toy or push it away? Does she swallow a new food or spit it out? Does she smile at a new person or cry and move away?

4. **Adaptability**—How does the child react to change? Does he have a hard time with changes in routines or with new people? How long does it take him to get used to new foods, new people, and other new circumstances?

5. **Sensory threshold**—At what point does a child become bothered by noise or light, changes in temperature, different tastes, or the feel of clothing?

6. **Intensity or energy level of reactions**—How does the child respond emotionally? Does she react loudly and dramatically to even the most minor disappointment, or does she become quiet when she is upset?

7. **Mood**—Does the child have a positive or negative outlook? Is she generally in a light-hearted mood, or does she take things very seriously?

8. Distractibility—Is the child readily distracted from a task by what is going on around her? When being fed her bottle, does she turn her head to look in the direction of every new sound she hears or movement she sees?

9. Persistence—How long does the child stay with a task when it is challenging? How does he react to interruptions or requests to clean up when he is playing?

Your Teaching Practice

Think about your own temperament and how it influences your teaching style and interactions with children. This can be particularly useful when a child's behavior challenges you. Consider each temperamental characteristic along a continuum (i.e., high activity level at one end, low activity level at the other). Place yourself on that continuum and then place the child. You may find that temperamental differences or striking similarities play a part in your relationship with the child and in your reactions to and feelings about his behavior.

Interests

Children demonstrate their individuality through their interests and preferences. Children have many interests that evolve and constantly change over time. One child may be fascinated by cats and another by airplanes or cars. One child loves to sing nursery rhymes; another enjoys dressing up in different costumes.

Children's interests motivate them and make them excited to continue learning. For example, if a child is interested in cats, you can engage her in reading, listening, and talking by offering a book about cats to look at or read aloud together. You can invite a child who loves to sing nursery rhymes to use puppets, props, or instruments in your home. You can supply your dramatic play area with a variety of costumes to encourage the child who loves dressing up to spend time there.

If a child is difficult to engage in certain tasks or does not use speech to communicate, try to find something that interests him. Try to use his interests to give him opportunities to interact with others and develop language skills. For example, a child who is interested in and skilled at using the computer and tablet can be encouraged to assist and talk with other children with less technology experience. Knowing the interests of the children in your care will help you build relationships and create an exciting environment to support each child's learning.

Children's interests will give you great topics for long-term studies. If a home is being constructed next door and you've observed that Nathan is fascinated by tractors and that Jorge and Tamika love to build towers using blocks and other materials, you might consider a long-term study of buildings. Understanding how children's interests evolve will also help you plan ways to extend the study over a longer period of time.

Whether or not you can use individual children's interests and preferences to inspire studies, continue to respond to their many interests. Doing this will show the children in your care that you value what is important to them. It also provides endless opportunities to guide children in developing new skills and knowledge.

Learning Styles

Every person has a preferred way of learning. Some people are visual learners. Some learn better by listening, while others have to handle something physically before they can understand it. One style is not better than another; it's simply the way a particular person learns best.

You will probably observe at least three styles of learning in your group of children:

Auditory learners, or children who learn best by listening, are attuned to oral language and other sounds. They solve problems by talking about them. Auditory learners can follow oral instructions and explanations. You can build their knowledge by describing and explaining what they did: "When you added coffee grounds to the paint, it changed the way the paint feels when it dries." You can also ask open-ended questions to encourage children to verbalize their thoughts: "What are you making for the baby doll's breakfast?" The more opportunities you provide for auditory learners to hear and verbalize concepts, the better they will understand them.

Visual learners, or children who learn best by seeing, are drawn to color, shape, and motion. They seem to think in images or pictures. Visual learners benefit when you show them how things are done, rather than just tell them verbally: "Jonetta, Kate can show you how to put the interlocking blocks together so that you can build with them." Visual learners also remember ideas and concepts better when they are presented as an image: "Let's make a graph of the different types of shoes we're wearing today." Children who learn by looking need to make visual representations of their thoughts and feelings: "Zach, I know that you're sad that your daddy had to go away. Why don't you draw a picture about the way you're feeling?"

Kinesthetic learners, or children who learn best by moving, are generally well coordinated and confident about their bodies. Touching things and moving help them process and recall information, and build understandings.

Have you ever seen a preschool child twirl around as she tries to remember something? This twirler might be a kinesthetic learner. Something about moving helps her learn a concept or process other information. Kinesthetic learners benefit by knowing that it is all right to get up and move around. You can facilitate their learning by relating concepts to their bodies, "When I push down on your head, you can feel the pressure, Setsuko. That's what a vise does to a piece of wood. It holds the wood in place."

Because children do not all learn in the same way, you should take all styles of learning into account. Traditionally, teachers in formal school settings have appealed primarily to auditory learners and, to a lesser extent, to visual learners. Kinesthetic learners have had to adjust their way of learning in order to do well in school. Rather than expecting children to adjust, it is important to make sure to present information so that all children—listeners, lookers, and movers—can be successful learners. Moreover, brain research shows that the more ways children explore a concept, the more likely they are to remember what they learn. You can maximize learning by offering learning opportunities for children of all learning styles.

Life Circumstances

In addition to other individual differences, varying life circumstances contribute to the uniqueness of each child. Consider how each of these factors affects the children you care for and teach.

- family composition, including the number and gender of parents, guardians, and other Intro sentencefamily members present in the home
- child's birth order, including the number and spacing of siblings
- presence of the chronic health problem or disability of a family member
- exposure to violence, abuse, addiction, or neglect
- home languages
- family cultural practices
- type of community in which the child lives
- kinds of work family members do
- age at which parents gave birth to or adopted their first child
- family economic status
- living situation, including history of moving
- parent's/guardian's level of education
- parent's/guardian's job history, including work-related travel
- special circumstances such as marital separation and divorce, absence of a family member for reasons not directly related to marriage, birth or adoption of a new sibling, how many different people and places the child experiences each day

Try to be aware of each child's circumstances when he or she enters your program. Your program's enrollment forms may be helpful in learning more about individual families. Talking with family members and taking notes about what you learn is an important first step. Encourage families to communicate with you about anything new taking place in children's lives, and honor their styles of communication. This process will take time as you develop a trusting relationship with family members. Remember to honor the confidentiality of information that family members share with you. If a family shares information with you that you do not know how to handle, seek advice from your supervisor or an outside expert.

Including All Children

An important aspect of best practice in early childhood education is the inclusion of all children. By incorporating the concept of Universal Design for Learning (UDL), *The Creative Curriculum*® shows how to implement a high-quality inclusive program. When you use UDL, you can support the learning of all children in your care, including English-language learners, advanced learners, and those who have disabilities and developmental delays. By providing a variety of formats and accommodations for instruction, learning, and assessment, you can offer children multiple ways of acquiring knowledge and skills and of communicating what they know (Division for Early Childhood, 2007).

English- and Dual-Language Learners

Children whose home language is not English are very likely to be in your care, if not now, then in the future. The number of children who speak a first language that is not English (English-language learners) or who are learning English at the same time they are learning another language (dual-language learners) has increased dramatically and continues to increase in the United States.

Young children in your program may be learning two or more languages simultaneously, English in your program and another language or languages at home. Children may arrive in your program without ever having heard English anywhere other than on television, which is not a very good teacher. You may have several children who share a common home language other than English, or you may have children whose first languages are rare in your community.

Just as all children have very different strengths and needs, children who are learning English while they are learning another language vary greatly. The extent of children's knowledge of their primary language can vary, just as it does for children who speak only English at home.

Some children have language-rich home environments and arrive with strong language skills in their primary language. Other children have a weaker foundation on which to build language skills. Immersing them in a language-rich environment while they are in your care can help them increase their skills.

A number of misconceptions about learning two languages can cause unnecessary anxiety for providers and families. The following chart dispels some of these common misunderstandings (Genesee, n.d.; Snow, 1997).

Misunderstandings About Dual-Language Learning

Misunderstandings	Reality
Children who are exposed to more than one language are at a clear disadvantage.	Bilingual children are often very creative and good at problem solving. Compared with children who speak one language, those who are bilingual can communicate with more people, read more, and benefit more from travel. Such children will have an additional skill when they enter the workforce.
Learning two languages at the same time confuses a child.	Children do not get confused, even when they combine languages in one sentence. Mixing languages is a normal and expected part of learning and speaking two languages.
Learning two languages during the preschool years invariably slows children's readiness to read.	Actually, the opposite is often true. English-language learners usually learn to decode words well.

Misunderstandings	Reality
When children are exposed to two languages, they never become as proficient in either language as children who have to master only one language.	As long as they consistently use both languages, children can become proficient in both languages.
Only the brightest children can learn two languages without encountering problems. Most children have difficulty because the process is so complex.	Nearly all children are capable of learning two languages during the early childhood years. While the process may be complex for adults, young children's brains are still developing the structures for language, so they are able to learn multiple languages.

Specific strategies for supporting dual-language learners are discussed in other chapters. Exposure to rich language experiences in two languages is a definite asset. All children can benefit from learning another language.

Levels of English Language Acquisition

Early childhood educators need to know about the process and stages of English language acquisition, methods to assess the overall language abilities of young English-language learners, and the influence of home culture and family values. As in all areas of development, children vary in their approaches to and rate of English language acquisition. Preschool children also vary in their readiness to use their new language to express what they know. There are many important differences among young English-language learners: the languages they speak at home, the social and economic resources available to their families, the amount and timing of their exposure to English, the timing and circumstances of the family's immigration to the United States, the family's literacy practices, similarities between a child's first and second languages, and so on. These factors influence the amount and type of instructional adjustment needed for children to learn the second language successfully (August & Shanahan, 2010; Snow et al., 1998). Teachers and providers need to find out about each family's unique circumstances in order to design individualized approaches that build on the child's strengths and prior knowledge.

The following chart explains the typical developmental sequence of English language acquisition by describing what you might observe children doing at each level (adapted from Tabors, 2008).

Levels of Learning a Second Language

What You Might Observe	
Home language use	Children continue to use their home language with providers and other children, even if it is not understood.
Nonverbal/observational period	Children limit (or stop) the use of their home language as they realize that it is not understood by others. They use nonverbal methods to communicate, such as gesturing or pantomiming, usually to get attention, make requests, protest, or joke. Children listen to and learn the features, sounds, and words of the new language (receptive language skills) but do not yet use the new language to express themselves. This period of active language learning can last from a few months to a year.
Telegraphic and formulaic speech	Children begin using one- and two-word phrases in English and begin to name objects. They may use groups of words such as "Stop it," "Fall down," or "Shut up," although they may not always use them appropriately. The children repeat a phrase they hear others use to achieve social goals, even though they probably do not know the literal meaning of the words and are repeating familiar sounds because they are functionally effective.
Productive/fluid use of language	Children begin to use simple English sentences like those they hear in meaningful contexts. They begin to form their own sentences by combining words they have learned. Like all young children, they gradually increase the length of their sentences.

Many factors, such as a child's temperament, amount of previous experience with English, and opportunities to use English, influence how quickly a child moves through each stage and develops expressive language skills in English. For example, with her quiet temperament, Rosa may stay in the nonverbal stage longer than a child who is more outgoing.

It is important for you to model grammatically correct English and to encourage the children's families to speak and read to them in their home languages. Bring the children's home languages into your program as much as you are comfortable doing. Research about Spanish-speaking children has shown that providers who speak even a little bit of Spanish to them promote the social skills that support learning a new language (Chang et al., 2007).

Special Needs

All children have strengths and needs of varying kinds. Some children have special needs because they have disabilities. You may work with a child or multiple children who have a documented disability or disabilities. **Always think of children with disabilities as children first**. Remember that a disability is only one aspect of a child's development. You need to be cautious when thinking about special needs and refrain from using labels such as gifted or disabled that may alter or obscure important information about children and hinder adults from considering the whole child. A child may be an advanced learner in some areas or have a disability in another, but it rarely influences every aspect of development. For example, a child who is an advanced learner might be ahead of his peers in reading but lacks social skills.

Advanced learners: There may be children in your program who are developmentally ahead of their peers. You may notice that their language is developing at a faster rate and is more complex. They may solve puzzles quickly, ask lots of specific questions, or have interests that seem unusual for their age.

Children with strong skills in one or more developmental area are called advanced learners. We tend to think first about intellectual and cognitive skills when we use that term, but children can demonstrate these skills in any number of areas. Gardner's theory on multiple intelligences shows that people can be talented in at least eight different ways. For example, a child in your program may be athletically advanced, a logical thinker, a talented musician, or an incredible artist.

Advanced learners are rarely gifted in all areas of development. In fact, they often have uneven development, but their strengths in other areas aid them in acquiring skills where they need extra support. For example, some children who have strong language skills can approach physical tasks better when demonstrations are accompanied by verbal instructions of what steps to take (e.g., how to throw a ball).

Adults might have a hard time understanding how a child could be advanced in one area of development and not in all. Why would a child who has a large vocabulary still have trouble socializing and interacting with peers? You need to note areas in which each child needs extra support and to assist with the continued development of strengths.

Like all children, advanced learners need to be challenged or they are likely to become bored and unmotivated. Challenging your advanced learners will help them be interested in what they are doing and become more confident in their growing skills. You can observe individual children, determine their strengths and needs, and create an environment where every child feels supported and challenged.

Children with disabilities: All children have strengths and needs of varying kinds. Some children have special needs because they have disabilities. While there are many types of disabilities, most can be described as developmental delays and medical, emotional, or physical problems. Increasing numbers of children are being identified as having attention-related disorders and autism.

Always think of children with disabilities as children first. Learn about each child's strengths and interests and then consider the child's special challenges. Remember that a disability is only one aspect of a child's development. It does not define the whole child. Children with disabilities have a wide-range of abilities and needs. A child may have a disability that affects one area of development, but he or she may be developing typically in other developmental areas. Children with disabilities usually follow the same pattern as children who are developing typically. However, they may develop at a slower pace, in a different sequence, or take smaller steps toward a developmental objective.

The first questions about a child's need for special services may be raised at the child's birth, during a later medical checkup, by the family, by a specialist, or by you. As a family child care provider, you may be the first person to become concerned about a child's development. Federal law requires each state to have a Child Find system to help identify children with disabilities and make sure that they receive appropriate services. If you are concerned about a child's development, talk with the child's family and help them learn how to access the local Child Find system.

Two federal laws govern services provided to young children with disabilities. One law governs services for children under age 3. The other specifies services for older children. Both laws require the development of a plan that answers basic questions about the nature of the child's disability and specifies what must be done to meet his educational needs. For children under age 3, the law requires the creation of an Individualized Family Service Plan (IFSP). Services must be provided in a "natural setting." A natural setting is one in which the child would spend time if he or she did not have a disability. This definition makes a family child care home an ideal setting for a child with disabilities. For children age 3 and above, the law requires that a child with a diagnosed disability who is eligible for special education services have an Individualized Education Program (IEP). The IFSP and IEP include goals and objectives, a description of how the disability affects the child's access to the general curriculum, and the types of special education services the child needs.

In addition to these two laws, the Americans with Disabilities Act (ADA) requires family child care homes and centers to make reasonable modifications to include children with disabilities. To meet the law's provisions, family child care providers must make simple, inexpensive changes, such as getting rid of physical barriers or providing adaptive equipment.

Special education legislation ensures that children with disabilities, their families, and their family child care providers are supported well. If a child in your family child care program has a diagnosed disability, the child's IFSP or IEP will identify the type and frequency of the services he or she needs. For example, if a child has a chronic medical condition, health care workers will assist you in learning to feed the child and provide medication. Additional service providers may include speech therapists, occupational therapists, or physical therapists. All of these specialists will provide services in the natural environment of your family child care home and help you include the child with disabilities in all aspects of your program.

Your Teaching Practice

Consider how a disability may affect the child's daily routines in your program. Gather information to help you decide what adjustments you need to make, if any. As you plan to individualize the curriculum, keep the following questions in mind:

- Do you need assistance or help during certain parts of the day?
- Do you need to make changes to your environment so a child can participate and be included in the program?
- Are there certain teaching practices that are more effective than others? How can you create a daily schedule that meets the child's needs?

Consider these questions when thinking about how you can effectively plan and implement the curriculum for all children in your care regardless of ability.

Summary

In your family child care program, you may care for infants, toddlers, twos, and preschool and school-age children. To understand how to organize your home and your day, what children are learning, and how to guide children's development and learning, you need to have a good understanding of what children are generally like at each stage of development and what developmental objectives to keep in mind. In addition to understanding how children develop and learn, you must also discover the unique qualities of each child and understand the importance of gender, temperament, interests, learning style, life experiences, language, and special needs. The more you know about each child, the more you can appreciate a child's special qualities and use that knowledge to build a positive relationship.

2

Organizing Your Home and Your Day

Organizing Your Home and Your Day

A family child care home is a unique environment for early childhood education. Part home and part child care program, it provides a relaxed environment for learning. However, the combination also poses special challenges. Providers meet these challenges in different ways. Some providers take advantage of the home's familiar environment for their program. They use the living room, with its comfortable couch and chairs, for reading and snuggling. They use the kitchen, where they can cook, serve meals, and let children play with pots, pans, and plastic containers. The bathroom becomes a place to smile, sing, and talk with children so that diapering and toileting are times to build relationships and support learning. Other family child care providers prefer to designate a separate space in their home. That space is used exclusively for family child care, not for the providers' families. Both models have strengths and challenges, so some providers use a combination of separate and shared spaces. To help you select the arrangement that works best for you and your family, these approaches are discussed below.

This chapter provides general information about creating an indoor environment that meets the needs of the children in your program as well as your family's needs. It also includes information about planning a responsive program. *Volume 2: Routines and Experiences* provides specific information about arranging the environment for daily routines and experiences.

This chapter includes three sections:

Setting Up Your Home discusses options for arranging your home for family child care. These include shared space, separate space, or a combination of the two. It includes information about how to furnish, equip, and organize your family child care home so that it is safe and welcoming for children and families. It explains how to arrange the environment to encourage positive behavior, and it suggests ways to store and display materials so that children can use and care for them easily.

Planning Your Day talks about how to develop a flexible daily schedule that helps structure the day's routines and experiences. It discusses the events of the day and shows how to plan so that your program runs smoothly.

Planning Your Week explains more about thinking ahead. It introduces the "Child Planning Form" and the "Group Planning Form," which help you use what you know about the children in your group to plan meaningful play experiences.

Setting Up Your Home

The way you arrange your family child care home can make it easier for children to learn, get along with others, and become independent. It can encourage positive behavior. It can also make it easier for you to care for children.

Many factors influence the way you set up your home for family child care. These include such considerations as the size of your home, whether you have a basement or another large room to set aside for the family child care program, and the type of flooring in your home. You also need to think about whether you have a safe place for children to play outdoors or whether you will take them to a nearby playground or park. Some family child care providers use areas throughout their homes during the day and convert the spaces back into family living areas at the end of the day. They store equipment in closets and move heavy items on wheels. Others designate parts of their home for family child care and always leave them set up that way. Your decisions will depend on the size and design of your home, as well as your family's feelings about sharing space. Many providers use a combination. For example, they reserve a family room in the basement exclusively for family child care but also use the kitchen and bedrooms as family child care space.

Shared Space

A home can be a stimulating but relaxed environment for learning. There are soft and safe places for children to explore. You may have plants and pets that the children can help care for. The kitchen is made for cooking activities and meals. The carpet or rug in your living room can be a place for "tummy time" for a young infant and a place where two preschool children can play a simple board game. Common kitchen items such as wooden spoons (to bang on pots) or measuring cups (to nest) make wonderful toys for children. Sharing your family space makes children feel comfortable almost immediately, and this homey environment is often one of the things that families are looking for when they choose family child care rather than center care.

When the place that is used to care for children is also your family's home, you have to consider not only the needs of the families you serve, but also your own needs and those of your family. Balancing needs can be a challenge, so you need to think about how to convert your home into program space during the day and turn it back into a space that your family uses and enjoys after program hours.

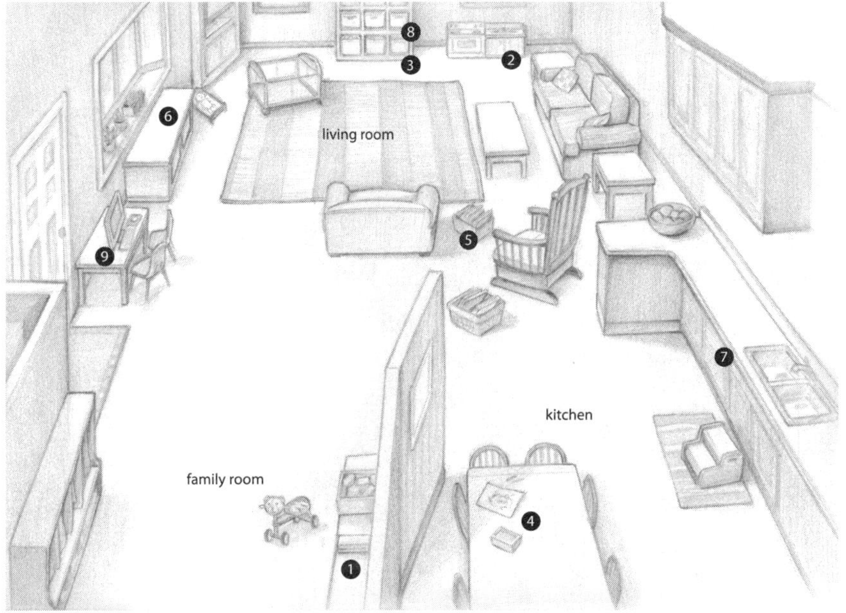

1. Blocks
2. Dramatic Play
3. Toys and Games
4. Art
5. Library
6. Discovery
7. Sand and Water
8. Music and Movement
9. Technology

The following guidelines will help you use shared family child care space effectively:

Identify which rooms of your home will be used for family child care and which are off-limits to the children. Decide where experiences can take place in your home. Is your living room a large space that can be used for active musical games, block building, and dramatic play? Will you offer water play in the kitchen or perhaps the bathroom? Look for comfortable places for quiet activities such as looking at books, drawing with crayons, and listening to music.

Close off places that are off-limits. For example, a tool shed or storage area can be locked, and your bedroom door can be closed. Rooms that you do not wish to use for your program can be blocked by a door, a gate, or a large piece of furniture. Childproof the space used by children. Breakable objects can be stored in areas that are off-limits.

Set aside a place for school-age children to be by themselves when they want and where you keep their games and special materials such as paper, scissors, markers, and glue.

Make taking out and putting away family child care materials as easy as possible. Identify places where these materials can be stored out of sight after program hours. Put the materials in wheeled carts so they can be moved easily.

Separate Space

If you reserve places in your home only for your family child care program, you can designate experience areas for particular types of play. For example, children need a protected space for playing with blocks, an easy-to-clean area for messy activities such as art or water play, and some cozy spots for reading or listening to music. A couch, armchair, rug, and curtains make the program space comfortable for you and the children.

The amount of space in your home will determine how many areas you can set up. Here are some arrangement guidelines:

Separate noisy areas from quiet ones.

Define each area clearly by using shelves, tables, or tape so children can identify physical boundaries easily.

Locate experience areas near needed resources. For example, set up art materials near a water source, and place a computer and digital audio player near electrical outlets.

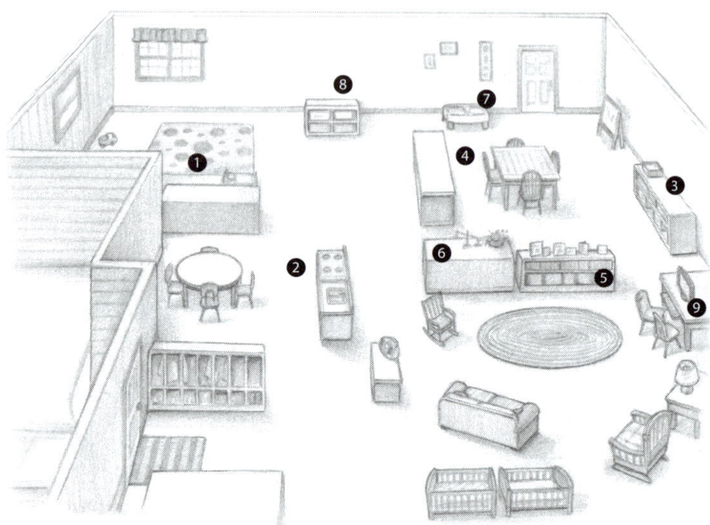

1. Blocks
2. Dramatic Play
3. Toys and Games
4. Art
5. Library
6. Discovery
7. Sand and Water
8. Music and Movement
9. Technology

Establishing Experience Areas

Experience areas with a variety of materials can offer children a range of clear choices. Throughout the day, some children will want to work in quiet areas, either alone or with other children. Areas that are conducive to looking at books, creating art, or playing with toys and games can encourage children to engage in these quiet activities. Areas that are set aside for dramatic play, building with blocks, woodworking, or large-muscle activities allow children to be more physically active. Dividing your home into spaces that accommodate a few children at a time addresses some children's preferences for a smaller group setting. It also allows some separation for the various age-groups within your family child care setting.

The Creative Curriculum® suggests that a child care environment have defined areas for dramatic play, block play, toys and games, art, looking at books and writing, sand and water play, and a discovery table. The amount of space in your home will determine how many areas you can set up. Your kitchen may be the perfect place for children to engage in cooking activities. If possible, try to include places in your home for children to play musical instruments and work with technology, e.g., a tablet or computer, if available. Ideally, children should have daily access to certain materials like musical instruments and art materials, but these items can be brought from storage if they cannot always be available.

Tips for Setting Up Experience Areas

To begin setting up experience areas in your home, note the location of electrical outlets, windows, doors, sinks, and storage space. Look for movable furnishings that can help define a space (e.g., shelves, tables, dramatic play furniture). Keep in mind the challenges you may have in your home environment: built-in cabinets and shelves, columns, heating and cooling vents, exposed pipes, the locations of doors that may be needed for emergency exits, and so on.

Here are some additional tips for setting up your home:

Establish traffic patterns for entering and exiting the designated spaces in your home, putting belongings away in cubbies or a closet, using the bathroom, and moving from one area of the home to another.

Cleary define areas that need protection by using furniture or shelves (e.g., a block corner and library nook).

Locate quiet experience areas away from noisier areas.

Decide which areas need tables and chairs. Try to minimize the number of tables in the space to allow children to use the floor and open spaces for their play. Keep in mind that you need enough table space to accommodate children and adults during mealtimes.

Be mindful of activities that are affected by floor coverings. Art, sand and water, and cooking are considered messy activities that should be in areas with a washable floor. Materials like drop cloths, pieces of vinyl, or shower curtains can be used to help with potential messes. Soft flooring is ideal for activities during which children prefer to sit or kneel comfortably.

Strategically place experience areas near needed resources. Art, water play, and cooking activities should be near a sink or water source. Lamps, CD players, computers, and printers need to be close to electrical outlets.

Reserve areas close to windows and light as places for children to explore and look at books, write and draw, and care for plants.

Organize the space so you can see each separate area. Safety and child abuse prevention regulations require supervision of children at all times. That means always having children in your sight.

Providing Materials in Experience Areas

Experience areas work well for the children in your care when the materials you select are attractive, relevant to children's experiences and cultures, and appropriately challenging. The materials you include in experience areas should introduce children to content, such as plants and animals for children to observe and care for (science); collections of materials, e.g., buttons, bottle caps, or balls, to sort and graph (math); books that children can use to look up information (literacy); gears, and clocks to take apart (technology); and more.

General Considerations

In addition to establishing areas for routines and experiences, there are other aspects of the physical setting to keep in mind as you set up your family child care environment. It is important to identify a place for group time, places for children's work, and storage areas for children's belongings and materials. Depending on individual children's needs and interests, you may have to change and adapt your home so that all children have access to experience areas and materials. Your setting should be as comfortable and attractive as possible so children enjoy being there.

A Place for Group Time

Establish a place in your home where all children can gather to talk about the day, listen to books and stories, be introduced to new materials, transition from one activity to another, and participate in music and movement activities. If your home has limited space, you can hold meetings in one of the large experience areas, e.g., the library or block area.

Here are some additional guidelines:

Try to use an area with large floor space to accommodate all of the children and adults in a circle.

Provide comfortable seating. If your group area does not have a carpet or rug, you might use carpet squares or pillows so everyone has a soft place to sit and participate.

Display charts or pictures that you want to discuss with the children, such as a job chart, the daily schedule, and charts for potential graphing activities.

Try to include an easel or chart stand so you can write down group discussions or display pictures or big books as you read to the children.

Choose a location near electrical outlets for audio equipment and near shelves or cabinets for materials such as CDs, scarves, puppets, and musical instruments.

Children's Work and Displays

Try to designate areas within your home to display and showcase children's work. Find special places for each child's work to go on your walls and allow the children to pick the items they want to display. Include the children's names and photographs to identify their work.

Invite children to talk about their artwork. Record what they say on a piece of paper and include it with their work. Writing down what children say is an oral language and literacy experience and gives children the impression that their work is important and worthwhile. Displaying work also gives children's families and visitors an opportunity to see what you are currently teaching and what children are learning.

Children's work should be displayed at their eye level so they are able to identify and discuss their work with others. Keep displays in your home simple and up to date. Try to display photos of the children's families and include photos of what the children are currently learning. Take photographs that show children participating in activities and include a note explaining what they are doing.

Consider the following places for displays:

- walls
- pillars
- the tops and backs of shelves
- a clothesline and clothespins or a net
- windows
- a binder

You need to be creative about displays if you have a limited space available in your home. Multiple binders placed in experience areas could be a great alternative for putting children's work and photographs inside. For example, if you have Nathan's drawing of his house and a photograph of Rosa and Keisha building a tower, those items could be placed inside a binder and kept in the block area for children to look at and talk about.

Places for Storage

Proper storage is essential to having an orderly family child care setting. Think in terms of three storage types: open storage for materials that you want easily accessible to children, secure storage for materials you want to limit, and personal or individual storage for children and adults.

Multiple shelves that are sturdy and safe for children to use are ideal for storing materials that children can access independently. An alternative to open shelving could be created by securing plastic milk crates together. If you allow children to take naps, you also will need to find storage for cribs, cots or mats, blankets, and pillows.

Secure storage for cleaning supplies and sharp utensils ensure that children are kept safe throughout the day. This type of storage is also useful for storing materials you do not want the children to use until a later date. Organize and label boxes or containers so you can find what you need easily.

For children's belongings, designate spaces that are easily accessed and clearly labeled with children's photos and names. Closets, bins, or crates can be used as cubbies for storing children's clothing and additional personal items. Labeled dishpans can be used to store toys or other materials brought from home and can be a place for work that children take home. Finally, set aside a place or room in your home where adults can store their belongings safely.

A Comfortable and Attractive Setting

As you set up your family child care environment, make sure it is comfortable, attractive, and homey. Here are some suggestions:

Take advantage of the natural light in different areas of your home. Use mirrors to reflect light to enable children to look at the environment from different perspectives. Add lighting to the space by using table or floor lamps to enhance the coziness of your home.

Incorporate soft items into the environment whenever possible. Add soft chairs, a crib mattress or futon covered with an attractive blanket or sheet, pillows, area rugs, and stuffed animals.

Include different textured materials to stimulate children's senses, e.g., bumpy, smooth, soft, hard, rough, squishy, and sticky.

Designate quiet spaces where children can work independently and away from the rest of the children. Consider a tent, a large box filled with blankets and pillows, a comfortable chair or couch near a window or fish tank, a book nook on a window seat, and access to a CD or digital audio player with headphones.

Allow the children to take care of your pets and plants. Children can observe, care for, and cuddle with the animals in your home. In the discovery area, include natural objects, such as bird nests, seashells, pinecones, feathers, an ant farm, or butterfly habitat.

Children With Disabilities

As you arrange furniture and choose your materials, think about the abilities and needs of each child, including those who have a physical or sensory disability. Ensure that all of the children are able to actively participate in all designated areas. Always keep in mind safety, comfort, and the use of materials and equipment. Seek out a special education consultant to help you evaluate your home and outdoor areas to determine what needs to be changed or added to encourage and accommodate each child's full participation.

Here are some suggestions:

Make sure that **traffic patterns and walkways** between experience areas will easily accommodate a wheelchair or walker. **Ramps and low toilets** may be required or preferred to make facilities accessible.

Use adjustable tables in your home so children's wheelchairs can fit underneath. Allow the other children to stand at the table.

Provide wedges so children can play comfortably on the floor.

Find a room or area to store adaptive equipment that is not being used.

Make easy-to-use materials available, such as puzzles with knobs and art or writing tools with easy-to-grip handles.

Provide different types of technology for children to use, e.g., large keyboards, touch screen devices, headphones, and trackballs.

Use visual, auditory, and tactile cues to help children effectively explore their environment. **Be aware** of children who are too close to **sources of loud sounds** that can interfere with hearing aids.

Special Considerations for Setting Up the Physical Environment

Whether your program is located in a space used only for family child care or takes place throughout your home, safety is the first consideration. In a family child care home, you—and you alone—are responsible for the safety of the children in your care. Supervision is critical. The National Association for Family Child Care (NAFCC) safety standards require that providers be able to see or hear all children at all times. Children under age 6 may not be left inside or outside by themselves. Children younger than age 3 must be in the provider's sight at all times, except when the provider is attending to his or her personal needs for as many as 5 minutes. When children age 3 or older are not in sight, providers must be able to hear them (NAFCC, 2013).

A childproofed home environment, designed in accordance with your knowledge of development and individual children in your room, can prevent or at least minimize injuries or accidents. Conduct a safety check of your indoor and outdoor environment each day before the first child arrives. Hazards can emerge overnight. Family members may leave an item out that might be dangerous for children. Litter may be blown or thrown onto the outdoor play area. Pay close attention to each area the children use to make sure it remains childproof and safe.

One of the challenges related to maintaining a safe environment in a family child care home is meeting the needs of a diverse group that may include infants, toddlers, twos, preschool children, and school-age children. Your knowledge of each child's development and needs will help you think about how to set up the environment. For example, if infants are in your care, you need a protected space where they can play on the floor without getting run over by an older child. You also need a place where older children can play actively without tripping over babies. A toy that is appropriate for a 4-year-old can be a choking hazard for an infant or toddler. Safety concerns change as children develop and grow, so your environment may need to change as young infants become mobile and as toddlers become preschool children. Evaluate your environment frequently, particularly when you begin caring for a new child. Make any changes needed to keep children safe.

Some safety hazards are unique to family child care programs because they are in a home setting. Fireplaces and firearms, for instance, are rarely found in a child care center, but they are in some family child care homes. Bathroom and bedroom doors may have locks. Although child care centers often have pet rabbits, guinea pigs, hamsters, or gerbils, they rarely have dogs or cats. Use a safety checklist to identify hazards in both your indoor and outdoor environments.

Here some suggestions to consider for providing a safe environment:

- Be aware of and maintain the staff–child ratios in your family child care home. Supervise children at all times.
- Provide safe and sturdy furniture and equipment that is sized for the ages and developmental levels of the children who use the space.
- Make sure that furniture and equipment is in good repair and will not tip over. Remove or fix anything that may be in need of repair.
- Verify that your home does not have lead-based paint or radon, that radiator and hot pipes are insulated, and that heaters or furnaces are enclosed by barricades.
- Check toys every day to make sure they are in good condition. They cannot have broken parts, chipping paint, or sharp edges.
- Cover all electrical outlets and use child safety locks on cupboards and drawers when appropriate.
- Keep electrical cords and devices out of children's reach. Make sure that cords from window blinds or coverings are also out of children's reach.
- Check all toys and other materials to make sure they are not choking hazards. Remove anything with small parts. If an object can go through a choke tube or fit entirely into a child's mouth, it is too small.
- Display heavy toys on bottom shelves so children do not have to lift them.
- Be sure that water from faucets will not scald children. It should be under 120 degrees Fahrenheit.
- Store any hazardous equipment and materials out of reach, including adult purses, plastic bags, and cleaning supplies.
- Check your outdoor space and make sure it is free of trash, broken glass, and animal waste.

- Keep a well-stocked first-aid kit easily available and take additional kits with you for outdoor play, walks, and trips.
- Keep emergency contact information current and make sure that emergency exits are easily accessible and free of obstacles.
- Keep the environment as clean and hygienic as possible. Make sure that all play spaces are clean, that bedding and soft toys are laundered, and that other plastic or hard-surfaced toys are cleaned and sanitized regularly.

When working with children, frequent handwashing is critical to maintaining everyone's health. Everyone who enters your home should wash their hands or have them washed before interacting with the children or beginning play. Hands should also be washed periodically throughout the day. Wash your hands before feeding an infant, before preparing or serving food, after diapering and toileting, after touching pets, and after blowing noses. Frequent handwashing can dramatically reduce adult and child illnesses. Post a sign to remind visitors, staff members, and families to wash their hands. Encourage families to wash their hands along with their children's hands as part of their hello and good-bye routine. It will give them something to do together every day to ease the separation.

Here are additional suggestions for providing a heathy environment for the younger children in your program.

- Make sure to wash and sanitize mouthed toys after each use. Set up a system that stores mouthed toys until they can be cleaned. Come up with a separate system for laundering dirty clothes, blankets, or toys.
- Mix a spray bottle with bleach solution daily. Store bottles in close proximity to your changing tables, eating areas, and other surfaces that need to be frequently sanitized.
- Follow universal precautions and wear gloves when dealing with blood or bodily fluids.
- Designate a quiet, comfortable, and supervised waiting area for sick children to wait for their families.

Inform children's families about your health and safety policies and procedures. This shows that health and safety practices are a priority in your program.

Sending Positive Messages in the Physical Environment

Have you ever observed children and their family members when they visit your home for the first time? They often look around trying to decide if your program is right for them and their child. They may be asking themselves:

- Do I belong here?
- Do these people know me? Do they like me?
- Is this a place I can trust?
- Will I be safe here?
- Will I be comfortable?
- Can I explore and move around?
- Is this an interesting and exciting place to be?
- Can I count on these people to take care of me?

The most important part of the learning environment is you! The daily interactions you have with children are the best way to answer any of these concerns. The arrangement of the physical environment also sends strong messages to children and their families. Think about whether your environment conveys the messages you intend.

You belong here. We like you.

- At children's eye levels, display photographs of them engaged in play and with their families. Change them over time. Laminate the pictures or cover them with contact paper so children can touch them without tearing them. Place photos in cube frames that are unbreakable so children can carry them around.
- Provide places for children to put their belongings.
- Make sure that displayed pictures and materials honor the cultural diversity of the children and families.
- Plan the environment or change it based on your observations of children. For example, when children begin climbing on shelves or other furniture, add large pillows or plastic boxes that children can climb on instead.
- Invite family members to bring interesting materials from home for children, such as colorful bandanas, bottle caps, or a musical instrument.

This is a place you can trust. You will be safe here.

- Arrange furniture with each child's safety in mind. Cushion surfaces where children are learning to move on their own, making sure that the cushioning does not interfere with balance.
- Store materials near the areas they will be needed or used. Label containers, cupboards, and shelves so adult visitors and family members can find things and put things away easily.
- Limit changes in the environment to help cautious children know they can depend on the room arrangement.

This is a comfortable place to be.

- Include familiar household objects in the environment, such as curtains on the windows, large floor cushions, and nontoxic plants.
- Make sure that children's comfort items are available to them.
- Provide soft furniture, such as stuffed chairs and couches.
- Have space for adults and family members to engage with children in their play.
- Place reading materials in different spaces around the room so children and adults can sit down and enjoy them.
- Use soft textures and furnishings to help minimize loud sounds. Soft light, colors, and sounds give the environment a peaceful and comfortable atmosphere.

You can explore and move freely on your own.

- Designate enough space so that children can turn over, crawl, creep, pull up, stand, cruise, and walk around as they grow and become more independent. Use extra space from other areas in your home when necessary.
- Block off areas that are unsafe for children.
- Store heavier materials on low shelves that children can access easily.
- Make sure that materials stored on low shelves are intended for children's use.
- Label containers and shelves with pictures and words so children can easily find and return materials.
- Display books, toys, and other materials in consistent places so children know their location.
- Change and rotate materials in experience areas as children's strengths, needs, and interests change.

We will take care of you.

- Set up areas for daily routines.
- Provide a crib, cot, or mat for every child.
- Provide a supervised, comfortable waiting area where sick children can rest until their families come.

Scan your child care space regularly to find ways the environment can be enhanced to convey these positive messages. Meaningful and special touches make the environment warm and welcoming to everyone who comes into your home.

Your Teaching Practice

Think about the impressions you give to children and families when they first enter your home. If they were describing your program to someone after their first initial visit, what would they say? Evaluate the designated areas used for your program. What messages does each room arrangement send to children and families? Are those the messages you intend to convey? What changes can you make to convey a sense of belonging, safety, comfort, and trust?

Setting Up Your Home to Encourage Positive Behavior

Children respond best to environments that make them feel safe and secure. When they are given a special place to keep their belongings, children feel respected. When they know where to play, they are less likely to wander. When they know which things they may play with and which are off-limits, they learn to respect the rights of others. Children who have a wide variety of interesting and age-appropriate toys are more likely to become involved in purposeful play. When the environment supports group living, fights are rare and the day goes well.

When the environment is set up poorly, children may become confused. They may fight over toys or cry because they want a toy that another child is using. While there are many possible reasons for children's unwanted behavior, it's always a good idea to check the physical environment first to see if it is contributing to the problem. Here are some examples:

Unwanted Behavior	Possible Cause	How to Change the Environment
Children running around your home	Too much space is open; the rooms are not divided into small enough areas; activity areas are not defined.	Use furniture or shelves to help divide up the space. Try to avoid open spaces that encourage children to run.
Fighting over toys	Too many toys are popular and one-of-a-kind; children are frequently asked to share.	Provide duplicates of popular toys. Help children know when it will be their turns (e.g., use a sand timer or stopwatch to help children create a waiting list for turns).
Wandering around from area to area; inability to choose an activity	The room is too cluttered or overstimulating; available choices are not clear; there is not enough to do.	Get rid of the clutter. Simplify the layout of the room and provided materials. Add more interesting activity choices.
Misusing materials and not helping with cleanup	Children do not know how to use the materials appropriately; toys and materials are not organized in containers and are not placed where children can find and return them.	Designate a place for everything. Use picture and word labels to help children know where things go. Provide consistent guidance on how to clean up. Make a job chart to help children approach caring for materials and furniture as a shared responsibility.
Infants, toddlers, and older children interfering with each other's activities	Younger children do not have a safe space for crawling or toddling; older children do not have areas large enough for moving freely.	Set up safe, protected spaces where young infants can have tummy time and where mobile infants can crawl and walk. Include low tables where preschool children can play without being interrupted.
Children crying or fighting a lot	Children may be overstimulated by always being in a group or by having too many choices.	Have a quiet, cozy place for a child to spend some time alone, with one other child, or with an adult.

Organizing, Selecting, and Displaying Materials

Whichever approach you adopt for your family child care home, you will need low shelves, bins, or cabinets to store toys and materials, along with child-sized tables and chairs. Here are some additional guidelines:

Select high-quality materials that are well-made and durable and will last over the years.

Provide open-ended toys and materials that children of different ages can use in different ways. For example, babies and 4-year-olds can both enjoy nesting cubes, baby dolls, and plastic measuring cups.

Supplement purchased toys and games with common household objects. Children delight in banging on empty coffee cans or oatmeal containers. Keep safety in mind when selecting and displaying materials, especially if you care for children of different ages.

Work with children's families and therapists to make sure that children with disabilities have toys and materials that they can use by themselves and with other children. For example, chubby, flat crayons and puzzles with knobs can be used easily by most children, including those with fine-motor limitations. A communication board or electronic device can help a child with a language delay communicate with friends.

Involve families in collecting materials. Ask families to help collect and donate materials, such as pretend play props or large, empty cardboard boxes to play in. Families can bring family pictures or magazine cutouts to make homemade books that you can display around the room. Ask families to bring items that they would otherwise throw away, such as empty juice or milk containers, coffee cans with lids, fabric scraps, buttons, and so on.

When materials are organized and displayed thoughtfully, children are more likely to use and care for them. Storing materials so children can see and reach them helps children become independent because they can select and return materials by themselves. When materials are stored in an orderly, uncluttered way, children can find what they need and learn to take care of them. Low bookcases or plastic milk crates make excellent storage places. You can turn a closet into a storage space by installing shelves. Materials can be organized in cans, shoe boxes, and dishpans.

Here are some additional guidelines for organizing and displaying toys and materials:

Display a few carefully selected toys so children can see what is available and choose what they want to use.

Use picture and word labels on containers and shelves. Labels show that everything has a place. They help children find what they want and later participate in cleanup. Make labels by using photographs, drawings, or catalog pictures. Labels should have both pictures and words in lowercase letters. Use one color for English and a different color for the second language that is mostly used in your program. If there are additional languages spoken by children in your program, include words from those languages in a variety of places so children see their home language.

Store toys and related materials where they will be used most often and group materials that are used together. Display them neatly on low shelves, making sure that children can only reach materials that are safe for them to use. Consider where to store materials that only school-age children use, materials that younger children use only with supervision, materials for adult use, and materials with small parts that are a choking hazard for infants and toddlers.

Provide multiples of favorite toys. Young children often want to play with the same toy at the same time as other children in the group, but may not be developmentally ready to share or take turns. Duplicates of popular toys minimize fighting, disagreements, and waiting time.

Rotate materials regularly. As children outgrow or lose interest in toys that have been displayed, exchange them for materials that have been stored away.

Try to incorporate materials that honor diversity. Materials provided should depict people similar to the children in the program as well as the diversity of our society, including people with disabilities. Photographs, books, puzzles, figurines, dolls, music, art supplies, and props for imitating and pretending should portray all people in a respectful and positive way.

Here are some creative ideas that family child care providers have used for storage:

- Stack wooden or plastic food crates, and glue or bolt them together. Paint them and use them as storage shelves.
- Add casters to an empty crate and use it as a movable trunk for dress-up clothes.
- Collect shoe boxes to store scissors, crayons, paper scraps, and puzzles. Be sure to label each box as described above.
- Keep toys with small pieces, such as table blocks, pegs, and figurines, in baskets or plastic containers.
- Store sensory materials, such as sand and rice, in covered containers.

Planning Your Day

Setting up for family child care means both arranging the physical space in your home and organizing your day. Having a consistent but flexible daily schedule, planning ahead, and preparing for the more hectic times of day can make your program go more smoothly.

Daily Events

Daily events in a family child care home include the routines of the day: hellos and good-byes, mealtimes, diapering and toileting, sleeping and resting, and getting dressed. They also include the experiences you offer each day. There will be times when you gather all of the children in your group for a meeting or read-aloud session, and times when you set up a small-group activity. There will also be choice times when children are free to choose where, with what, and with whom to play. You will also have outdoor play whenever weather conditions are not extreme. Of course, every day also includes transitions, the times when children change what they are doing. This section describes the events of the day and offers strategies for promoting children's development and learning during each.

Arrival

Children arrive at different times, and you may be caring for your own children as well as getting school-age children (both your own and the children in your program) to the bus or school.

Plan something interesting for children to do independently. Books, audiobooks, CDs, and table toys are good choices for the early part of the day. Children can use them in the kitchen while others are having breakfast. Some family child care providers have special "hello" toys that they make available only at this time of day.

Include children in setting up for breakfast. This will help make breakfast a relaxed, unrushed time.

Encourage children to begin choice time when they finish eating breakfast and have cleaned up their places at the table. They do not need to wait until everyone has finished before they help clean up and decide what to do.

Make sure school-age children have everything they need to start their school day.

Use arrival time as a learning time. Having a sign-in sheet or creating a "Who's Missing?" chart helps children learn to recognize their names and build other literacy skills.

Group Meetings

At times throughout the day, you may want to gather all the children in your group together for a meeting or read-aloud time. Large-group meetings are most successful when they are kept short, usually 10–20 minutes depending on children's ages. Be ready to stop when children begin to lose interest. An infant may be happy to sit on your lap or play nearby during a group meeting. Allow toddlers to come and go (and maybe come back again). You may see them watching and listening as they play nearby.

Meetings are an important time of the day and provide opportunities for children to experience a sense of belonging to a group. Children can practice developing their communication skills as they express their thoughts, feelings, and ideas and share the work they have been doing. It is also a time for them to get to know their peers and practice their listening skills. Group meetings allow children to discuss topics that are of interest to them and can be a time to solve problems that affect the whole group.

Most providers plan group meetings for the mornings and at the end of the day. You might want to gather the children together at different times, such as to do a read-aloud before rest time, discuss plans or directions for your next activity, or welcome a special visitor. Plan group meetings ahead of time and make sure they are interactive and engaging for the children.

The first meeting in the morning can set the tone for your day. Children come in eager to talk about a variety of things: what happened at home, a new shirt or pair of shoes, or what they are excited to do today. Begin the meeting the same way each day, by singing a good morning song or doing a favorite fingerplay. Routines in the morning give the day predictability and consistency.

A group meeting just before children go home encourages them to reflect on the day's events and provides closure. Briefly review the highlights of the day and what you have planned for tomorrow. End this meeting with a closing routine, such as singing a good-bye song or reciting a favorite rhyme.

Small Groups

In your program, consider planning for and working with small groups of children every day. Small-group time gives you the opportunity to work with different age-groups and are designed to meet particular instructional goals. Small-group times enable you to

- introduce a concept or new materials,
- teach a specific skill or task,
- encourage conversations and the sharing of ideas,
- guide children's thinking and problem-solving by asking questions and posing new challenges, and
- observe individual children and document what they know and can do.

During small-group time, children who are not participating can be assigned a specific task, directed toward some materials to explore, or asked to choose from a variety of quiet activities. Depending on the children's ages, the length of time for small-group experiences will vary. A small-group activity planned to introduce new concepts or materials, address a particular skill, or conduct a focused observation typically lasts 10–15 minutes. Some small-group activities, such as cooking, engage children for a longer period of time and can take place during choice time.

Small groups change and are not the same every day. You might invite children to be part of a group when you want them to practice developing a specific skill. One day you might invite a group of children to explore open-ended materials such as leaves, shells, or buttons. The next day you might read rhyming books with a few children to help promote phonological awareness. In small-group settings, you can address multiple objectives with children at different age-groups and levels.

When planning small-group activities, think about each child's progress in terms of the curricular objectives and form your groups based on their interests, strengths, and needs. *The Creative Curriculum® for Family Child Care Intentional Teaching Cards™* give directions for meaningful, engaging small-group activities.

Choice Time

During choice time, children choose what they would like to do, with whom to play, and what materials to use. Choice time is the most important teaching and learning time of the day. It typically lasts for an hour or more, not counting time to clean up. During this period, most experience areas are available to children: blocks, dramatic play, toys and games, sand and water, library, art, and so on. When children are finished with one experience, they choose another. While all children will not usually be doing the same thing during choice time, you might plan a small-group activity, such as a cooking project in which children take turns participating. You can also conduct a planned literacy or math activity geared to children of a particular age. While children are engaged, you observe them, talk with them about what they are doing, ask open-ended questions, and make suggestions that extend their play and support learning. Here are some strategies for promoting children's development and learning during choice time:

Plan choice time. Use the information about children's interests and skills that you gain by observing them. Think about how choice time experiences help children learn concepts and skills in literacy, math, science, social studies, technology, and the arts.

Help children learn to make choices. During your morning meeting, talk about what you and the children will be doing during choice time that day. A chart with pictures can help children make choices. Give each child his or her name card to place on the chart to show where he or she will play. You can refer to *Intentional Teaching Card* SE23, "Making Choices," for additional guidance.

Allow enough time. Meaningful learning cannot be rushed. A longer choice time lets children become engrossed in what they are doing. They engage in more complex play.

Observe and interact with children during choice time. Pay attention to what the children are doing and decide whether to become involved. Some of your children will be engaged in meaningful play independently. If you decide to interact, ask open-ended questions and make suggestions that extend children's play and support their learning.

Add new materials, equipment, and props as children's skills and interests change.

Consider the individual needs and preferences of the school-age children and set up appropriate activities and choices for them. Some may want to do something very active after sitting for most of the day. Others may want to relax with a book or listen to music. Some may want to start their homework immediately, while others may want a break from academic work first.

Handle cleanup playfully. Make it fun. Adapt a song and sing, "This is the way we wash the paintbrushes, wash the paintbrushes, wash the paintbrushes." Play cleanup games. For example, you might invite one child to put away all of the long rectangular blocks while another puts away all of the cylinders.

Remember that cleaning up is a learning experience for children. They learn math as they match blocks to the shapes outlined on the block shelf labels, and they use literacy skills as they look at the word and picture labels on the various containers for toys and other materials. Cleanup also promotes self-regulation. Children learn to stop one activity and begin another.

Mealtimes

Mealtimes are a great time for children to learn and develop important skills. Children can learn about different kinds of food, how to serve themselves, and how to carry on conversations with others. These experiences at mealtimes help children develop positive attitudes toward food and nutrition. Food is something that often plays an essential role in family life and many cultural traditions, so take some time to talk with families about their children's eating habits and food preferences. Find out which children have food allergies or other health conditions that require certain dietary restrictions, and make sure that everyone in your program is informed.

Here are some additional suggestions:

Be prepared and plan ahead. If you constantly get up from the table to get what you need, children will have a hard time staying seated. To minimize your need to get up from the table, keep extra food and items on a nearby cart. Try to have extra napkins, sponges, utensils, and paper cups.

Invite children to help. Use small plastic pitchers and sturdy serving utensils and serving bowls so children can pour their own beverages and serve their own food. Provide children with plenty of time to practice using pitchers during water play and be sensitive to spills and accidents. Keep a roll of paper towels and a sponge handy to clean up. Children can assist during mealtimes by setting the table, clearing off the table after eating, and emptying food or trash from their plates into a garbage can.

Allow enough time. Some children take their time and are slow eaters. Children should not feel rushed or pressured to start or finish their meal. Make sure there is plenty of time for setting up, eating, and cleaning up. Food should never be used to reward or punish behavior. Making threats to withhold food or giving special treats for good behavior contributes to unhealthy attitudes about food. If you notice a child acting in a challenging way during a meal, the best way to respond is to deal directly with the behavior.

Rest Time

Rest time is an important routine for children and provides time for adults to plan, organize materials, call parents, and get a much-needed break. The length of rest time can vary each day. For children who attend longer than 6 hours, rest helps rejuvenate children for the afternoon. Infants and young toddlers may need more rest than preschool- or school-age children. Even in half-day programs, children can benefit from quiet time or rest time. Because sleeping is often associated with the child's home, some may have a difficult time calming down and sleeping in your home. This response is normal and can be expected. Follow a consistent routine at rest time so children feel secure and comfortable so they can relax. Here are some suggestions for rest time:

Prepare children for resting. Plan a quiet activity to calm the children down before rest time: a story, fingerplay, or quiet song or listening to relaxing music. *Mighty Minutes*® activities such as *Mighty Minutes* 17, "Dream," provide a relaxing transition activity. Children can help set up the cots or mats as they finish eating, toileting, and brushing their teeth. Allow children to bring comforting toys or soft, cozy blankets from home.

Give children time to settle down at their own pace. Sleeping patterns and ways children prefer to fall asleep will be different. It is important to accommodate children with their sleeping patterns to help them feel comfortable and secure. Playing soothing music, rubbing or patting a child's back, or just sitting next to a restless child often helps.

Supervise rest time. Many providers use this time to organize the room, complete their observation notes, and plan. Completing these tasks is fine as long as there is an adult supervising the children at all times. Plan and expect some children to wake up early and for children who do not want to sleep. Allow children who are awake to get up after 15 minutes or so to engage in quiet activities. You might create "nap bags" with quiet activities such as books, puzzles, and small toys or games that children can play on their cots or mats.

Allow children to wake up at their own paces. Children who sleep longer than most children may need additional rest. If you move their cots to an area away from the center of activities, they can get the amount of rest they need. These children may also need extra attention when they get up. If you are struggling with a child during rest time, discuss the situation with the family. Perhaps they can offer some insight or advice that will help you meet the child's needs and make rest time less challenging.

Going Outdoors

Going outdoors involves a lot of details and two transitional times: going out and coming back in. Before you go out, coats, hats, snowsuits, and mittens go on. When you come in, they come off again. Bathroom breaks are a must before and after outdoor time. Here are some strategies to help these transitions go more smoothly:

Store children's clothing near the door and within their reach. Provide coat hooks, cubbies, and storage containers for items that children can put on by themselves.

Encourage older children to help the younger children with their buttons, zippers, or mittens.

Have extra hats, scarves, and mittens available for children who do not have their own.

Help children stay engaged once they have on their outerwear. Choose a *Mighty Minutes®* activity to make the most of time spent waiting. Invite children to sing, do fingerplays, play simple games, or look at books while you help other children get dressed.

Minimize waiting time and do not expect children to line up to go outdoors.

End of the Day

Children are picked up at different times, and some will become anxious when they see other children leaving with their parents. Children, family members, and you are tired. You need to greet and exchange information with families while making sure that children are still engaged. Here are some end-of-the-day strategies that providers have found useful:

Plan some quiet activities for this time of day. Select toys and materials that can be put away easily, such as puzzles, table toys, crayons and paper, books, and CDs. Some providers offer special end-of-the-day toys the same way as they offer morning toys.

Spend a little time alone with each child, talking about the day and plans for the next day, reading a story, or playing together with one of the special toys. Some providers help children dictate a letter to their families about what they did that day.

Schedule additional outdoor time at the end of the day.

Urge parents to try to keep a regular schedule so that their children and you can anticipate their pickup time.

Stay calm and help children stay calm if families are unavoidably late because of heavy traffic or an emergency.

Greet families as they arrive. Talk about their child's day and your plans for the next day. Find out about the family's plans for the evening. Send home a *LearningGames®* activity or a book for the family and child to read together.

Transitions

Transitional times can be stress-free, relaxed and provide endless opportunities for learning and reinforcing concepts and skills. These times can also be confusing and chaotic if not guided or structured properly. If children do not know what your expectations are and have to wait with nothing to do, they may direct their attention to other things that may be distracting or challenging for you to address. Here are some examples of ways to structure transitions so they go smoothly and encourage learning:

Allow sufficient time. Treat all transitions as valuable experiences and allow enough time so children do not feel rushed.

Be clear and consistent. Provide directions that children understand and make sure that your expectations of them are age-appropriate. Keep transitions predictable and the same each day so children learn what to do and how to do it without a lot of adult guidance.

Give children a warning. Before a change takes place, tell the children that it is coming. For example, before cleaning up and washing hands for lunch, you might say, "Five minutes until clean up time. Finish what you are doing, and then we'll help each other put the toys away. It's almost time for lunch."

Meet individual needs. Try to avoid moving all children from one activity to another as a group or requiring children to wait and do nothing until everyone is finished. Give children who have completed their tasks something else to do, such as getting a book from the library or helping clean up, until everyone is ready to move to the next activity.

Give children specific tasks. Make sure your instructions are appropriate for the developmental level of the child. For example, a child who can follow only one-step directions will be confused if, in one set of directions, you tell her to put the balls in the shed, go inside, hang up her coat, and wash her hands.

Be flexible. If possible, give children additional time to complete special projects or activities in which they are particularly involved. For example, give some children time to complete their block tower while others begin cleaning up the art materials or musical instruments.

Use transitions as opportunities to teach. Think of different ways to guide children from one activity to the next in ways that teach and reinforce skills. For example, invite all children who are wearing a specific color or someone who is wearing shoes with laces to go to the next activity. Alternatively, you might say, "If your name begins with the same beginning sound as *cat*, *cap*, *car*, or *coat*, you may choose an experience area now." It is not easy to come up with new ideas every transition, so keep a set of *Mighty Minutes*® cards with you. These cards include many ideas for those moments of the day between activities that make transitions an enjoyable time for everyone.

The Daily Schedule

A consistent daily schedule helps children learn the order of their day. Young children like to know that they can depend on daily routines. This helps them feel secure. When you say things like "We will play outside after your nap," children learn what to expect. The daily schedule helps you organize your day and plan a good balance of routines and experiences for children. It also helps you balance active play and quiet activities.

You may wonder how it is possible to establish a daily schedule when you care for children of varied ages and when each child has different strengths and needs. For example, infants need to eat, be changed, and sleep according to individual schedules. Toddlers and preschool children can play for longer periods of time, but they still need quiet times and naps. In fact, toddlers may need a morning and afternoon nap. School-age children come and go. They may be with you in the morning, go to school, and then return, sometimes full of energy but sometimes as tired as can be.

Here are some guidelines for developing a daily schedule:

Be aware of children's individual needs for sleeping, eating, and toileting. Follow an individual schedule for each infant in your group.

Include time for active play and quiet play.

Offer opportunities for children to play in small groups or by themselves, and time to interact just with you.

If time allows, plan at least an hour a day for choice-time experiences so children can become deeply involved in their play.

Allow enough time for unrushed daily routines.

Schedule time to go outdoors in the morning and afternoon. Allow 40–60 minutes for each outdoor period.

If possible, schedule nap time directly after lunch. Children tend to be sleepy after eating.

Include times to intentionally teach literacy and math skills.

Provide materials for children to use quietly after they nap. That way, tired children can continue to nap while those who are awake play with table toys or look at books.

The "Individual Care Plan" (ICP) forms you complete with the help of each family will also help you create your overall daily schedule (see Chapter 5, "Partnering With Families"). The ICP forms give you information about when each child will arrive and go home (on most days), and when and how long each child naps or otherwise rests. For infants, the plan includes information about when the child eats, sleeps, and has his or her diaper changed. Once you have completed an "Individual Care Plan" form for each child, you can develop an overall schedule for your group that shows the approximate times of daily routines for each child. The actual times may vary from day to day, but a general schedule for routines will help you plan your day. For instance, it will help you avoid planning outdoor time when two infants are sleeping. Post the daily schedule so families can see it and know what to expect.

Sample Daily Schedule

Many factors influence your daily schedule. What time does your program open? When do families arrive? What time do school-age children leave for school? How old are the children in the group? Do you provide meals, or do families send food? What time do school-age children return? What are families' work schedules? How late are you open? Do you provide care around the clock?

The following chart gives suggestions for each daily event, including the approximate amount of time to allow for each. Your schedule will vary according to the needs of the children in your care, but the guidelines will help you think about your day.

Daily Event	What Happens
Preparation, arrival, and choice activities (60 minutes)	Before the children arrive, review the plans for the day. Conduct a quick safety and health check (e.g., refill cleaning and bathroom supplies, clean and sanitize tables, remove any broken or torn materials, check outside for trash). Prepare experience areas (e.g., add new materials, mix paint, collect all materials needed for small groups). Prep and have breakfast ready to serve. Greet each family and child as they arrive. Help children and families store belongings; have children select an activity (e.g., play with toys and games, draw, look at books, listen to recorded stories, or use the tablet or the computer).
Hand-washing and breakfast (30 minutes)	Sit and talk with the children as they eat breakfast. Set up a self-service breakfast for the older children to access. Feed infants if needed and assist young toddlers with eating. After breakfast, check and change infants' diapers and put infants down to nap on their individual schedules. The children can help clean up after breakfast and continue with the independent activities suggested above. School-age children leave for school.
Group meeting (10–20 minutes)	Give a signal to gather the group together. Start with a welcome song, discuss attendance, invite children to share news, lead a *Mighty Minutes®* activity, discuss plans for the day, and introduce any new materials added to experience areas. Keep group time short and stop if you see any children losing interest and who are ready to be more active.
Choice time (70 minutes)	Transition toddlers and preschool children gradually to choice time activities. Guide children in selecting where they want to start and what they want to do. As they finish one experience, they move to another. Some infants and toddlers nap during this time. As infants wake up, you bring them to join the other children's play experiences or put them in a safe place to explore. Some providers offer a special project or work on a study with preschool children during choice time. Observe and interact with individual children to extend play and learning. Also offer small-group literacy and math activities several times a week for preschool children. Give a 5-minute warning before cleanup time and help children put materials away in each experience area.
Small groups (10–20 minutes)	Gather a few children for small-group activities to introduce new concepts and tasks that reinforce skills children are developing. If you have other adults in the room, you may choose to conduct two or more small groups at once. Children who are not participating in a small group can select a quiet activity (e.g., play with toys and games, draw, look at books, listen to recordings, or use the computer). Guidance and ideas for conducting small-group activities is provided in *Intentional Teaching Cards™*.
Hand-washing and snack (15 minutes)	Sit with children and lead discussions about what they learned or noticed during choice time and small-group activities. Try to have a conversation with each child. Those who finish early can help clean up and go to the large-group area and look at books while others are finishing.

Daily Event	What Happens
Read-aloud (15 minutes)	Focus children's attention by beginning with a song or fingerplay that ends quietly. Read a story or discuss a book related to the topic of interest.
Outdoor choice time (1 hour)	Children get ready to go outside. They use the toilet, wash their hands, have their diapers changed, put on outerwear, and so on. Outdoors, children play in your yard or at a nearby playground. Supervise children closely as they use the playground toys and equipment (e.g., swings, climbers, and slides). Interact with and observe children as they dig in the sand, play ball games, ride bikes, blow bubbles, explore nature, and so on. Lead games and activities with movements that promote large-muscle development.
Transition indoors and to group read-aloud time (30 minutes)	Children come inside, use the bathroom, and wash hands, or they have their diapers checked and changed. Children participate actively in a short read-aloud time. They continue looking at books or do other quiet activities as you prepare lunch.
Lunch (30–45 minutes)	Wash hands. Involve children in setting the table and serving food. Sit with the children and eat family style. Eat with the children to encourage conversations about the day's events, the meal, and other topics that interest them. Bring infants' high chairs to the table so they can be part of the social experience. Guide children in cleaning up after lunch, using the toilet or changing diapers, brushing teeth, setting out cots or mats, and preparing to rest.
Read-aloud (15 minutes)	Read a new story or one that the children are familiar with, asking questions and involving children in the reading. Refer to your *Book Discussion Cards*™ or *Book Conversation Cards*™ for read-aloud guidance.
Nap time and afternoon snack (1–2 hours)	Everyone (except perhaps a baby who just woke up) has a rest period. Help children relax and get comfortable. Supervise the rest area at all times. Preschool children who cannot sleep rest quietly and look at books. After resting or playing quietly for 30–40 minutes, they get up and begin a quiet activity. Adjust the length of rest time to suit the age of the group and the needs of individual children. As children wake up, they use the toilet and wash their hands. Infants' diapers are checked and changed. Children eat a snack when they wake up. School-age children arrive and help themselves to a snack. Everyone cleans up from snack and chooses an afternoon activity.
Afternoon choice time and outdoor play (2 hours)	This is time for active indoor and outdoor play for all children, including school-age children. Some family child care providers take children outdoors right after nap time and then come indoors for afternoon experiences. Other providers schedule indoor experiences after nap time and go out in the late afternoon. Some offer a special project or work on a study.

Daily Event	What Happens
Transition and afternoon meeting (15–20 minutes)	Children either clean up from choice time or transition back indoors. Gather children together for group meeting and lead a movement activity, teach children a fingerplay, or involve them in an activity using musical instruments. Invite children to talk about the day, including what they liked and want to remember about it. This is also a great time to talk about plans for the next day.
End of the day	Children go home at different times. Involve the remaining children in quiet activities, such as hanging up their artwork and preparing materials for the next day. Greet families and involve children in sharing the experiences they had that day.
Planning and reflection (As time allows)	Review and reflect on how the day went along with your observations about individual children (skills, needs, and interests). Use this time to work on portfolios and observation notes.

Display a word and picture schedule at children's eye level so they can learn the order of the day. An example is provided earlier in this section.

Children need a daily schedule that is regular enough to be predictable, but flexible enough to meet their individual needs and interests and to take advantage of unexpected opportunities that arise. Although you can follow your schedule in a general way, you will want to use it flexibly. On a beautiful summer day, for example, stay outside longer and have a picnic lunch outdoors. Invite all of the children to join a group movement experience, following a child's lead as she whirls around to lively music. Take advantage of unplanned events that present learning opportunities. A sudden thunderstorm, the mail carrier at the door with a package, or the discovery of a caterpillar in your play yard may interest the children and change your plans and schedule for the day.

Remember, too, that every infant has an individual schedule for eating, sleeping, diapering, and playing. Each infant is fed when hungry, sleeps in a familiar place when tired, and has his or her diaper changed when it is wet or soiled.

Planning Your Week

Weekly planning includes both planning for individual children and planning for your whole group. Taking each child's individual strengths, needs, and interests into consideration as you plan is called *individualizing* care and teaching. With its small group size, family child care provides an ideal setting for individualizing your program.

To plan purposefully, you need to observe children carefully, think about what you learn about each child, and use what you know about their interests and skills. As (or very soon after) you observe children during daily routines and experiences, you write brief notes about what they do and say. For example, if an infant has been having trouble going to sleep, plan to organize his sleeping routine so you can rock him until he is very drowsy. If you and a toddler's family agree that it is time to begin toilet learning, note that on his individual plan.

Here are some examples of questions to guide your observations:

- What materials does the child use?
- How does the child use the materials?
- How long does the child stay engaged in the experience?
- Does the child play with other children or alone?
- What do you notice about his or her social–emotional skills? Physical development? Cognitive and language skills?
- What literacy and math skills are emerging?

When you collect this information, you can use it to offer play experiences that address each child's developmental levels and interests. If your plans are flexible and you feel free to revise them as often as you think best, you are more likely to take advantage of learning opportunities that arise during the course of daily life in the program. If you see that a child is fascinated by different sounds during a musical experience, you can provide homemade musical instruments so that the child can experiment with making musical sounds. To help a child develop fine-motor skills, you can plan experiences such as cutting paper, sifting sand, or playing with lacing and zipping boards. By knowing individual children's abilities in different developmental areas, you can build on and extend their skills. You can consider which *Intentional Teaching Cards*™, *Mighty Minutes*®, and *Book Conversation Cards*™ you will use with the group or with small groups of children.

To help you prepare for each day and respond to children's changing interests and skills, *The Creative Curriculum*® *for Family Child Care* includes two weekly planning forms: the "Child Planning Form" and the "Group Planning Form."

The "Child Planning Form"

The "Child Planning Form" is used on a weekly basis to record current information about each child. It helps you use what you know about each child to plan experiences that support his or her development and learning. Each week, take a few minutes to review your observation notes; examine portfolio samples; and think about recent events, interactions, and conversations with families. Record the most important facts in the "Current Information" section. Then note how you will use this information in the coming week. For example, describe changes you might make to routines and list materials you might introduce to the child.

The following example of a partial form shows current information and plans for two of the family child care children profiled in this book.

The Creative Curriculum® for Family Child Care

Child Planning Form

Week of: 5-15-2017

Child: Jeremy (8 months)	**Child:** Tamika (19 months)
Current information: At breakfast, Jeremy has been picking up pieces of cereal one by one. Karen mentioned that she is going to start using a sippy cup with Jeremy soon, although she's not planning to wean him completely from breastfeeding yet. This week Jeremy has been pushing up on his hands and knees. He looks like he's about to crawl. He squeals with delight every time he finds the rattle that I hide under a towel. We play that game repeatedly.	Current information: Tamika liked listening to and turning pages in *The Itsy-Bitsy Spider* board book. She started to try to do hand motions. At group time, she said, "Sing itsy spider." She played with the animal puzzle but needed a little help getting the pieces back into the right holes. She likes to play with containers in the kitchen while I'm getting lunch ready. She played with the big beach ball in the backyard.
Plans: Coordinate with Karen to add other finger foods for lunch and snack. Play a game where he hands me a clutch ball and I give it back to him. Put a toy a little out of his reach and encourage him to crawl to it. Play toy-hiding games and let Jeremy find them. Hide a toy behind my back and encourage him to creep or crawl to find it.	Plans: Continue rereading the book. Get out the spider puppet to use with the book. Do another simple fingerplay (maybe "Two Little Birds"). Clap while I sing. Look for other songs and fingerplays that have book versions. Put out some more simple puzzles. Let her play with containers and lids in the kitchen.

The "Group Planning Form"

The "Group Planning Form" helps you think about all of the children in your group and decide what changes to make to the environment, daily schedule, and routines. It also helps you determine what activities to offer during the week. It gives you an overall sense of direction for the week and a list of the materials you want to use. To complete the "Group Planning Form," think about the following questions:

- What interests the children now?
- What materials are the children using?
- What skills are the children developing?
- What is working well? What is not working well?

The following example of a completed form shows how to incorporate information from the "Child Planning Form" as you plan your week.

The Creative Curriculum® for Family Child Care

Group Planning Form

Week of: 5-15-2017

Changes to the Environment:

Add a clutch ball and a picture/word lotto game to the toys area.
Add spider puppet, song and fingerplay books, books with simple pictures, and books about exercise to the library area.
Add whistles and kazoos to the music and movement area; add feathers, cotton balls, and pinwheels to the toys and games area.
Set up obstacle course outdoors.
Bring out some simple exercise equipment (light weights, hula hoops, jump ropes).
Add birthday party prop box to the dramatic play area.

Changes to Routines and Schedule:

Add finger foods for Jeremy's meals and snacks.
Add 15 minutes to outdoor time for children to use the bubbles, pinwheels, obstacle course, and exercise props.

Family Involvement:

Coordinate Jeremy's new food with Karen.
Talk to Karen about coming next week to do yoga with the children.
Send home *LearningGames:*
- Jeremy—Game 32, "Sing Together"
- Jorge—Game 88, "In, Out, and Around"
- Nathan—Game125, "Move and Say"
- Rosa Maria—Game 147, "Props for Pretending" (in Spanish and English)
- Keisha—Game 105, "Match and Name Pictures"

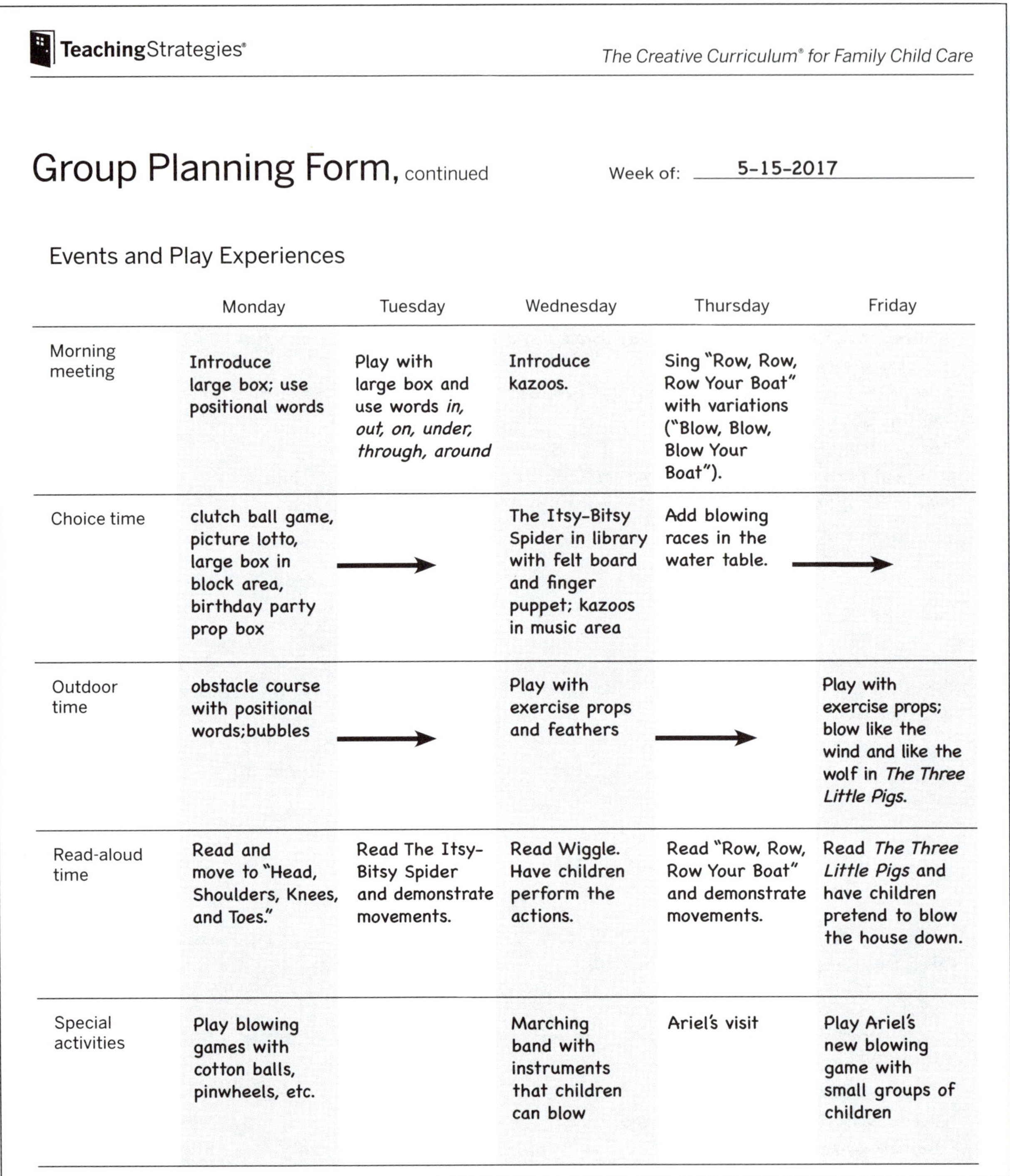

TeachingStrategies® *The Creative Curriculum® for Family Child Care*

Group Planning Form, continued

Week of: 5-15-2017

Events and Play Experiences

	Monday	Tuesday	Wednesday	Thursday	Friday
Morning meeting	Introduce large box; use positional words	Play with large box and use words *in, out, on, under, through, around*	Introduce kazoos.	Sing "Row, Row, Row Your Boat" with variations ("Blow, Blow, Blow Your Boat").	
Choice time	clutch ball game, picture lotto, large box in block area, birthday party prop box	→	The Itsy-Bitsy Spider in library with felt board and finger puppet; kazoos in music area	Add blowing races in the water table.	→
Outdoor time	obstacle course with positional words;bubbles	→	Play with exercise props and feathers	→	Play with exercise props; blow like the wind and like the wolf in *The Three Little Pigs*.
Read-aloud time	Read and move to "Head, Shoulders, Knees, and Toes."	Read The Itsy-Bitsy Spider and demonstrate movements.	Read Wiggle. Have children perform the actions.	Read "Row, Row, Row Your Boat" and demonstrate movements.	Read *The Three Little Pigs* and have children pretend to blow the house down.
Special activities	Play blowing games with cotton balls, pinwheels, etc.		Marching band with instruments that children can blow	Ariel's visit	Play Ariel's new blowing game with small groups of children

Allowing Flexibility

Although you develop a plan for each day, be ready to set your plan aside to address children's needs and to support their interests. If your plans are flexible and you feel free to revise them as often as you think best, you are more likely to take advantage of unexpected learning opportunities that arise during the course of each day. Remember that being responsive is more important than sticking to a plan. Always keep in mind that your positive interactions with children are more important than particular activities. Here are some suggestions for adapting your plans in response to children's needs and interests:

Think about the day before the children arrive. Review your weekly planning forms. Try to imagine how all parts of the day will fit together.

Assess the realities of the day. Will an infant need extra time and attention because she is teething? Did a family bring a bag of fresh apples, tempting you to make applesauce for snack? Is a sudden downpour making you rethink the walk you planned?

Remain flexible and adapt your plans as needed. No matter how carefully you prepare, you must always be ready to change your plans. Perhaps the children will be frightened by an ambulance siren or excited by a helicopter overhead.

Be responsive to individual children's needs and interests. For example, if you know that Tyrone is studying recycling at school, you might consider doing a study about trash and garbage. If Keisha loves to cook and has been sequencing the parts of stories by using felt pieces in the library area, you might help her follow a word and picture recipe.

Plan for bad weather and poor air quality. Even when conditions are too extreme for the children to go outdoors, they still need to move. Find ways to encourage indoor movement on those days. (Do not forget that going outdoors in the snow or a little rain can be fun!)

Expect the unexpected. Backup plans will also help you get through the day when you have to clean up after a sick child or your own child is home sick.

Taking Care of Yourself

Being a family child care provider is both demanding and rewarding work. You work a long, long day. You're awake, thinking about and getting ready for the day long before the first child arrives. When the children leave at the end of the day, you still have family responsibilities. You cook dinner, help your own children with homework, spend time with your spouse and other adults, and find a little time to review how the day went and think about your plans for the following day. Remember to take care of yourself and your family. Only by taking care of yourself will you have the resources and energy to care for the children and families in your program.

Summary

The learning environment is the starting point for implementing *The Creative Curriculum*®. Your family child care home needs to be a place where children feel safe to explore and where providers feel supported and competent. A well-organized environment guides children to make choices, encourages them to use materials appropriately, and teaches them to take responsibility for maintaining their surroundings. A well-structured daily schedule and consistent routines let children know what to expect throughout the day. The plans you create and follow help you feel prepared and intentional about the experiences you offer each child. The next chapter explains the content areas of literacy, math, science and technology, social studies, and the arts.

3

What Children Are Learning

What Children Are Learning

When you work with children under age 5, you witness more learning and development than anyone will observe during any other period of their lives. What and how children learn during this period become the building blocks for school readiness. For older children who spend time with you, learning does not stop when they leave school each day. Just watch a school-age child experiment to see what a caterpillar likes to eat!

Providers who know what kinds of experiences to offer children at each stage of development are able to help children build a strong foundation for lifelong learning. Physical development and aspects of social–emotional, cognitive, and language development are addressed in Chapter 1, Knowing How Children Develop and Learn." This chapter ("What Children Are Learning") will help you understand how to support learning in the content areas. At the end of each content area section you will find the objectives for development and learning that relate to the topic of that section.

The Foundation of All Learning discusses the social–emotional characteristics and approaches to learning that are critical to future school success.

Building Language and Literacy Skills describes how children acquire communication skills. It talks about how they learn to hear, understand, and produce the sounds and rhythms of language; engage with books and stories; and learn about print concepts, cues for reading, letters, and writing.

Discovering Mathematical Relationships discusses children's beginning understandings about numbers and operations, geometry, measurement, patterns, and collecting and organizing information.

Exploring Like Scientists explains that young children are scientists who are curious about the physical and natural world around them. They are eager to find answers to questions, try their ideas, observe what happens, and make discoveries.

Learning About People is social studies: where and how people live, how they get along with others, how they solve problems, and how they lived in the past.

Creating Through the Arts explains that dance, music, drama, and the visual arts are media through which children can express their ideas and feelings. They also learn to appreciate the artistic expressions of others.

Integrating Learning Through Studies describes how you can lead children in studying a topic of interest by helping them raise questions and conduct firsthand investigations.

The Foundation of All Learning

School readiness is an important topic that most families want to investigate before enrolling their child in any program. Children who have strong social–emotional skills and a positive attitude toward learning enter school ready and motivated to learn. The ways children feel about themselves and they ways they relate to others influence what and how they learn. This kind of school readiness begins as early as infancy.

For young children, learning depends on the trusting relationships they build with the important adults in their lives. The research on relationships, especially the importance of secure attachments, finds that young children develop strong social–emotional skills when their needs are met consistently by trusted adults and when they have positive interactions. Children who know that they are safe, loved, and cared for are eager to venture out to explore everything around them. When adults encourage these explorations and share children's excitement about new discoveries, children gain confidence in themselves as learners.

Children are more likely to be successful in learning content if they are building on a solid foundation of social–emotional and general cognitive skills. Children who have developed these skills are more self-confident, deal with stress in healthy ways, are persistent, and solve problems both independently and in groups.

The foundational skills below are essential to providing opportunities for school readiness within your program.

Regulating emotions and behaviors: Without self-regulation skills the ability to learn content can be a struggle. Children who control their impulses develop the ability to manage their emotions and behaviors; cope with strong emotions like anger, fear, and excitement; tolerate frustration; follow limits and expectations; and delay gratification. These important skills are acquired over time and continue to develop well beyond the early childhood years. In order for a child to regulate her own emotions and behaviors, she must 1) develop a basic understanding that actions have a positive or negative response, 2) know what behaviors are considered acceptable, 3) understand that she is capable and in control of her behavior, and 4) know that she is responsible for managing her emotions. When adults are considered trustworthy and responsive to every child's needs and create an environment that is positive and nurturing, children learn how to manage their emotions and regulate their behaviors.

Establishing and maintaining positive relationships: The ability to enter into ongoing social interactions successfully is a needed skill that begins with an infant's early interactions with their primary caregiver and quickly develops into an interest in watching other children play. A child's ability to form positive relationships with adults is essential not only to their social–emotional development but to their academic success (Palermo et al., 2007). The quality of provider–child and parent–child relationships can support or limit children's development and learning (Howes et al., 2008). When children have these strong, positive relationships, their learning and development flourishes. Children with secure attachments have an easier time interacting with peers, forming positive relationships, and being part of a group.

Participating cooperatively and constructively as a member of the group: Being able to successfully function as a member of a group requires an understanding of other people's feelings, personal needs, and desires. When an infant coos or babbles to the children while playing, he is showing an interest in belonging to the group. When a 3-year-old waits patiently for a turn on a trike, she is developing the understanding that other people's needs are important, too. When children are in a group, they gradually learn to cooperate, negotiate, lead and follow, and express their feelings and ideas. By intentionally creating a caring, nurturing, and cooperative environment, you support children in building these needed skills.

Developing positive approaches to learning: When children have a positive approach to learning they are enthusiastic, **and are eager to learn more.** These positive approaches of learning consist of attention and engagement, persistence, problem-solving, curiosity and motivation, flexibility, and inventiveness in thinking, which are all essential to children's future success. They can be easily observed each day when interacting with your children. For example, when watching a 2-year-old build a block structure, you will notice how she stays engaged for a long period of time, and demonstrates problem solving skills as she carefully selects the blocks to use as a base, and uses her curiosity and motivation to manipulate and explore different ways to create her structure. By providing children with age-appropriate challenging tasks or activities, supporting them through the problem-solving process, and offering a variety of opportunities to make choices, you are supporting these positive approaches to learning.

Children easily develop these foundational skills when they are with adults who sincerely care about them, are kind and respectful, take joy in their discoveries, have appropriate expectations, and guide behavior in positive ways. The interactions you have with your children are great opportunities to nurture these skills that are important to children's success as learners.

Building Language and Literacy Skills

Children begin developing language and literacy skills as soon as they are born. When responsive adults talk with them, engage them in conversations, read to them every day, and teach them songs and rhymes, children are eager to communicate in all of the ways that you do: talking, listening, reading, and writing.

In your family child care home, children need many experiences that enable them to acquire vocabulary and other language skills, including discriminating the sounds of language; enjoying books and stories; and exploring cues for reading, print concepts, letters, and writing.

Vocabulary and Language

One of the greatest achievements in the first few years of life is the development of oral language. This includes the ability to understand the words that they hear (receptive language) and to put their own ideas and feelings into words so they can share them with others (expressive language). A child with a good vocabulary and language skills can engage in conversations, share ideas and feelings, ask and answer questions, and work through problems.

People once had the misconception that it was not important to talk to young infants because they might not understand what we say. We know now that adults and caregivers should use every opportunity from birth to talk to infants, describe things, reassure them, and sing to them. Children who have rich, meaningful language and literacy experiences early on usually have twice the vocabulary of children who do not.

Children communicate in a variety of ways. In addition to spoken words, they use other vocal sounds, approximation of words, facial expressions, gestures, and signs. If you care for children whose primary language is not English, you should encourage them to continue using their home languages as they also learn English. Dual-language learners are more likely to become better readers and writers of English if they also understand the words and ideas in their home languages.

Language and Literacy Content	What Providers Can Do	What Children Might Do
Vocabulary and Language (Acquiring new words and using them to communicate)	**Young and Mobile Infants** Explain what you are doing during routines: "I'm going to change your diaper now. You will feel much better when we're finished. First, I'm going to..." Use a high-pitched, sing-song voice and talk face-to-face with infants to get their attention. Speak slowly and use short sentences and simple speech. Describe what a child is doing: "You like those nesting cups, don't you? You like banging them together. Now you're banging them on the floor. Look! You put one inside the other, and it fit!" Converse by listening attentively and engaging in back-and forth exchanges. Use gestures, facial expressions, or other cues to increase their understanding.	**Young and Mobile Infants** Say, "Ma-ma" and "Da-da." Turn her head toward you and smile when you speak to her. Point toward and look at an object he wants, saying, "Uh, uh," then look at you and back at the object, repeating the sound until you hand him what he wants. Understand some words (for example, wave her hands when you say, "Bye-bye," or point to a ball when you ask, "Where's the ball?"). String sounds together and repeat the sounds in a sing-song voice that begins to sound like speech (for example, "Ba-ba-ba-ba-ba-ba-ba-ba"). Use 10–50 single words that refer to people, objects, and events, simplifying some words (for example, *ba* for bottle or *ma* for more).

Language and Literacy Content	What Providers Can Do	What Children Might Do
Vocabulary and Language (Acquiring new words and using them to communicate)	**Toddlers and Twos** Expand on what a child says: When he says, "Go out," you can say, "Do you want to go outside to play?" If she says, "More milk," you can say, "You finished all of your milk. You must have been thirsty. Now you want more milk. Here it is." Share picture books with photos or objects that children can point to and name. Ask open-ended questions to encourage children to verbalize their ideas. If a toddler points to her shoes and says, "New shoes," you can say, "I see that you have new shoes. They are blue. How did you get those shoes?" Listen carefully and wait patiently as children express themselves. Do not rush them. Label storage containers and shelves with picture and word labels. Describe and talk about what children see, hear, feel, taste, and smell, for example, on a walk outdoors.	**Toddlers and Twos** Combine words into two-word sentences (for example, "Daddy car," or "More milk"). Use a questioning intonation to ask questions (for example, "What dat?" or "Go out?" or "Where mommy?"). Use signs or pictures in a sequence to express an idea (for example, baby + cry). Begin to use language to get information by asking who, where, what, and why. Begin to use prepositions (in, on); pronouns (me, he, we); negatives (cannot, do not); and conjunctions (and, but, or). Understand and follow simple directions and stories. Use language to express ideas and feelings: "No go outside." Use 2- to 5-word sentences to communicate. Learn 50–200 words by age 2.

Language and Literacy Content	What Providers Can Do	What Children Might Do
Vocabulary and Language (Acquiring new words and using them to communicate)	**Preschool Child** Engage in frequent one-on-one conversations with children. Provide children with many firsthand experiences and talk with them about what they are doing. Introduce new words by using various strategies: explaining, pointing to pictures, using facial expressions and other body language, or changing your tone of voice. **School-Age Child** Offer a dictionary and help a child look up the meaning of a word. During a read-aloud, have children share and discuss words that they may not know. Provide opportunities for children to talk and share ideas with each other.	**Preschool Child** Point to a toy truck and say, "That's a front loader. It picks up heavy things." Say at group time, "I'm going fishing with my dad tomorrow. We're going to bring fishing poles and a big net and catch 100 fish." Describe a scary dream as a nightmare after the provider reads *There's a Nightmare in My Closet.* **School-Age Child** Ask you for a dictionary to look up an unfamiliar word in a book he or she is reading. Give a lengthy description of something that happened at school. Show you a list of new words she has to learn for homework and ask for your help. Use or experiment with large words in daily vocabulary.

Language Sounds (Phonological Awareness)

The ability to hear and distinguish the sounds and rhythms of language is another important literacy skill. *Sound awareness,* the ability to notice and distinguish different sounds, is the first step in developing phonological awareness. In the first three years of life, the brain is receptive to learning the sounds that make up language. Each language has its own set of sounds that are used to form words. These sounds are called phonemes. When children interact with adults and caregivers who talk, sing, and interact with them, they pay attention to the sounds and rhythms of the languages they hear. Even newborns have the ability to distinguish their mother's and father's voices from other voices or noises they hear around them. You may have noticed that a baby pays particular attention to the type of speech called *parentese.* When you speak slowly in a high-pitched, sing-song voice, face-to-face with an infant, he is likely to pay attention to you long before he understands what you are saying. You may feel a bit silly talking this way, but it is very effective in getting infants to listen to your voice. By around 6 months of age, infants have learned to babble and repeat the sounds that make up the languages they hear. Everyday experiences and routines help children develop sound awareness. When you interact with and talk to children, sing the lyrics of a song or nursery rhyme, and do fingerplays, you are helping children become aware of the sounds and rhythms of their language. When you give children the opportunities to be involved in these types of experiences, they will develop this very important awareness.

During the preschool years, most children develop *phonological awareness,* the ability to hear the small units of sound in spoken language. It includes the various ways oral language can be broken down into parts, for example, words, syllables, and letter sounds. Research has shown the importance of developing phonological awareness during the early years. The skills that make up phonological awareness follow a developmental progression. The simplest level of phonological awareness can be promoted by strategies such as reciting rhymes; calling children's attention to beginning word sounds; and helping children clap out words or syllables of a song, rhyme, or chant. Playing with speech sounds aids in the development of phonemic awareness, which is the most advanced level of phonological awareness. Phonemic awareness is the ability to hear, identify, and manipulate the basic sounds—phonemes—of spoken words (National Institute of Child Health and Human Development, 2007). You can promote the phonological awareness in preschool or school-age children by drawing attention to the separate sounds of spoken language through playful songs, games, and rhymes.

Children who are learning to speak English as a second language are also developing phonological awareness through the activities and experiences that you provide. They may not say English sounds correctly, however. These children are learning how to hear and discriminate the sounds of the English language, so it is important to support (rather than correct) their efforts while you continue to help model correct English pronunciation.

Everyday experiences help children learn about the sounds and rhythms of language and eventually to distinguish among language sounds. Here are examples of what you will observe:

Language and Literacy Content	What Providers Can Do	What Children Might Do
Sounds and Rhythms of Language	**Young and Mobile Infants** Imitate an infant's babbling and encourage her to imitate the sounds you make: "I hear you saying, 'Ma-ma-ma-ma.' Now you're saying it back to me." Recite nursery rhymes, clapping along with the beat: "Patty cake, patty cake, baker's man. Bake me a cake as fast as you can." Talk about the sounds animals make: "What does a cow say? Moo. What does a dog sound like? Woof-woof." **Toddlers and Twos** Sing songs that encourage children to listen for and anticipate an action: "Ring around the rosie... ashes, ashes, we all fall down!" "Open, shut them...but do not put them in." Read stories with rhyming refrains and pause when you get to the rhyming word so children can fill it in: "Brown Bear, Brown Bear, what do you see? I see a red bird looking at..." Play with words: "See you later, alligator," "Let's comb your hair, you little bear."	**Young and Mobile Infants** Recognize his mother's or father's voice before he sees them. Put sounds together ("da-da-da"), listen intently when you imitate them, and then repeat the sounds again and again. Calm when she hears you sing the same lullaby she hears at home. String sounds together in a sing-song voice. Attempt to voice the sounds of animals and things (for example, "baa-baa"; "choo-choo"). **Toddlers and Twos** Repeat familiar phrases from songs and rhymes. Fill in the rhyming word in a predictable refrain when you pause before saying the word. Recognize familiar environmental sounds (for example, a fire truck siren, a chirping bird, a car horn, and the ring of a phone). Play with the sounds of familiar words (for example, "Nanabana"). Repeat words he or she enjoys hearing and saying (for example, "Pop, pop, pop"). Repeat the refrain from a song she has heard many times: "E-I-E-I-O."

Language and Literacy Content	What Providers Can Do	What Children Might Do
Sounds and Rhythms of Language	**Preschool Child** Lead children in singing, saying rhymes, reciting fingerplays, and playing language games. Read books that play with the sounds in words, such as those by Dr. Seuss. Talk about words and language sounds during daily activities (e.g., "Tasheen and Tyrone, your names both start with the same sound, /t/."). **School-Age Child** Display and talk about how words are pronounced, focusing on beginning and ending sounds. Read and help children sound out unfamiliar words. Provide children with poems with rhyming words for children to read.	**Preschool Child** Fill in the missing rhyming word in a phrase. Make up nonsense words or silly names (e.g., Silly Willy and Funny Bunny). Clap as designated words or syllables are said (e.g., clapping twice while saying the name Kelly during the recitation of a rhyme). Notice that several names or other words begin with the same sound (e.g., Jonelle, Juwan, and Jonetta). **School-Age Child** Notice that different words start and end with the same sound. Sound out a written word she does not recognize and sometimes ask you for help. Explore rhymes (for example, say, "I need a word that rhymes with *flower* for my poem.").

Enjoying Stories and Books

Reading books and sharing your pleasure in language and stories are among the most important ways you can help children become readers. Children who regularly hear stories read aloud develop a foundation for literacy, including the motivation to learn to read. This is a key ingredient for children being successful in school. Most children who enjoy being read to develop a love for books that will last throughout their lives, enriching their experiences and stretching their imaginations.

Before an infant can focus his eyes on the pictures, turn the pages, and understand the words you are saying, he can begin to associate books with the pleasant feelings he has when you hold him on your lap and read him a book. Understanding books and other forms of texts also involves learning how to handle books in particular ways, such as holding the book right-side up, progressing from front to back, and knowing book-related words such as author and illustrator. As children get older, you can begin to help them learn about different forms of literature by offering a variety of books and calling children's attention to their particular characteristics.

The Creative Curriculum® provides many additional resources that give children opportunities to read, discuss, and enjoy books. *Book Conversation Cards*™ offer strategies for you to use as you engage children in learning experiences during read-alouds. The cards include age-specific guidance for sharing the vocabulary, illustrations, and activities found in the program collection of *Highlights Hello*™ and *Highlights High Five Bilingüe*™.

Vocabulary and language—Children learn new words as you read and share books about a variety of objects, actions, events, and places. Books for young children contain words that are less commonly heard and often include more complex sentences than the language used in daily conversations. The descriptive language and synonyms for familiar words included in books help further develop children's language skills. Rich vocabularies and background knowledge are essential for children's later comprehension of more challenging school texts.

How print works—Young children learn about print when you point out words and letters, run your finger under print, and discuss what you are doing as you handle and read a book (for example, "Let's turn to the next page"). Children gain the understanding that pictures and print are meaningful and learn that they can manipulate books in different ways to follow a story.

Letters and words—Young children begin to recognize a few letters, typically the first letters of their names and letters in environmental print, such as on signs for restaurants, cereal boxes, toy logos, or the *S* in a stop sign. They may also enjoy finding and talking about the letters in simple alphabet books. Older children begin to recognize beginning letters and are learning how to sound out unfamiliar words.

Comprehension—This refers to understanding what is heard or read. Infants show that they comprehend print when they point to pictures they see in a book. Toddlers begin to relate events in a story to their own lives, and older twos begin to retell stories they are familiar with. Older children who comprehend what has been read aloud may ask questions and make comments about the story or act it out in a play.

Understanding books and other texts—When reading stories to young children, they become aware that stories have beginnings and endings. They begin to understand that "Once upon a time" starts some stories and "The End" is the end of some stories. Understanding books and other texts can also involve learning how to handle books, such as holding the book right-side up; turning pages front to back; and knowing book-related words such as *title*, *author*, and *illustrator*.

Phonological awareness—The types of books you read to children help children gain awareness of the sounds of language. The first step in the development of phonological awareness is discussed in the previous section.

Literacy Content	What Providers Can Do	What Children Might Do
Enjoying Stories and Books	**Young and Mobile Infants** Provide cloth and soft plastic books that young infants can grasp, chew, and manipulate and cardboard books for mobile infants. Hold infants on your lap as you read and show them books with simple, bright pictures. Talk about the pictures. Label pictures a child points to: "That's a bottle, just like yours." Ask the child to find a picture, and ask questions about it: "Does he look happy?"	**Young and Mobile Infants** Snuggle into your lap and watch intently as you turn each page. Point correctly to the picture of a familiar object when you ask where it is (for example, "Where's the dog?" and "Can you show me the baby's eyes?"). Gaze at the bright pictures in a book you are holding or one that is propped up where she can see it. Wave, suck, chew, and manipulate the pages of a cardboard or cloth book. Vocalize as you read a book with simple, repetitive language.
	Toddlers and Twos Let children play with and manipulate the book as you read, and encourage them to help you turn the pages. Encourage children to chime in as you read a predictable book with repeated phrases. Read books to children and tell stories every day, one-on-one and with small groups. Reread familiar books and talk about the different things they notice each time.	**Toddlers and Twos** Make the sounds you have modeled as animal speech or other environmental. Pretend to read the story, talking as if she were reading the text. Make connections between the content of a story and what he sees around him (for example, get a toy truck after seeing a picture of one in a book). Ask you to read a favorite book repeatedly.

Literacy Content	What Providers Can Do	What Children Might Do
Enjoying Stories and Books	**Preschool and School-Age Child** Add storytelling props to the Library area for acting out stories. Omit a word at the end of a sentence when reading a highly predictable book. Ask questions as you read a story to preschool children: "What do you think will happen next?" and "Did that ever happen to you?" Encourage children to recall the important events of a story (e.g., "Do you remember what happened when the wolf blew on the house of straw?"). Provide a variety of age-appropriate fiction and nonfiction books for children to choose from. Discuss books that school-age children are reading to find out what topics they are thinking about and what their ideas are.	**Preschool Child** Anticipate and recite refrains in a familiar book. Listen to a story and ask questions or comment about it. Make up stories with a beginning, a middle, and an end. Select books to look at and read independently. Use books to find answers to questions (for example, to identify a caterpillar found in the yard). Act out a familiar story. **School-Age Child** Seek a quiet place to read a book after school. Read a story to younger children and act out the parts. Use books to do research for homework Enjoy having you read a chapter book to him.

Exploring Writing

Reading and writing go together. A group of letters is a symbol for a word, just as letters are symbols for sounds. Long before children can recognize letters and read or write letters and words, they begin to understand that one thing can represent something else. For example, a picture of a banana represents a real banana, a block can stand for a car, and logos mean a company name or a product.

Children are inspired to write if they often see print, hear it read aloud, and see you writing for different reasons. Young children are fascinated when they see you writing. They want to imitate what you and their families do. At first, they have no idea what you are doing; they just notice that you are holding an object, moving it across paper, and leaving marks. Over time and experience, they start to understand the purposes of writing.

Literacy Content	What Providers Can Do	What Children Might Do
Exploring Writing	**Young and Mobile Infants** Let infants see you writing and talk about what you are doing: "I'm making a list of what I need to buy so we can make me pancakes tomorrow." Use picture and word labels on containers for toys and materials. **Toddlers and Twos** Show and talk about pictures: "This is a picture of your mommy and daddy," and "Can you find the picture of the puppy on this page?" Use picture and word labels on containers for toys and materials. Provide large crayons, water-based markers, paint and brushes, and large chalk for toddlers and twos. Offer plenty of plain paper so they can use these tools to make marks, scribble, paint, and explore writing.	**Young and Mobile Infants** Watch you as you write a note. Make random marks on paper with large crayons. **Toddlers and Twos** Move a paintbrush across a large sheet of paper until it is almost completely covered with paint. Experiment to see what kinds of marks she can make, like lines, dots, zigzags. Make a series of looped scribbles and tell you, "This my mommy." Begin to recognize common symbols in the environment and some letters, especially the first letter in his name. Draw lines and make marks that begin to look like letters. Ask you to write something for her, such as a story or letter that she dictated or her name on a picture.

Literacy Content	What Providers Can Do	What Children Might Do
Exploring Writing	**Preschool and School-Age Child** Talk about features of print while writing with children (e.g., the top-to-bottom and left-to-right progressions). Occasionally run your finger under the words as you read a story. As you write with children, draw their attention to punctuation marks such as periods and question marks (e.g., "I'd better put a period here because it's the end of the sentence."). Post a sign with pictures and words about what to take for snack. Post sign-up sheets for activities. Provide writing prompts for children to work on. Read and ask questions about children's writing (e.g., "What is your story about? Who are the characters? What's going to happen next?").	**Preschool Child** Scribble across a piece of paper, include some letters, and then read aloud what she wrote. Write a sign for a building he made with blocks. Look at an alphabet chart and tell you which letters are in her name. Write his name, using an initial capital and writing the rest of the letters in lowercase. Identify a letter by its name as you read a book together (for example, say, "That is a w," and point to the first letter of each word in the phrase "Wishy-washy, wishy-washy."). Arrange the magnetic letters on your refrigerator to spell her name. **School-Age Child** Write a book review for a homework assignment. Use the computer to write a social studies report. Write a description of a picture. Make signs or write plays.

Objectives for Literacy

Objective 15. Demonstrates phonological awareness, phonics skills, and word recognition

a. Notices and discriminates rhyme
b. Notices and discriminates alliteration
c. Notices and discriminates discrete units of sound
d. Applies phonics concepts and knowledge of word structure to decode text

Objective 16. Demonstrates knowledge of the alphabet

a. Identifies and names letters
b. Identifies letter–sound correspondences

Objective 17. Demonstrates knowledge of print and its uses

a. Uses and appreciates books and other texts
b. Uses print concepts

Objective 18. Comprehends and responds to books and other texts

a. Interacts during reading experiences, book conversations, and text reflections
b. Uses emergent reading skills
c. Retells stories and recounts details from informational texts
d. Uses context clues to read and comprehend text
e. Reads fluently

Objective 19. Demonstrates writing skills

a. Writes name
b. Writes to convey ideas and information
c. Writes using conventions

(The objectives related to language were listed in Chapter 1 "Knowing How Children Develop and Learn" as part of the discussion of language development.)

Incorporating Language and Literacy in Daily Experiences

The chart below gives examples of ways to enhance the experiences you provide for children by including materials that promote language and literacy learning.

Blocks	Dramatic Play	Toys & Games
Provide paper, markers, and tape for children to make signs for buildings. At the children's eye level, hang charts, artwork with captions, and photos that show environmental print.	Offer books and magazines for children to use while playing house. Introduce a variety of purposes for print (e.g., recipes, shopping lists, receipts, greetings, etc.).	Talk about colors, shapes, and pictures in a board game. Provide matching games to promote children's visual discrimination skills.

Art	Sand & Water	Library
Invite children to dictate stories to go with their artwork. Share books about famous artists and their work.	Add literacy props to the sand area, such as letter-shaped molds and toy road signs. Encourage children to describe how the sand and water feel.	Offer an assortment of recommended children's books. Set up a writing area with pens, markers, pencils, paper, rubber stamps, ink pads, envelopes, etc.

Discovery	Music & Movement	Cooking
Offer books about scientific topics (e.g., insects, plants, seeds, etc.). Provide paper and markers for children to record their observations.	Write the lyrics of a favorite song onchart paper. Encourage children to use instruments for sound effects as you tell stories together.	Make recipe cards with pictures and words. Talk about words and letters on the food containers.

Technology	Outdoors
Write and illustrate the steps for using a computer. Use a drawing or simple word-processing program to make a book with children.	Bring colored chalk and other writing materials outside. Have children examine street signs in the neighborhood.

Discovering Mathematical Relationships

Mathematical thinking involves noticing similarities and differences; organizing information; and understanding quantity, numbers, patterns, relative position, and shapes. Learning the concepts and language of math—*more, fewer, smaller, the same as, how many*—gives children a sense of order, a way to make predictions and comparisons, and ways to solve problems.

Children discover mathematical relationships every day when they explore space, compare amounts, and sort and match objects. As Jean Piaget explained, young children need many opportunities to explore and manipulate interesting objects. Lev Vygotsky emphasized the important role of adults who take an interest in what children are doing and who talk with children about their discoveries (Geist, 2003).

To promote children's mathematical thinking, it helps to know which math concepts are basic and what experiences are appropriate. While it may have been a long time since you studied math, you can provide experiences to help children explore numbers and operations, geometry and spatial sense, measurement, patterns, and sorting and classifying (National Council of Teachers of Mathematics, 2000).

Number and Operations

This aspect of mathematical thinking involves learning about and using numbers. Number and operations include

- counting (numbering items in a particular order)
- matching the appropriate number with each of the items being counted (one-to-one correspondence)
- figuring out how many objects are in a group
- comparing groups and figuring out which groups have more and which have fewer

- understanding rank order (first, second, third, last)
- recognizing numerals
- putting groups of objects together to find out "how many in all"
- making equal groups
- understanding that fractions are parts of wholes (for example, halves, thirds, and fourths)

You help children understand number concepts when you use numbers in everyday activities, sing songs that include numbers, invite children to help you set the table, and provide materials for them to explore.

Math Content	What Providers Can Do	What Children Might Do
Number and Operations	**Young and Mobile Infants** Talk with infants and use mathematical language: "You have one nose, two ears, and five fingers." Provide toys that engage children in exploring size, such as nesting cups and stacking rings. Sing songs and fingerplays that use numbers, such as *Mighty Minutes* 21, "Ten Little Toes."	**Young and Mobile Infants** Look at you intently as you put on her socks and say, "Here's one sock for this foot and one sock for your other foot. Two feet, two socks." Smile when you bring more cereal and ask, "Do you want more cereal? You must be hungry!" Reach for more objects with which to play.
	Toddlers and Twos Teach children counting songs, rhymes, and chants (e.g., "One, two, three, four, five. Once I caught a fish alive."). Use comparison words: "You picked out the heaviest rock" and "You're telling me that you want a smaller ball." Count with children, touching each object as you count: "Let's see how many trucks we have. One, two, three, four. We have four trucks." Encourage children to compare quantities: "Do we have more red balls or more green balls?"	**Toddlers and Twos** Stomp around the room, singing, "One, two, one, two, five." Notice that another child has a larger lump of dough and ask you for more. Line up a set of cars and place one block next to each car. Build a tower with blocks and announce, "Mine bigger." Hold up two fingers and say, "I two," when you ask, "How old are you?"

Math Content	What Providers Can Do	What Children Might Do
Number and Operations	**Preschool Child** Use words that indicate order: "Who wants to be first to stir the pancake batter? Who wants to be second?" Count during daily activities (e.g., the number of children who are present, the number of cups needed for each child to have one, or the number of paintbrushes needed so that there is one for each paint container). Encourage children to compare quantities: "Do we have more red caps or more blue caps?" Use numbers as you talk with children about what they are doing: "You had two apple slices, but you ate one. Now you have one slice left," and "You have three markers, and I have three. We have the same number of markers." **School-Age Child** Offer materials and manipulatives that encourage counting and problem-solving. Provide more complex board games. Have them keep score during games or use math games that require keeping score. Encourage children to solve simple word problems.	**Preschool Child** Notice that it takes five scoops of sand to fill a cup. Respond, "I'm four," and show you four fingers when you ask how old he is. Organize a collection of bottle caps by color and say, "There are more white ones." Stand by the door to go outside and say to a friend, "I'm first, so you can be second." Count five children and then set the table with five plates, five napkins, and five forks. **School-Age Child** Use numbers to identify quantities, for example, count 10 plastic bears and write the numeral *10*. Figure out how to distribute 15 marbles to three children so each has the same number of marbles. Keep score in a card game. Solve simple math problems.

Geometry

Geometry involves recognizing shapes, size, position in space, direction, and movement. Children learn about different shapes when you encourage them to create designs with pattern blocks, draw, paint, cut shapes for their artwork, sort blocks as they put them back onto shelves, and identify shapes outdoors. You can help support their understanding by describing the shapes that children create or find inside and outside of your home.

An understanding of geometry and spatial sense begins with recognizing similar shapes and understanding body positions in space. Children gain spatial sense as they become aware of themselves in relation to objects and people around them. They learn about location and relative position (for example, *on, off, under, below, in, out, near, far, next to*). When you are able to describe what children see ("The orange looks like a ball."), you help children develop a basic understanding of geometry. Opportunities to build and explore structures of various sizes enables children to develop an understanding about spatial relationships.

Math Content	What Providers Can Do	What Children Might Do
Geometry and Spatial Sense	**Young and Mobile Infants, Toddlers, and Twos** Play body games such as pat-a-cake and "This Little Piggy." Include materials and toys with different shapes and talk about what they are called. Provide large cardboard boxes and tunnels so children can crawl in and out and over and under and experience different positions in space: inside, outside, over, under. Provide toys that children can manipulate by putting items inside, taking them out, or moving them around. Use positional words: "Let's put all the balls in the box" and "Keisha is sitting next to Tyrone." Talk about 2- and 3-dimensional shapes and link them to common objects: "That block is shaped like a train car." Include materials that children can use to build structures.	**Young and Mobile Infants** Place his hands around a bottle, feeling its shape. Experience being wrapped in a blanket. Run her hands back and forth along the edge of a table. Crawl through a tunnel, enjoying the feeling of being in an enclosed place where she can see out. Bang blocks against different slots in a shape-sorting box until they fall through. **Toddlers and Twos** Try to put a teddy bear into a box that is too small, then find a larger box and put the bear into it. Play with various shapes and put all the cubes in a bucket. Decide whether to go around or through a structure in order to get an object. Learn the names of some shapes (for example, explain, "This is a circle. Like a pizza."). Bend down to look when you say, "Your shoes are under the table."

Math Content	What Providers Can Do	What Children Might Do
Geometry and Spatial Sense	**Preschool and School-Age Child** Talk about geometric shapes as children use unit blocks and pattern blocks. Provide empty boxes, tubes, and containers for children to use for constructions. Take children on a walk to look for shapes in the environment. Describe spatial relationships as children play (e.g., "You're putting the horse inside the fenced area you made."). Help children explore the attributes of shapes by encouraging them to cut food into various shapes, such as cutting toast into triangles and squares. Have a theme for the day: for example, serve circular foods like crackers, cucumber slices, and tortillas. Offer geoboards, tangrams, pattern blocks, and computer programs that involve drawing shapes and manipulating them.	**Preschool Child** Use a geoboard to create geometric shapes with rubber bands. Use empty boxes, tubes, and containers to build an imaginary playground. Say, "I made a square," after putting two triangular blocks together. Show his friend how to build a block boat and tell him, "Do it this way. You need a square block like this. You have to turn it up to make it fit." **School-Age Child** Explore ways to fill an area (for example, use pattern blocks and put 5 diamonds or 10 triangles inside the outline of a flower). Classify shapes by attributes (for example, explain that squares, other rectangles, and diamonds are all four-sided shapes). Use geometric language to describe shapes and spaces (for example, "A rectangle has four lines and four angles."). Build shapes by using other shapes (for example, use two small tangram triangles to build a parallelogram, a square, and a larger triangle).

Measurement

Measuring involves such skills as figuring out how long or short something is or how much something weighs. When young children say things like "I'm bigger than you" or "This rock is heavy. I can't move it," they are using the language of comparison and measurement. They may begin measuring with nonstandard tools, such as a piece of string or their feet, before they use a ruler or tape measure.

Knowing about measurement includes

- describing how long or tall something is, how much a container holds, how heavy an object is, how much space is covered, and much time a task takes;
- comparing two objects by particular attributes (characteristics);
- comparing three or more objects or events and putting them in order; and
- choosing a useful tool to measure something.

As infants, toddlers, and twos examine, play with, and compare toys and objects, their explorations lay the foundation for learning about measurement. By the time they are preschoolers, children begin to show interest in measuring things. At this stage, children will begin learning how to use nonstandard tools, such as a shoe, a piece of string or ribbon, or even their hands, to measure objects. Formal instruction in the use of standard tools such as rulers, scales, clocks, thermometers, and measuring cups is typically taught toward the end of kindergarten and in the primary grades.

Math Content	What Providers Can Do	What Children Might Do
Measurement	**Preschool Child** Use a sand timer or kitchen timer to let children know that there are only 5 minutes left until cleanup. Show children how to use common objects as measuring tools (e.g., "Look. This table is five blocks long."). Ask open-ended questions during measurement activities (e.g., "What is the best way to measure the height of your pumpkin?"). Use words like *before, after, next, yesterday, today,* and *tomorrow* throughout the day (e.g., "Tomorrow is Leo's birthday."). **School-Age Child** Provide standard measuring tools for older children to use, such as scales, rulers, yardsticks, measuring tapes, clocks, timers, and measuring cups. Encourage children to compare: "Are you trying to figure out who is taller? Stand back-to-back so we can compare." Invite children to estimate things like how many cups will fill the bowl or how many steps it takes to walk across the living room. Make picture and word recipes for children to follow. Show how many cups, tablespoons, teaspoons, and so on are needed for each ingredient.	**Preschool Child** Realize that only a short time is left for cleaning up when you turn the sand timer over. Measure a table by using a unit block. Count how many cups of sand it takes to fill a small bucket. Use a piece of ribbon to measure the length of a rug. Compare similar objects: "This leaf is big, but that one is even bigger." Use measurement words and talk about relative amounts: "You are getting so heavy, I can hardly pick you up!" and "This red sock is longer than the blue one." **School-Age Child** Use a ruler to measure earthworms he found in the garden and determine which is the longest. Ask you for a scale to see how much she weighs. Use a tape measure to determine how long a piece of wood needs to be for a project. Look at the clock and tell you the time. Use measurement vocabulary (e.g., inches, centimeters, feet, ounces, pounds). Read and follow a recipe.

Patterns

Patterns are the arrangements of such things as objects, shapes, and numbers in a particular order. As children learn and begin to recognize regular repetitions of basic units, they figure out relationships among objects and begin to generalize about number concepts. For example, there might be a pattern of sizes, such as large, small; large, small; large, small; and so on. There are color patterns, such as red, blue; red, blue; red, blue; and so on. When daily schedules are consistent, children also begin to understand the pattern of daily events: "After my cereal, I get a bottle."

Recognizing patterns is important to science and literacy learning as well as to mathematics. To begin to develop the ability to recognize, continue, or create patterns, young children first need many opportunities to explore and manipulate objects, notice their similarities and differences, and describe their relationships. With guidance, preschool and school-age children learn to recognize and analyze simple patterns, copy them, create them, make predictions about them, and extend them.

Math Content	What Providers Can Do	What Children Might Do
Patterns	**Young and Mobile Infants, Toddlers, and Twos** Provide a variety of different print materials and textured fabrics for infants to touch. Sing repetitive songs, follow consistent routines, and talk about events of the day: "First we put away the toys. Then we can go outside. When we come in, we'll read a story." Use a *Book Discussion Card*™ for guidance on drawing attention to the predictable and repetitive language while reading. Provide toys that children can use to make patterns, such as colored wooden blocks, large beads and laces, and pegboards with large pegs.	**Young and Mobile Infants** Focus on the color or texture of your clothes. Wave her arms in anticipation when you arrive with her bottle. Open his mouth when you lift a spoon toward his face. Stroke a rough carpet and feel a smooth tile floor. Play with nesting cups, trying different sizes until she finds one that fits inside another. Place several small blocks in a line, scatter them around the floor, and then collect and line them up again. **Toddlers and Twos** Use a small cup to fill a larger one with sand. Say a repetitive phrase from a storybook while you read it aloud. Point to the Papa Bear in a book when you ask, "Which bear is bigger?" Line up cars of different sizes, grouping the big ones together and the little ones together. Group all the green pegs together and the red pegs together in a pegboard. Place the graduated rings of a stacking toy in correct order so they all fit on the post.

Math Content	What Providers Can Do	What Children Might Do
Patterns	**Preschool Child** Clap hands and then pat thighs in a pattern (e.g., clap, pat; clap, pat; etc.). Later move in a more complex pattern (e.g., clap, clap, pat; clap, clap, pat; etc.). Draw children's attention to various patterns (e.g., "I see a pattern in your shirt today: red stripe, blue stripe; red stripe, blue stripe…"). Describe patterns you see children creating (e.g., "You made a pattern with the felt pieces: square, triangle; square, triangle…"). **School-Age Child** Encourage children to share the pattern they have created. Help children notice more complex patterns, for example, on a number chart. Continue a pattern that repeats some units and grows, for example, one, two; one, three; one, four; one, five; and so on.	**Preschool Child** Beat a drum as you do (e.g., loudly, softly; loudly, softly; loudly, softly; etc.). Line up small cars in a pattern of red, black; red, black; red, black; etc. Sponge paint a patterned border around a picture. Add interlocking cubes correctly to continue a pattern that they are shown (e.g., white, blue, green; white, blue, green; etc.). **School-Age Child** Describe a pattern made with blocks: "Red, blue, yellow; red, blue, yellow; red, blue, yellow…" Continue counting by fives after you prompt, "Five, ten, fifteen…" Order a group of objects according to size, quantity, texture, or weight (for example, put a collection of balls in order from largest to smallest). Recognize a pattern in a pattern block design and be able to continue it.

Sorting and Classifying

We think mathematically whenever we organize information in a logical way in order to make comparisons. Infants, toddlers, and twos become aware of similarities and differences when they use their senses as they explore their surroundings. They learn by watching, listening, touching, smelling, and tasting. When they manipulate objects, children discover how they are the same and different. When you describe and talk with them about what they are discovering, you help them become aware of different characteristics. Preschool children might make a collection of leaves, sort them into piles according to type, and organize them on a three-dimensional graph to compare how many they have of each type. School-age children are able to conduct surveys and make graphs to show the results. They organize collections into categories and count the number in each set, and they roll dice, make predictions about which sums will occur most often, and record their findings.

Collecting and organizing information includes

- recognizing how objects are the same and different;
- separating objects into groups by features such as size, color, shape, sound, and use;
- presenting information by using objects, drawings, pictures, charts, and graphs; and
- describing information by using words like *more, fewer, the same number as, smaller than,* and *not* (e.g., "The shapes in this group are circles. The shapes in that group are *not* circles.").

Math Content	What Providers Can Do	What Children Might Do
Sorting and Classifying	**Young and Mobile Infants** Meet the daily needs of each individual child and provide them with items they prefer. Provide toys young children can sort and manipulate in a variety of ways. (e.g., soft blocks, balls, etc.). **Toddlers and Twos** Display toys on shelves and in containers labeled with a picture and word and explain how you organized them and why. Point out how children organize things: "You put all the red pegs in a row" and "You lined up all the blue cars." Provide older toddlers and twos with collections that they can organize in different ways, such as large plastic bottle caps, plastic animals, pinecones, and shells.	**Young and Mobile Infants** Recognize your voice and stop crying when he hears you say, "I know you are hungry. I am coming right now with your bottle." Distinguish between familiar and unfamiliar adults. Show a preference for a particular blanket or toy. Pick out all the banana slices from a fruit salad. Collect wooden blocks and put them in a box. **Toddlers and Twos** See a picture of a donkey and say, "Horsie." Place blocks of various shapes into the matching opening in the shape-sorter box. Pick out all of the round beads from a pile of assorted beads. Select all of the cubic blocks from a pile of different shapes and then build a tower.

Math Content	What Providers Can Do	What Children Might Do
Sorting and Classifying	**Preschool Child** Pose a "question of the day" (e.g., "Do you like to wear your shoes during nap time?"). Show children how to make tally marks under the headings *Yes* or *No* on a chart of responses. Graph collections of objects found in experience areas, such as stickers, leaves, rocks, shells, buttons, etc. Ask questions such as "How did you make your group?" and "Where does this one go?" and "How are these alike?" **School-Age Child** Ask questions such as "How did you sort these items?" "What attributes does each group have?" "How many are in each group?" Offer school-age children graph paper to keep track of data and make comparisons. Also encourage them to make predictions, for example, ask, "When you flip a coin 20 times, how many times will it land heads-up?"	**Preschool Child** Sort a collection of dolls into a group with shoes and a group without shoes. Make a graph of a sticker collection, sorting them by color. Make tally marks under the headings *juice* and *milk* on a piece of paper while surveying which beverage children prefer for snack. Draw a picture of each object that floats and each that sinks after testing them in the water table. **School-Age Child** Sort by several attributes (for example, gather a set of large red plastic circles). Use a tally system to find out which ice-cream flavor people prefer: chocolate or vanilla. Observe the weather and collect data about the number of rainy days during a particular period. Predict an outcome and test the prediction (for example, predict which sum of two faces will occur most frequently and then roll two dice 50 times).

Objectives for Mathematics

Objective 20. Uses number concepts and operations

a. Counts
b. Quantifies
c. Connects numerals with their quantities
d. Understands and uses place value and base ten
e. Applies properties of mathematical operations and relationships
f. Applies number combinations and mental number strategies in mathematical operations

Objective 21. Explores and describes spatial relationships and shapes

a. Understands spatial relationships
b. Understands shapes

Objective 22. Compares and measures

a. Measures objects
b. Measures time and money
c. Represents and analyzes data

Objective 23. Demonstrates knowledge of patterns

Incorporating Mathematics in Daily Experiences

Blocks

Suggest cleanup activities that involve sorting by shape and size.

Use terms of comparison when you talk with children about blocks (e.g., *taller*, *shorter*, and *same*).

Dramatic Play

Add telephones, menus, and other items with numerals on them.

As you participate in the children's play, talk about prices, addresses, and times of day.

Toys & Games

Provide collections for sorting, classifying, and graphing.

Have children extend patterns with colored cubes, beads, etc.

Art

Use terms of comparison, e.g., "That piece of yarn is longer than your arm."

Provide empty containers of various shapes for creating structures.

Sand & Water

Provide measuring cups and spoons, and containers of various sizes.

Ask estimation questions (e.g., "How many cups will it take to fill the container?").

Library

Add numeral stamps to the writing area.

Include books about math concepts (e.g., size, number, comparisons, shapes, etc.).

Discovery

Offer tools for measuring and graphing.

Provide boxes and materials for sorting by size, color, and shape.

Music & Movement

Play percussion games that emphasize patterns (e.g., soft, loud, loud; soft, loud, loud; etc.).

Use language that indicates spatial relationships (e.g., *under, over, around, through*).

Cooking

Use a timer for cooking.

Provide measuring cups and spoons.

Technology

Include apps that focus on number concepts, patterning, measurement, shapes, etc.

Offer a drawing program that children can use to create patterns.

Outdoors

Have children look for natural patterns.

Invite children to collect items during a walk and then sort, classify, and graph the items.

Exploring Like Scientists

Science is way of searching for explanations and understandings about the physical and natural world. It involves finding answers to interesting questions: What does this feel like? How does this work? Why did this happen? What would happen if we tried it another way? How can we make this work better?

Scientists are curious and eager investigators. They wonder about what they see, try their ideas, observe what happens, and draw conclusions. A new discovery often leads them to investigate more. Opportunities to explore and investigate are everywhere for those who are interested.

Young children are born scientists. They are curious about everything and want to figure out how things work. Infants explore and investigate their environment by using all of their senses. They spend a lot of time gazing at things, but, once they are mobile, they begin to find out for themselves how things also feel, taste, smell, and sound. Toddlers and twos experiment, to discover to how things work, what things do, and what they can make happen. They are fascinated by animals, people, and how plants grow. Just like scientists, children are curious and want to investigate the world around them.

You don't have to be a scientist, yourself, to be an effective science teacher for young children. Science is all around you. You can take advantage of daily routines and everyday experiences indoors and outdoors to encourage children's curiosity and desire to investigate the world round them. Young children can explore three aspects of science: the physical world, life science, and Earth and the environment.

Physical Science

Physical science involves exploring the physical properties of objects and materials. Young children gather information about the physical world by using all of their senses. When children explore the materials you provide they learn about weight, shape, size, color, and temperature. They discover how things move and change. What does that feel like? Is it slimy, squishy, hard, or sticky? How does it smell? Is it loud or quiet? Is it fast or slow? How can I make it move? Can I roll it, twist it, blow on it, or push it? What will happen if I drop it on the floor? When children make a block ramp to race cars, look through a kaleidoscope, or pick up objects with magnets, they are learning about the physical properties of objects.

Throughout the day, you will see children touching, tasting, smelling, listening to, looking at, manipulating, and experimenting with objects to learn about the physical world around them.

Science Content	What Providers Can Do	What Children Might Do
Physical Science	**Young and Mobile Infants** Place objects in infants' hands that they can hold, manipulate, and mouth safely. Give a baby a spoon to hold while you feed her with another spoon, explaining, "You can hold a spoon, too. Soon you will feed yourself." Offer a basket with colorful fabric scraps of different textures for children to examine. **Toddlers and Twos** Provide collections of objects for children to explore and play with, such as large plastic bottle caps, plastic containers, and balls. Show interest in children's discoveries: "That dough feels soft and squishy, doesn't it?" and "You figured out how to make music with those bells. You just shake, shake, shake them."	**Young and Mobile Infants** Bat at a hanging toy to make it move (testing cause and effect). Raise his bottle and continue sucking when the milk level drops. Pull aside a blanket you used to hide a toy (understand object permanence). Push the buttons on a pop-up toy to make various items appear; then push the items down and start again. Watch you make a soft toy squeak; then squeeze it to reproduce the sound. **Toddlers and Twos** Try using different tools at the water table (e.g., watering cans, cups of different sizes, funnels, scoops, sponges, basters). Use a plastic screwdriver and hammer to turn bolts and pound pegs on a toy workbench. Use words to describe the properties of objects (e.g., *hard*, *smooth*, *heavy*, *sticky*).

Science Content	What Providers Can Do	What Children Might Do
Physical Science	**Preschool Child** Provide tools such as magnets, magnifying glasses, balance scales, pulleys, and mirrors to encourage children's explorations. Use open-ended questions to extend investigations (e.g., "Why does this big toy boat float and the penny sink?"). Describe physical changes that children can observe (e.g., "When the blue paint ran into the yellow paint, it turned green!"). Include old, small appliances or broken toys on a "take apart" table to help children learn how things work. **School-Age Child** Plan activities where children are able to observe change occurring (e.g., freezing water, melting a piece of ice, boiling water to make steam).	**Preschool Child** Use a magnet to pick up metal objects buried in sand. Tilt block ramps more steeply to make cars go down faster. Use a pulley to lift a basket of books into the reading loft. Use a balance scale to weigh rocks and see which are heaviest. Sort a collection of buttons. Take apart an old clock to see how it works. **School-Age Child** Notice that materials can be changed from one state to another: solid, liquid, and gas (e.g., observe frozen and boiling water, or cook an egg and see that it changes from a liquid to a solid). Experiment with the variety of sounds that can be produced by putting different amounts of water in bottles and striking them gently with a spoon. Test objects to see which ones a magnet will pick up and figure out what else the objects have in common.

Life Science

Life science is learning about living things. You are teaching life science when you give children opportunities to care for plants and animals. They want to answer many questions: What does the rabbit like to eat? How loud can I make my voice? What will happen if I pick this flower? Where did all these leaves come from? Which animals lay eggs? What do animals and plants need to grow? How does my body work? What is a life cycle?

Science Content	What Providers Can Do	What Children Might Do
Life Science	**Young and Mobile Infants** Take infants for walks outside in strollers and allow mobile infants to explore outside in safe designated areas. Place multiple plants out of reach, but allow opportunities for infants to look at and enjoy. Have a fish tank with a covered top and place it where children can watch the fish. **Toddlers and Twos** Take children outdoors each day to experience plants and animals, the weather, and an entirely different environment. Point out what is happening: "I see that you are watching the clouds move in the sky." and "What did you find? Those are acorns. Do you want to put them in a bucket?" Provide natural materials for toddlers and twos to explore and examine: shells, pinecones, feathers. Plant a small garden outdoors or have indoor plants that toddlers and twos can help care for. For older toddlers and twos, have a pet like a rabbit or guinea pig that they can help care for.	**Young and Mobile Infants** Discover her toes, grab her feet, and try to put them into her mouth. Touch your mouth as you sing. Play with your hair as you hold him. Look into a tree when she hears birds chirping. Play with the grass and dandelions in the yard. **Toddlers and Twos** Get excited when he sees a squirrel scamper across the yard and up a tree. Pretend that a doll is a baby and take her for a walk in a stroller. Fill a pail with damp sand, pat it down, and turn it upside down to make a pretend cake. Watch a line of ants march along the sidewalk and try to figure out where they are going. Ask you, "Where snow go?" when she sees that the snowman she helped build the day before is no longer there. Help you water the plants in the garden. Hold a carrot for the pet rabbit to eat and say, "He hungry."

Science Content	What Providers Can Do	What Children Might Do
Life Science	**Preschool and School-Age Child** Add living things, such as plants and pets, to your home and show the children how to care for them. Provide markers and paper so children can observe and record the growth of plants that they started from seeds. Talk with children about different kinds of animal homes, such as bird nests, beehives, anthills, etc. Observe and discuss the life cycles of animals, such as butterflies and frogs. Help children learn about health and their bodies every day (e.g., "Can you feel your heart pounding after running so much?" and "The carrots you're eating are very good for you.").	**Preschool Child** Comment, "Our gerbil sleeps all day long. I wonder if it stays awake at night." Water plants after observing that their leaves are drooping. Notice that she breathes more deeply while running on the playground. **School-Age Child** Do research to learn about the habits and needs of a pet in order to care for it. Help you plant a garden, weed it, and keep it watered. Collect insects from the garden, examine them with a magnifying glass, and look them up on the Internet to find out what they are and what they do. Look in a book to identify various birds that he sees in the neighborhood.

Earth and the Environment

For children, this aspect of scientific study involves learning about the immediate environment, including natural materials like rocks, sand, and dirt, and about less concrete things like weather, seasons, the moon, and the stars. Your location will influence the kinds of experiences you can provide for children to explore Earth and the environment. Even very young babies take an interest in their immediate environments.

Science Content	What Providers Can Do	What Children Might Do
Earth and the Environment	**Young and Mobile Infants, Toddlers, and Twos** Play shadow tag. Take children outdoors each day to experience an environment that is entirely different from the inside of your home. Point out what you observe: "See how the wind is blowing the trees? Look, the clouds are moving, too!" Set up a compost system in the backyard and use the material in a garden. **Preschool and School-Age Child** Lead a discussion about things we do during the day and things we do at night. Paint the sidewalk with water and talk about why the water disappears. Talk about the seasons as children notice environmental changes (e.g., "I can tell that fall is here. The leaves are turning red, yellow, orange, and brown." Discuss the weather each day while preparing to go outdoors (e.g., "Rosa, will you please check the outside temperature today? Do we need to wear sweaters?"). Create a large calendar on which children can keep track of the weather. Provide a variety of books that focus on weather, seasons, planet Earth, etc.	**Young and Mobile Infants** Notice moving shadows on the wall or a curtain blown by the wind. Reach toward falling leaves. Pat the water in a puddle. **Toddlers and Twos** Collect sticks in the backyard, put them in a bucket, and then play with them. Pick up a small rock, place it on the slide, watch it roll down, run after it, and then repeat the same actions many times. Fill a bucket with snow, bring it inside, and then wonder why the snow disappears and the bucket has water. Collect vegetable and fruit scraps to put in the compost pile. **Preschool Child** Talk about what they do during the day and at night. Add water to dirt while making mud pies. Paint with water on the sidewalk and notice that the picture soon disappears. Examine a prism and see that colors appear on the wall when he turns it. Create shadows by using a flashlight and various objects. **School-Age Child** Check the weather forecast on the Internet and report it to you. Bring a newspaper story about a tornado and talk to you about what happened and how to stay safe. Suggest that you set up a recycling system. Notice what animals are doing to prepare for winter.

Objectives for Science

Objective 24. Uses scientific inquiry skills

Objective 25. Demonstrates knowledge of the characteristics of living things

Objective 26. Demonstrates knowledge of the physical properties of objects and materials

Objective 27. Demonstrates knowledge of Earth's environment

Incorporating Science in Daily Experiences

Blocks	Dramatic Play	Toys & Games
Talk with children about height, length, width, weight, and balance. Encourage children to investigate momentum, velocity, and incline by experimenting with ramps, balls, and marbles.	Introduce props such as a stethoscope or binoculars. Model hygiene skills by washing dolls and toy dishes.	Talk about balance and weight as children use table blocks. Sort, classify, and graph natural items such as rocks, leaves, twigs, and shells.
Art	**Sand & Water**	**Library**
Describe the properties of materials, especially as they interact (e.g., *wet, dry, gooey, sticky*). Use water and brushes for outdoor painting so children can explore evaporation.	Make bubble solution and provide different kinds of bubble-making tools. Put out magnifying glasses and sifters so children can examine different kinds of sand. Provide a variety of objects for floating and sinking experiments.	Include books about pets, plants, bodies, water, inventions, etc.
Discovery	**Music & Movement**	**Cooking**
Include nontoxic plants that children can care for. Offer tools, such as a magnifying glass and a microscope, that children can use to observe the properties of objects.	Set out bottles with different amounts of water so children can investigate sounds by tapping the bottles. Record children's voices as they sing; play them back for children to identify.	Encourage children to taste, smell, touch, listen, and observe during each step of the cooking process. Discuss how heating and cooling change substances.

Technology	Outdoors
Have children observe cause and effect by hitting a key or touching a screen. Explain how you use technology tools to make a job easier.	Take pictures of a tree or bush that the children see every day and discuss how it changes during the year. Have children listen to their heartbeats or feel their pulses before and after running or exercising.

Learning About People (Social Studies)

Social studies involve learning about people: where and how people live, work, get along with others, solve problems, and lived in the past, and how their lives are shaped by their surroundings. Even infants are social scientists; people are more fascinating to them than any toy or object. They recognize the sound of their parents' voices and can distinguish familiar people from strangers. Before long, they can identify the people in their families and people who belong to other families.

Children often learn about time (history) from daily routines you establish, such as a story before rest time, large-group time after choice time, and outdoor play after lunch. When you talk with them about what they see on a walk with you around the neighborhood, children begin to learn about geography. They notice how people are the same and different. They learn firsthand about responsible citizenship: to make choices, understand different points of view, resolve conflicts peacefully, and treat others respectfully. When you provide props for children to enact experiences at the grocery store or clinic, they gain a better understanding of various jobs and how people do them. This learning will continue outside of your program as they visit the supermarket, the doctor, the hardware store, and the shoe store. As young children develop and learn, they look back on how they have changed and what has changed in their environment.

Social studies topics to be explored with children include

- spaces and geography,
- people and how they live, and
- people and the past.

Spaces and Geography

Geography for young children involves learning about the physical characteristics of the place in which they live. They also discover relationships among places they know well and places that are less familiar. They begin by exploring the environment around them and take an interest in getting from one place to another. A beginning understanding of mapping includes learning how to get to the bathroom and playground and learning which direction to walk on a trip to the store. That kind of learning is supported when children build roads and structures with blocks. Older children learn to make and read maps, understand that a globe represents Earth, can identify continents and countries, and appreciate how physical conditions affect all aspects of life.

These types of questions can help children understand spaces and geography:

- Where do you live? What is your community like?
- How do people move from one place to another?
- Where are you positioned in relation to other people and objects (e.g., near, far, next to, outside, or behind)?
- What is a map, and how can it help us?

Social Studies Content	What Providers Can Do	What Children Might Do
Spaces and Geography	**Young and Mobile Infants, Toddlers, and Twos** Talk to children and explain where they are going and what they are doing (e.g., "I see Jorge climbing under the slide, and Tamika is climbing up on the chair to sit down".) Take children on neighborhood walks and talk about what they see: "We're going to walk two blocks to the library. Let's notice what there is to see." **Preschool Child** Point out the physical characteristics of places you visit: "Look how tall the apartment buildings are on this block." Provide a variety of open-ended materials for children to build roads, houses, etc. Play board games that involve children traveling on a game board, which helps children with directionality and understanding maps. Create an obstacle course for children to follow outdoors. **School-Age Child** Offer older children maps and a globe and talk about various countries. Help school-age children find and use the online mapping games offered by the National Geographic Society.	**Young and Mobile Infants, Toddlers, and Twos** Crawl, walk, climb, jump off, crawl through, and investigate spaces and structures in the environment. Begin to understand words that describe position (for example, next to, on, and under). Point to an apartment building and exclaim, "Mine!" **Preschool Child** Say on a walk, "I know where the mailbox is. It's right around the corner." Build a road with houses and a gas station and explain, "This is a city. The cars go here on the road. If they need gas, they come to the station, and I fill them up." Look at a picture of a bridge and try to make one like it with blocks. Tell you, "We went on a plane to Mexico. It was far away. It was hot there, so we didn't need our jackets. We even went swimming!" Look at a map with you and identify land, rivers, lakes, and oceans. **School-Age Child** Understand that maps are representations of actual places. Draw a map of the neighborhood. Use a globe to find countries. Talk about how climate affects the way people live and what they do. Complete a puzzle of the United States and identify most of the states.

People and How They Live

"People and how they live" is an important aspect of social studies that includes the physical characteristics of people; similarities and differences in habits, homes, and work; family roles and relationships; and the jobs people do. Older children begin to explore these concepts by studying themselves and their families and making connections about how rules in the program help children and providers get along and live together.

These questions about people and how they live will guide you in creating different ways for children to learn these ideas:

- Who are the people in your family? What do they do?
- How do you make and keep a friend?
- What are the jobs of people in our community?
- How do people use money to get goods and services?
- What are some of the rules in your home, school, and community?

Social Studies Content	What Providers Can Do	What Children Might Do
People and How They Live	**Young and Mobile Infants** Keep photographs of children and their family members in an album so children can look at them. Place mirror on the wall near the floor so infants can look at themselves. **Toddlers and Twos** Take walks and talk about the different jobs of people in your neighborhood (for example, mail carrier, firefighter, store clerk, and librarian). Read stories about people and familiar situations, and help children relate the stories to their own lives. Provide paint, crayons, markers, and construction paper in various skin tones. Explain to children what rules are, look like, and why they are important.	**Young and Mobile Infants** Get excited when she sees familiar people enter the room. Gaze at photographs of family members. Watch other babies with great interest. Point to himself in the mirror when you ask, "Where is the baby?" **Toddlers and Twos** Act out family scenarios, such as feeding a baby, pushing a doll in a carriage, or talking on the phone. Understand the sequences of routines (e.g., get a special blanket when you say it is nap time or go to wash hands when you announce that lunch is almost ready). Pretend to be a firefighter when playing with a fire truck. Show an understanding of the rules (e.g., say, "No!" instead of hitting a child who tries to take something from her).

Social Studies Content	What Providers Can Do	What Children Might Do
People and How They Live	**Preschool and School-Age Child** Create rules about getting along and cooperating in the context of real problems as they arise (e.g., "There was a problem at the sand table today. What rule can we make so everyone has enough room to play?") Invite families to participate in the program and share aspects of their cultures. In the dramatic play area, introduce new props that focus on jobs (e.g., jobs in a flower shop, auto repair shop, restaurant, and grocery store). Visit different businesses in the neighborhood and discuss people's jobs.	**Preschool Child** Talk about family members and their roles. Describe their family members' jobs. Point out that their hair color is the same as someone else's. Use a toy cash register to pretend to sell shoes. **School-Age Child** Talk about similarities and differences in family structures, lifestyles, customs, and habits. Recognize the basic needs of all people for food, water, clothing, shelter, and clean air; look at a book about different kinds of homes around the world. Talk about the kinds of work people do and the skills and tools they need in order to perform their jobs.

People and the Past

Learning how people lived in the past is history. Young children focus on the here and now. They do not have much understanding of the concept *long ago*. They learn about time in relationship to themselves, including their daily schedule, what they did yesterday, and what they will do tomorrow. Gradually they come to understand concepts about time and events that have already happened. Consider the following questions as you think about how to teach children about people and the past:

- How do things and people change over time?
- How do we measure time?
- How do we talk about time? How do we talk about the past, present, and future (e.g., by using terms such as *this morning*, *after lunch*, and *tomorrow*)?

Social Studies Content	What Providers Can Do	What Children Might Do
People and the Past	**Preschool Child** Follow predictable routines and a consistent schedule so children learn that there is an order to each day. That helps them begin to develop understandings about time. Ask children to bring in pictures of themselves as babies or to bring articles of their baby clothing. Discuss how the children have changed over time. Use words like *today, tomorrow, yesterday, next week, before*, and *long ago* as you talk about events and routines. **School-Age Child** Invite grandparents to talk about their lives as children. Point out things that change in your neighborhood: "This used to be a small grocery store, but they made it much bigger." Ask children questions that help them recall events: "What did you do last time we had a big snow storm?" Offer school-age children stories about long-ago times and far-away places.	**Preschool Child** Remembers the daily schedule and can tell you what routine comes next. Say, "My daddy took me to the park last weekend." Hold up a baby shoe and say, "My foot used to be this little, but now it's big!" Say, "A long, long, long time ago I went to my Aunt Susie's house." Tell a friend, "I used to live in New York, but now I live here." **School-Age Child** Enjoy reading stories about people who lived long ago and talk about the differences between their lives and people's lives today. Make a book about his life and family, beginning with his experiences as a baby. Interview grandparents about life when they were young and what they did differently from today.

Objectives for Social Studies

Objective 29. Demonstrates knowledge about self

Objective 30. Shows basic understanding of people and how they live

Objective 31. Explores change related to familiar people or places

Objective 32. Demonstrates simple geographic knowledge

Incorporating Social Studies in Daily Experiences

Blocks

Include figurines that represent persons who have various jobs and cultures.

Display pictures of buildings in the neighborhood.

Dramatic Play

Include props related to different jobs and social roles.

Add multicultural dolls and props such as cooking utensils, play foods, empty food containers, and clothing.

Toys & Games

Select puzzles and other materials that show or are related to diverse backgrounds and jobs.

Play board games that encourage cooperation, following rules, and taking turns.

Art

Include paint, crayons, markers, and construction paper of various skin tones.

Encourage children to paint, draw, and write about what they saw on a field trip you took together.

Sand & Water

Invite children to talk about roads and tunnels they make in sand.

Hang pictures of bodies of water (rivers, oceans, lakes, ponds, and streams).

Library

Include books that depict diverse cultures, genders, and persons of different abilities.

Show children how to use nonfiction books, including picture dictionaries and encyclopedias.

Discovery

Set up a recycling area where children sort paper, cardboard, glass, metal, and plastic into bins.

Music & Movement

Show videos that present the languages, music, and dances of many cultures.

Include instruments from different cultures.

Cooking

Encourage parents to bring in favorite recipes.

Visit stores that sell foods of different cultures.

Technology

Encourage children to work together to research a study topic or represent their learning.

Develop rules with the children for using tablets or computers. Post the rules in the Technology area.

Outdoors

Take many trips in the neighborhood and talk about what you see.

Invite children to make maps of outdoor environments by using chalk on concrete.

Creating Through the Arts

The arts involve creating, designing, expressing, and exploring ideas and feelings by using a wide range of materials. Children mix paints; pound and shape molding dough and clay; build structures with blocks, boxes, and construction toys; dance to music; dramatize stories; chant; and sing. The arts are a joyful part of their lives and another language with which to express themselves.

You will find many practical ideas for offering children enjoyable and meaningful experiences in movement, music, drama, and visual arts in *Volume 2: Routines and Experiences.* By offering children open-ended materials and encouraging them to use them freely, you convey that their ideas, feelings, and self-expression are important.

Dance and Movement

When children dance, they express feelings and ideas by moving their bodies in response to music. Most children are able to move easily; you only need to encourage and appreciate their enjoyment. As they get older, they may be a little more inhibited and may prefer to learn and follow a dance routine.

Arts Content	What Providers Can Do	What Children Might Do
Dance and Movement	**Young and Mobile Infants, Toddlers, and Twos** Sing and play music as you hold an infant and dance around the room with a toddler. Teach simple dance routines such as "Head and Shoulders." Incorporate songs that have children jump up and down, clap their hands, or stomp their feet. **Preschool or School-Age Child** Have children move as if they were large elephants, slithering snakes, hopping toads, or graceful birds. Play different kinds of music that inspire children to move quickly (e.g., polkas) and slowly (e.g., lullabies). Provide opportunities for children to dance freely.	**Young and Mobile Infants, Toddlers, and Twos** Rock back and forth to music. Imitate your movements as you dance. Participate in a simple dance routine like "Hokey Pokey." Clap, jump, and stomp feet while listening to music. **Preschool or School-Age Child** Use scarves and streamers as they move to music. Imitate movements of animals they watched on a trip to a farm. Move quickly and slowly as the tempo of a march changes. Enjoy creating her own dance movements.

Music

Music involves combining voices and/or instrumental sounds to create melodies and pleasing rhythms, or just listening to and enjoying different kinds of music. Music can affect both emotions and behavior. A lively melody can inspire children to get up and move around. A quiet, slow melody can calm children and help them relax. Children learn about music by listening and responding to the sounds they hear. To develop an understanding of music, you can provide children with opportunities to play musical instruments, learn and make up songs, listen to recordings, and talk about sounds. When children listen to the different types and genres of music, explore instruments, create melodies, learn songs, and make up songs, they develop an appreciation for music and enjoy different forms of musical expression. You will find a variety of music and movement activities in your collection of *Mighty Minutes*®.

Arts Content	What Providers Can Do	What Children Might Do
Music	**Young and Mobile Infants, Toddlers, and Twos** Record or learn lullabies that are familiar to infants and use them to comfort a child. Rock, pat, and move with children to the beat and melodies of different musical pieces. Sing and teach children different kinds of songs: fingerplays, folk songs, singing games, story songs, songs about routines, and so on. Set up an area where children can explore and play various instruments. **Preschool or School-Age Child** Play different types of music and talk about the differences: classical, marches, folk, rap, etc. Set up an area where children can explore instruments and listen to and create music. Introduce children to simple musical terms (e.g., *tune, melody, rhythm, beat, quickly, slowly, loudly, softly*). Teach children songs that are or might be familiar to their families.	**Young and Mobile Infants, Toddlers, and Twos** Relax against your shoulder as you sing a lullaby. Smile and make noises as you sing an up tempo song. Repeat "row, row, row" as you sing "Row, Row, Row Your Boat." Beat a drum, trying to keep time with the music on a CD. Sing and hum parts of a familiar song as he finger paints. **Preschool or School-Age Child** Make different sounds with musical instruments. Play musical games, such as "The Farmer in the Dell" and "Hokey Pokey." Say, "That music makes me think of a bee." Sing a song on her own. Learn to play a simple song on a xylophone. Identify different instruments by sound (for example, a saxophone, a piano, a guitar). Play an instrument and read music.

Drama

Drama involves telling stories through action, dialogue, or both. By acting out familiar stories and making up their own plays, children develop language skills and an understanding of story structure. They also learn to cooperate with others. Drama is a wonderful way for children to learn and have fun.

Arts Content	What Providers Can Do	What Children Might Do
Drama	**Young and Mobile Infants, Toddlers, and Twos** Play peek-a-boo and other social games with infants. Encourage children to imitate and pretend by playing with them. Provide props for dress-up and dramatic play and take on a pretend role, yourself. Provide puppets and props, and encourage children to put on a play. **Preschool and School-Age Child** Participate in and encourage children's pretend play. Gather props and invite children to act out familiar stories, such as *The Little Red Hen*. Have children show you the facial expressions of people who are happy, sad, angry, tired, excited, or afraid. Provide puppets and props and encourage children to act out a story you read with them.	**Young and Mobile Infants, Toddlers, and Twos** Imitate your gestures as you sing "The Wheels on the Bus." Hold and rock a baby doll. Crawl across the floor and bark like a dog. Pretend to talk on a toy phone. Use different props to to take on pretend roles. **Preschool and School-Age Child** Gather props and act out *Goldilocks and the Three Bears* in the dramatic play area. Show the facial expressions of the troll as they retell *The Three Billy Goats Gruff.* Write and direct a play, giving out parts and explaining what each person should do and say.

Visual Arts

The visual arts include painting, drawing, making collages, sculpting clay or molding dough, weaving and stitching, print making, and more. Children need opportunities to work with different kinds of paint and paper; draw with crayons; cut with scissors; mold dough; and clean up with mops, sponges, and brooms. They learn to use different kinds of materials to express their ideas and show what they know.

Arts Content	What Providers Can Do	What Children Might Do
Visual Arts	**Young and Mobile Infants, Toddlers, and Twos** Collect soft, textured fabrics and crinkled tissue paper for infants to explore. Offer toddlers and twos a variety of art materials: jumbo crayons; large colored chalk; stubby, short handled brushes; paint; molding dough; and finger paint. **Preschool and School-Age Child** Provide materials children can use to represent their ideas (e.g., markers, crayons, paints, paper, clay, collage supplies, wire, wooden scraps). Talk about book illustrations and explain techniques such as torn-paper pictures, watercolors, and pastels. Add mirrors to the art area and encourage children to look at their own facial features when they draw people. Encourage children to draw pictures to show what they have learned.	**Young and Mobile Infants, Toddlers, and Twos** Make crayon marks on a large sheet of paper. Enjoy the feel of finger paint. Roll molding dough and pretend it is a snake. Use large chalk to draw on the sidewalk. Paste collage materials on construction paper. **Preschool and School-Age Child** Create a torn-paper collage after looking at books illustrated by Leo Lionni. Use brightly colored paint at the easel. Try different ways to balance a mobile. Create a get-well card for a friend. Mix blue and yellow paint to make green paint. Draw a picture of something they have learned and describe it. Create a structure using "beautiful junk."

Objectives for the Arts

Objective 33. Explores the visual arts

Objective 34. Explores musical concepts and expression

Objective 35. Explores dance and movement concepts

Objective 36. Explores drama through actions and language

Incorporating the Arts into Daily Experiences

Blocks

Encourage children to build simple scenery, such as a bridge for acting out *The Three Billy Goats Gruff.*

Display posters that include geometric shapes and patterns.

Dramatic Play

Display fine art posters that inspire dramatic play.

Provide props to help children explore different roles.

Toys & Games

Include materials that have different art elements (e.g., games that involve patterns, textures, and colors).

Add building toys for children to manipulate and explore.

Art

Provide a variety of media for children to explore, including clay, paint, collage, and construction materials.

Invite a local artist to share his or her work.

Sand & Water

Display photographs of sand sculptures and encourage children to sculpt sand.

Offer tools for drawing in wet sand.

Library

Talk about art techniques used by illustrators (e.g., Leo Lionni's torn-paper pictures).

Include children's books about famous artwork.

Discovery

Provide kaleidoscopes and prisms and encourage children to draw the designs they see.

Collect natural materials when you take neighborhood walks with the children. Encourage the children to use the materials for collages.

Music & Movement

Provide a variety of musical instruments to explore.

Add scarves, streamers, and costumes to encourage dancing.

Cooking

Encourage children to be creative while preparing their snacks.

Dramatize foods being cooked (e.g., a kernel of corn popping or cheese melting).

Technology

Include drawing and painting apps for touchscreen devices.

Include software that enables children to create music.

Outdoors

Bring art materials outdoors.

Provide streamers and scarves for outdoor dance and movement activities.

Integrating Learning Through Studies

One interesting and exciting way to promote children's learning is through in-depth, long-term studies. This is sometimes called the *project approach.* Studies enable you to involve children of all ages (particularly those ages 3 and older) in a common effort. Studies are a great opportunity to dig deeper into topics that children already have some prior knowledge of and show interest in. Working from children's everyday experiences, their observations, and sources you have available can help you create a several-week study that challenges children to test predictions, find more information, represent their findings, and make conclusions.

Whether you call it a *study* or a *project,* this approach involves organizing learning experiences in a way that is both relevant and exciting for children. In the past, a common approach to tying content learning together was through the implementation of themes. Providers often used the same themes every year, whether or not the topic or experiences suited the interests and skills of their children. Although some worked well and providers were able to implement them in a developmentally appropriate way, other themes were not appropriate for all programs. For example, in Hawaii, an autumn theme in October when the local temperature is 80 degrees and the leaves on the palm trees outside do not change color or fall off—won't be meaningful or relevant to children's experiences.

Building on children's knowledge and interests is a more meaningful way to teach. This approach is referred to as *integrating content studies.* Educators Lilian Katz, Sylvia Chard, and Judy Helm use the term *project approach.* Similar to a study, a project is

> an in-depth investigation of a topic worth learning more about.... The key feature of a project is that it is a research effort deliberately focused on finding answers to questions about a topic posed either by the children, the teacher, or the teacher working with the children (The Project Approach.org, 2014).

The study or project approach involves organizing your program in ways that are relevant and exciting for children. One of the most important features of a study is its support of children's disposition to be curious, explore the world, and make sense of their experiences.

Throughout a study, you can observe and record children's comments and questions, their involvement with materials, and their interactions with each other. To help you reflect on each child's development and learning, you can collect samples, photographs, and photocopies of their work. Remember to date each piece and write a short note about the context in which it was created.

Selecting a Good Study Topic

Begin by selecting a topic that is appropriate for your group. Ideas may originate from any source—you, the children, or the children's families. You might choose to develop a study around something that children are curious about (e.g., balls), a social concern (e.g., food we eat), or an unexpected event (e.g., ants in the kitchen). The best topics are relevant to children's experiences (topics that build on what children already know). The following questions can help you select a good topic:

- Do enough of the children have experience with the topic that they can come up with questions to investigate and explore? Does the topic build on what children already know?
- Can children explore the topic firsthand, in a variety of ways over an extended period? Can objects be manipulated? Can it be explored easily in your home?
- Are resources available, such as people to talk with, places to visit, objects or living things to observe and explore, and books to read? Can children do some research for this topic independently, without depending entirely on you?
- Can the topic be explored in a variety of ways over an extended period?
- Will the topic permit children to learn skills in literacy, math, science and technology, social studies, and the arts in real-life contexts?
- Will the children be able to represent their learning about the topic in a variety of ways (for example, through pretend play, by writing, and by making constructions)?
- Will family members want to get involved with the study? Is the topic respectful of cultural differences?
- Can the topic be explored by children of different ages?

When you decide on a topic that will work, you can begin figuring out how content might be addressed. It is also important to collect resources on your topic and find experts and ideas for informative field trips. You will also want to consider how the children's families can get involved.

The length of time spent on a specific study depends on many factors, including the children's ages and interest level. The length of a study should be determined by how engaged and excited children are about the topic, not by a calendar. In general, a study should be able to maintain children's interest for 3–4 weeks.

Your Teaching Practice

You can brainstorm study topic ideas with other family child care providers and talk about whether those ideas are good topics for studies. Consider any themes that you currently teach or have taught in the past. Is there a way to expand that theme and adapt it into a meaningful study full of hands-on investigations? For example, a theme about apples that includes cutting out and coloring paper apples could be a study in which children learn about each stage of an apple's life cycle, compare and contrast different types of apples, learn whether or not they can grow an apple tree, and investigate what happens to an apple core after it is thrown away.

As an example, the following scenario illustrates why you might conduct a study about trash, garbage, and recycling in your family child care home.

> On a walk one day, the children in your program were fascinated by the garbage truck. They watched and listened as the truck stopped at each house along your street. They imitated the sound of the truck when it crushed the trash. When they came inside, they built houses in the block area and rolled toy trucks in front of them to pick up the garbage. They also brought the wastebaskets from various places in your family child care home into the dramatic play area to dump into a large box. On the next several neighborhood walks, the children became aware of trash on the streets and soon expressed an interest in picking up litter along the route. Coincidentally, Tyrone's class at school began a recycling project. The students, who were learning about which items are recyclable, began collecting newspapers and plastic containers.

You realize that the children are curious about trash and garbage. You review the guidelines to determine whether it would be a good study topic. After saying yes to each of the questions, you decide to build on the children's interest by engaging them in a study. Here is an explanation of how you might help children in your family child care home study trash, garbage, and recycling.

1. **Find out what children already know.** Observe children as they explore objects and pictures related to trash, garbage, and recycling. Listen to what they say. Then ask them, "What do you know about trash and garbage?" Record their answers on chart paper. Post the paper on the wall.

   Here are some examples of what children might say:

   "Garbage is dirty and smelly."

   "Some people throw their trash on the ground."

   "Garbage can make you sick. My mother says not to pick it up."

   "At my house, we recycle newspapers every week."

   "In my house, the sink grinds up the food we don't eat. It makes a lot of noise."

2. **Learn what children want to find out.** During a group time, ask, "What do you want to find out about trash, garbage, and recycling?" Record the children's questions on chart paper and post the paper on a wall. Add to the list as the study progresses.

   Here are some examples of the questions children might ask:

   "Who collects the garbage from this home?"

   "When is the garbage collected?"

   "Where does the garbage truck take the garbage?"

   "Why do we separate newspapers, glass, and plastic?"

   "Why do we put some food in the compost bin?"

   "Why do we put some food in the sink?"

3. **Think about what children can learn.** Consider how you will address literacy, math, science, technology, social studies, and the arts during this study. Here are some suggestions for a study of trash and garbage:

   Literacy

   Keep lists of observations, discoveries, and new vocabulary related to trash and garbage.

   Read and discuss books about trash and garbage, such as *The Day the Trash Came Out to Play*; *The Garbage Truck; I Stink*; *Too Much Garbage*; *Recycle!: A Handbook for Kids*; and *Trash! Trash! Trash!*

   Look for the recycling symbols on empty containers.

   Encourage children to draw, write, and talk about trash and garbage.

   Start a list of the kinds of litter children find, such as paper, plastic, and metal containers or other objects. Add to the list throughout the study.

   Math

   Count, sort, categorize, and measure trash and garbage.

   Take a neighborhood walk and compare the shapes of different kinds of trash and garbage containers in the neighborhood.

   Use a stopwatch to see how long it takes each of several children to move a pile of newspapers into a wagon. Make a chart to compare the children's times.

Science and technology

Encourage the children to examine and compare trash and garbage items by using their senses of touch, smell, sight, and hearing.

Find out how garbage trucks and sink disposals work.

Consult Web sites related to trash, garbage, and recycling.

Social studies

On a trash-collection day in your neighborhood, take the children outdoors to observe the collection.

Visit a recycling center or landfill.

Involve children in picking up litter on neighborhood walks, in local playgrounds, or in other locations. (Provide gloves and bags and make sure that children don't pick up broken glass and other hazardous materials.)

Interview the trash collector. Find out what he or she likes and does not like about the collection job.

The arts

Ask families to save and send in newspapers, clean food containers, and other recyclable materials, and have children use throwaways for art projects.

Reuse clean plastic spoons, foil pans, cardboard tubes, and cans to make musical instruments.

4. **Add materials:**

blocks—toy garbage trucks and small containers to use as miniature trash cans

dramatic play—props to create a recycling center

toys and games—a bottle cap collection for matching and sorting, and a sanitation worker or garbage truck puzzle

art—objects to recycle as collages and constructions, and newspapers for papier-mâché

library—fiction and nonfiction about trash and garbage, and an audio recorder to use during interviews with sanitation workers

discovery—old phones, clocks, and small appliances to take apart

cooking—a container to collect garbage scraps to compost

outdoors—trash collected on a neighborhood walk to use for sorting, counting, and predicting

5. **Investigate the children's questions.** Assign children to investigate particular research questions. Ask open-ended questions to encourage further discoveries. Observe how children are investigating, and suggest additional materials and resources. Decide whether to teach particular content material directly.

   Here is a sample investigation:

   Question: What do we throw away here?

   What To Do:

   Tell children that they are going to sort the trash in one of the trash containers in your family child care home to find out what kinds of things get thrown away. Give children rubber gloves to wear and tell them that it will be a safe task.

   As children take turns taking objects from the trash bag, help them categorize the items. They might sort the trash by its source, such as the kitchen or the art area, or they might sort it according to what it is made of, such as plastic, paper, metal, cloth, rubber, or wood.

   As they sort, place the items on large pieces of paper or cardboard. When the sorting is finished, write the names of the categories on each large background piece and have the children glue the items onto the paper or cardboard. Ask children what they discovered about trash by sorting it. They might notice the least and most common types of trash. They might notice some things that should not have been thrown away at all. They might be surprised at the quantity of trash. Record their discoveries on chart paper.

   Weigh the trash on the bathroom scale. Repeat the task on other days. Encourage children to predict how much the trash will weigh and then to check their predictions.

6. **Involve families.** Families may think that trash, garbage, and recycling is a strange topic, so it is important to help them understand why you selected this topic and how they can participate in this study. You might wish to send a letter to families about the children's study of trash and garbage. Families can do many things at home with regard to this topic, from starting a compost heap to avoiding the purchase of overpackaged goods. This study can really benefit your community!

7. **Celebrate learning.** When you notice that children are losing interest, bring the study to a close. Plan a special way to celebrate the children's learning and accomplishments.
   - Invite families to come for a festive cleanup day at a local park or recreation area. After picking up trash, have a trash-free picnic.
   - Have a "beautiful junk" art show. Everything must be made from objects that would otherwise be put in the trash.

When you conduct studies with preschool and older children, simplify study-related experiences for **toddlers and twos**. Toddlers and twos can participate in a study if they are interested in the topic. Choose simple, appropriate experiences for them that relate to the topic.

- Go on a neighborhood walk to pick up trash. Give toddlers or twos a paper grocery bag and help them collect items during the walk. When you get back home, talk about what they found.
- Let toddlers and twos help you empty the trash containers on trash day and put the containers out for the trash and recycling collectors.
- Go outdoors when the trash collectors come and watch how they put the trash into the truck. Describe what you see.

Offer more complex study-related experiences for **school-age children.**

- Encourage school-age children's interest in the environment and focus on recycling. If you have a garden, start a compost heap and add table scraps.
- Have school-age children learn about recycling in your local community. Where are the recycling sites? What does your community do with the paper and other recyclables that it collects? How much does it collect? Encourage the children to design posters and other marketing materials to encourage their families, neighbors, and schools to recycle.
- Have the children learn about Earth Day and design an Earth Day celebration for your family child care home.
- Investigate how products are packaged in the United States and in other countries. Compare the amount of trash generated. Learn how other communities and countries handle trash, garbage, and recycling.

Summary

This chapter focused on what children are learning and the role you play in building a strong foundation for their success as learners. It showed how the daily routines and the experiences you plan are opportunities for supporting children's learning in language and literacy, math, science, social studies, and the arts. This is not the only chapter where you will find suggestions for promoting children's learning. In *Volume 2: Routines and Experiences*, routines and experiences are discussed in detail. You will find many specific suggestions for selecting materials and for interacting with children as they learn through play. The positive relationships you build with the children in your care are the base from which children acquire cognitive and language skills and knowledge about the world around them. The next chapter, "Caring and Teaching," begins with the important topic of relationships and explains how providers use a range of teaching strategies to guide children's development and learning.

4

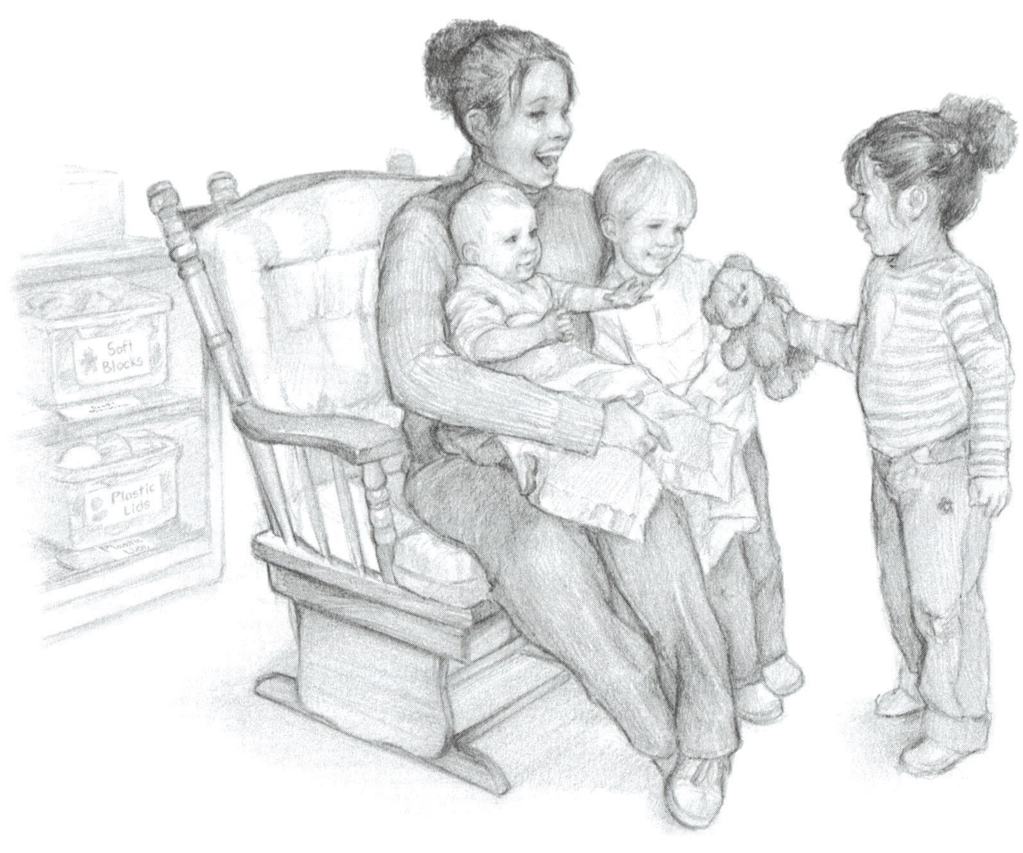

Caring and Teaching

Caring and Teaching

Being a family child care provider is interesting, fun, joyful, challenging, educational, inspiring, and often exhausting. No two days are alike. You soothe a crying baby and walk with her snuggled close to your body, letting her know she is safe. You invite some toddlers and twos to sing a song with you, and then you all shout the lyrics together and dance enthusiastically to the music's beat. Outdoors, you hand a preschool child a magnifying glass, show him how to use it to observe the worms under a rock, lead him through the scientific process, and help him test hypotheses. You sit with a school-age child at the computer, helping her locate Web sites that will assist her in doing her homework. During all of these experiences, you use your skills and knowledge to support children's development and learning.

This chapter explores four aspects of your role as a family child care provider:

Building Relationships explains how to build trusting, responsive relationships with and among children while maintaining positive relationships with the members of your own family.

Guiding Children's Behavior suggests ways to help young children express their feelings and regulate their behavior in age-appropriate but acceptable ways. The section describes positive guidance strategies, including creating rules and helping children learn to solve problems. It also provides information about responding to children's challenging behaviors.

Teaching Intentionally and Responsively presents a range of approaches and strategies to support children's development and learning. Recognizing the many benefits of learning through play, we explain how providers support children's learning in experience areas as well as during routines, transitions, and planned small- and large-group activities. It offers strategies for including all children.

Assessing Children's Learning offers guidance about observing children in order to get to know and understand them. This section explains how and why to observe children, what to look for, how to use the information to guide children's progress, and how to share information with families. There are four steps in the assessment process: 1) observing and collecting facts; 2) analyzing and responding; 3) evaluating; and 4) summarizing, planning, and communicating.

Building Relationships

Young children thrive when they have close, supportive, and trusting relationships with the important adults in their lives. Secure relationships are children's foundation for learning. Their connection with you enables them to feel safe enough to move, explore, experiment, and learn. You are in an ideal position for building positive relationships with children because you care for a relatively small number of them in a warm, comfortable environment.

In *The Creative Curriculum*® family child care home, providers accept and respect each child, seeing all children as skilled and competent learners. Providers support and encourage children to become problem-solvers by exploring and experimenting within a comfortable and safe environment. Mistakes are considered an opportunity to reflect and learn. For these reasons, children can gain a sense of belonging to a community, and that sense gives them the self-confidence to take on new challenges and seek answers to questions. It is important to learn about children's unique qualities—what they like to do, how they learn best, what skills they are developing, what challenges they face, and with whom they like to be. Understanding the whole child can help you appreciate and respect children. That appreciation becomes the foundation for gaining and building upon a child's trust.

Building Trusting Relationships

Every interaction you have with children provides an opportunity to build relationships that enable children to flourish. Here are some strategies for building positive relationships:

Make sure that children's basic needs are met. If you take care of infants, this means feeding them when they're hungry, changing them when their diapers are wet or soiled, and allowing them to rest or sleep when tired. Babies need to be cared for according to their individual timetables, not yours. When infants' needs are met consistently and lovingly, they feel safe enough to explore their environments and get to know new people.

Relate in ways that encourage trust. Be dependable. Let children know that they can count on you. Greet them at the door each morning. Respond promptly to a child who is crying or unhappy. Keep your promises, for example, "Yesterday I said you could help make our snack today. Are you ready?" If you are unable to follow through on a promise for some reason, take time to explain why. Remember that building relationships is a central part of your work. Slow down and spend time with each child individually, every day.

Delight in children's uniqueness and make them feel special. Show that you enjoy every child's company. Laugh with infants as they take their first halting steps, fall, and get up again. Smile at the toddlers' emerging sense of humor. Enjoy the closeness of reading a preschool child's favorite book with her and talking about the story together. Show your pleasure in a school-age child's artistic skills. Express your affection for the children in obvious ways.

Use caring language to let children know that they are respected, understood, and valued. Think about what you say and how you say it. Even infants who cannot yet talk and who do not know the meaning of your words are sensitive to the tone and volume of your voice. Use the children's home languages whenever possible. Practice using caring words and a caring tone. For example, when comforting an upset child, you might say, "You're having a hard time. I can tell by your tears that you're feeling sad. Let's sit together and figure out how to help you feel better."

Be flexible enough to meet individual needs. Offer an infant a bottle when she is hungry, regardless of whether it is the scheduled time for a snack or meal. Give a toddler time to finish his puzzle before you change his diaper. Allow a preschool child to complete the spaceship he is building with blocks, even if it means he will not join you as you read a book aloud to a group. Lengthen your outdoor time to accommodate a game the school-age children are playing.

Offer children opportunities to make decisions as often as possible. Give children clear alternatives when a choice is theirs. For example, at snack time, ask younger children to choose banana slices or graham crackers. Allow a school-age child to decide whether to do homework right away or relax for a while before getting started. This shows that you respect children's ability to make decisions on their own.

Observe children closely to decide how to respond. Give the child your full attention. Observe the child's facial expressions and body language. Learn to distinguish an infant's cries so you will know whether the child needs to be fed or needs a different kind of attention from you. Learn how to calm a toddler who is having a tantrum, how to encourage a preschool child to wait for a turn on the tricycle, and how to listen well when a school-age child confides in you about a problem at school.

Build relationships with all children, including those with whom you do not have an easy rapport. You may find that you do not bond with some children as easily as with others. As a professional, you need to understand why. Perhaps you and the child have very different temperaments or personalities. Analyze your feelings and see whether you can change your own attitude or approach to strengthen your relationship with the child. Look for and focus on the child's positive characteristics. Providers often find reward in developing strong relationships with children with whom they do not have a natural rapport. Make a commitment to relate in a positive way with every child in your care, each and every day.

Know yourself. Having self-awareness allows you to ask yourself questions such as, "Why am I acting this way? Where are these feelings coming from?" For example, you would want to identify and address why you are overly involved with one child or shying away from another. Be aware that your feelings shape the interactions you have with children. Recognizing your feelings will help you in forming positive relationships and responding to children individually. Take time out of your day to take care of yourself so that you will have the focus and energy to give the children your full attention.

Helping Children Get Along With Other Children

The trusting relationships you build with each child form the foundation for their having other positive relationships. When you treat children in loving, respectful, and consistent ways, children feel good about themselves and their ability to relate well with others. Daily life in a family child care setting can be stressful for some children. Interacting with individual children or in a small group will allow you and the children to have a break from the intensity that comes from being part of a large group. One-on-one and small-group interactions also allow you to give individual children attention and provide opportunities to make personal connections that are not as easily made within a large group.

Limit group activities for infants and be flexible when responding to individual needs. Although you still need to respond to individual needs, toddlers in groups can begin following the same schedule for meals and naps. Toddlers and twos tend to start in one group and regroup themselves throughout the day as they play and explore different activities and experience areas.

Preschool and school-age children are often eager to engage with others and enjoy doing so. They likely have the acquired skills needed to enter groups successfully and sustain positive interactions with a small group of children. Children at this age begin to show preferences among their peers and often play regularly with children they prefer. As they begin to learn the skills needed to make and keep friends, they seek out specific children for certain activities.

Here are some strategies for helping children get along with other children in family child care:

Model friendliness. Young children look to you as a model. They are very aware of what you do, what you say, how you react, and what is important to you. The way you interact with each child, with their families, and with visitors to your program teaches children more powerfully than the words you use. As the old saying goes, "Actions speak louder than words."

Coach children. Show children how to join a group activity. "Nathan, you look like you want to blow bubbles with the other children. I bet they do not know that you want a turn. Try saying, 'May I take a turn?' Go ahead and try it."

Acknowledge children's positive interactions. Comment when you see children engaging positively with each other. Acknowledge when a child uses kind words or otherwise comforts another child. For example, if a toddler comes over to you while you are holding a crying baby, you might say, "You are worried about Jeremy, so you touched his face very gently. You're helping him feel better."

Help children understand the consequences of their actions. Some children do not understand that their actions upset other children. By describing their actions in words, you help children become more conscious of and better able to manage their behavior. For example, you might say, "Keisha, did you notice that you were in the other children's way when you sat down in the middle of the floor? Next time, try asking, 'Where can I play so I'm not in your way?' Let's see if that works better for everyone."

Encourage children to help one another or pair them to work on tasks. Throughout the day, offer children opportunities to assist each other by sharing a job. For example, you might have occasions to invite one child to help look for another's missing shoe, or you might ask two children to set the table for lunch.

Talk with children about making friends. You can spur discussions by reading aloud one of the many wonderful children's books about friendship, such as *Will I Have a Friend?* by Miriam Cohen. Children also love homemade books and storytelling about familiar events and people they know, such as a story about one child in the program helping another find his jacket on the playground.

Point out the benefits of caring behaviors. When you tell a child, "Look at Rosa's smile. She is happy because you invited her to make pretend cupcakes," the child experiences the positive consequences of what he does. Over time, children who practice caring behaviors learn to use them more frequently and without adult prompting.

Provide interesting materials and experiences throughout the room. Purposeful room arrangement and thoughtful organization of toys and materials often helps avoid challenging behaviors. When children are given enough space to engage with materials of interest, they are more likely to be content and get along with their peers.

Include equipment and materials that promote interaction and cooperation. Show children how to play with and use materials together. This guidance will help them learn how to share, engage, and learn from one another. Provide large sheets of butcher paper for children to color or paint on together and offer opportunities for group water and sand play. Building with blocks is also a great opportunity for small groups of children to take turns and use the same materials.

Arrange the environment to help children begin to experience turn-taking and sharing. Younger children need opportunities to practice taking turns and sharing within your family child care environment. Placing three chairs around a small table helps children figure out whether there is a place for them or whether they should come back. Providing duplicates of toys can minimize conflict over sharing, which is an unreasonable expectation for toddlers and twos.

Allow children time to work out their differences, but be ready to step in if needed. For example, when you wait a few minutes before stepping in, you give two children a chance to realize that there is room for each of them to sit on the sofa together. Watch carefully and stay close by so you can intervene if you need to.

You may find that some children need more assistance from you than others in making friends. Children who are particularly shy, who are aggressive, or who do not understand other children's emotional cues may need more help from you in building positive relationships. You can help children enter play with others by pointing out how to join the action in a positive way. For example, you might suggest, "When it's time to play outside, let's get your jacket on more quickly so that the other children aren't waiting for you." Model language for children to use when they want to join other children's play, such as saying, "What are you doing? May I help you build a bigger airport?" or "May I help you clean up?" With your guidance, all children can form the positive relationships that are very important to their development and learning in all areas.

Balancing Your Relationships

Providers sometimes worry that their own family will suffer if they get very attached to the family child care children. Indeed, their own children may have moments of jealousy if they see their parent hug and laugh with other children, compliment other children's behavior, and cheer about other children's accomplishments. Even your spouse may experience pangs of jealousy, feeling that you are giving all of your caring and energy to the children in your program.

How do you deal with these feelings, which are quite normal and not unexpected? It often helps to discuss the situation with your family. You need their support and agreement that opening your home and caring for children outside the family is a good decision. It enables you to be at home with your own children and still have a profession. Reassure them that they are your first priority and that the affection you feel for the children in your program is very different from the love you have for them.

Ask your family members to tell you their concerns so that you can address them. Here are a few ideas for helping family members feel more secure.

Invite your family to be part of your family child care program. Family child care is a family affair. Talk about what it means to them to be part of a family child care business. The business will certainly affect their lives. Reassure them that you understand their need for privacy. Help your children see the ways that they benefit from your family child care business, such as having more family income or more children with whom to play. Encourage them to assist as they can, perhaps by helping you put away toys at the end of the day or prepare food for the next day.

Talk to your spouse about his or her role in your family child care program. Will your spouse sometimes be home while children are in your care? If so, does your spouse interact with children easily? How will he or she express affection comfortably? Does your spouse understand positive guidance strategies, and is he or she willing to use them? Would your spouse prefer not to interact with the family child care children but be willing to support you in other ways, such as by grocery shopping, helping with paperwork, repairing broken materials and equipment, cooking dinner, or spending more time with your own children?

Make your family's needs a high priority, especially after program hours. You will undoubtedly have program-related things to do after the family child care children leave. These may include thinking about how the day went, reviewing your plans for the next day, tidying up, and preparing meals for the next day. As important as these tasks are, it is essential for you to have time with your family. Do not forget to line up a substitute for the times you may have to take care of important family business or when you or a family member becomes ill.

Maintain your family's rituals and routines. Put your children to bed and wake them up by following your family's established routines. Give your own children special attention every day, whether by reading a book together, watching a video, or going outside at night to look at the stars.

Help your own children understand how they belong to the family child care program. If your own children are part of the program, help them manage sharing their home, their toys, and their parent's attention with others. For example, if most toys are to be shared, consider letting them choose some that will not be shared. Help them understand that, even though they are your own special children, they must follow the family child care rules during the program's hours.

Take care of yourself. Despite the hard work, being a family child care provider should be an enjoyable experience. Find ways to relax and reduce your stress when you are having a difficult day or things do not go as well as planned. Take a deep breath. Do yoga with the children. Although you strive to be an excellent and professional family child care provider, it is realistic to expect missteps from which you can learn.

Guiding Children's Behavior

Children learn what is expected of them by observing the behavior of the people around them. Children sometimes behave inappropriately when they do not understand or cannot meet adult expectations. Some children act out when forced to follow a schedule that conflicts with their natural rhythms. Others are confused when rules and routines are different from those at home. With adult guidance, children learn to identify their emotions, use language to express strong feelings, and think about consequences before acting.

The words *punishment* and *discipline* are sometimes mistakenly used to mean the same thing. They are actually very different. Punishment is a response to unwanted behavior that places a penalty on the child. Punishment may stop children's negative behavior temporarily, but it does not teach them to manage their behavior themselves. Discipline means directing children toward acceptable behavior so they learn to control their own actions. Because discipline is often confused with punishment, the early childhood field often uses the word *guidance* instead of *discipline.* Guidance requires an understanding of child development.

Age-Appropriate Expectations

Knowing what is reasonable to expect of young children at each stage of development helps you know how to respond to children and how to help them understand their feelings and manage their behavior. Some child behaviors that bother family child care providers are actually signs of typical development.

Infants are just beginning to understand that their actions affect other people. As they explore the world, some of their explorations have results that adults do not want. For example, a 5-month old child who rolls from back to tummy may cry because he cannot turn back over again. Infants do not yet have the ability to think consciously about what they are doing or how to express their feelings in acceptable ways. Until they are at least 6–8 months old, infants cannot control their own behavior. They cry to let you know they are hungry, tired, or uncomfortable. They are not crying to annoy or control you deliberately. Comfort them by meeting their needs consistently and lovingly. That helps them learn how to calm themselves and regulate their emotions.

Mobile infants begin to realize that adults do not approve of some of the things they do. They begin to use your facial expressions, body language, and "I" statements to guide their behavior. A simple smile gives the message, "Yes, it's alright to splash in the tray of water that is on the floor." Even from across the room a frown can stop a child from throwing a block.

Toddlers are full of energy and eager to assert their independence. They are just beginning to use language to express their feelings. They want to do things independently even if they are not skilled enough. They often test limits and enjoy the power of saying, "No!" even to something they want. They can be possessive and are not yet ready to share. They need adults who understand them; have a sense of humor; and who set clear, realistic limits about which behaviors are acceptable and which are not. Positive reminders help toddlers behave appropriately.

Preschool children are beginning to understand the difference between right and wrong. They can use speech to express their feelings and to solve problems, although they do not always do so. They sometimes act out their feelings or lose control without considering the consequences of their actions. Preschool children need understanding adults to help them use speech, not their hands or feet, to express anger and frustration.

School-age children know the differences between appropriate and inappropriate behavior. However, they are still children, and they sometimes act irresponsibly. At about age 8, they gain an understanding of right and wrong. They are interested in rules and are very concerned about whether problems are handled fairly. They are usually able to tell an adult what is bothering them, and they often offer solutions.

Supporting the Development of Self-Regulation

An important part of growing up is learning how to behave in the ways expected by one's family and community. Children need a lot of time and experience to develop self-regulation, which is the ability to manage feelings and control actions. Young children have intense feelings of joy and excitement as well as feelings of anger and frustration. They do not always have the ability to stop and think about how to express their feelings in appropriate ways.

You can do many things to help children develop and practice self-regulation skills.

Give children opportunities to plan and to follow guidelines. Planning helps children decide what they will do and when. Playing games with rules, using recipe cards to cook, and making wooden bead necklaces with color patterns also support children's self-regulation skills.

Encourage children's sense of independence. Invite them to actively participate in daily routines. Give them opportunities to make choices. Organize the environment so children can easily access and put away materials.

Offer acceptable choices. Choices give children some control over events. Offer them many opportunities to make choices about what to play with, wear, and eat so that they know that they have the power to make choices and that their choices are important to you. Make sure that the offered choices are acceptable to you and reasonable for the child. For example, you might ask, "Would you rather play with the cardboard blocks or paint at the easel while we wait for the other children to finish their naps?" Limit choices for very young children to two alternatives.

Give children plenty of opportunities to develop competence. Invite children to help you with everyday chores, such as setting the table, preparing food, and sorting laundry. Label shelves so children can find what they want and help put materials away. Interpret children's cues to understand what they want to communicate, and respond to children's attempts to express themselves.

Understand that young toddlers and most twos are not yet ready to share. This does not mean that they are selfish or mean. Children at this age need time and opportunities to develop a sense of ownership and learn first to take turns and then to share. Encourage and model taking turns and sharing, but do not insist or force children into it. To help avoid conflicts with turn-taking and sharing, provide duplicates of popular toys.

Plan the day so there are no long waits between routines and experiences. If children have to wait for a few minutes, be intentional about what you are doing in those in-between times. Share a *Mighty Minutes®* activity, do a fingerplay, or tell a short story to help pass the time in a meaningful, interesting, and relaxed way.

Read aloud books that are related to self-regulation. Choose time-honored books that children love, such as *Please, Baby, Please*, by Spike Lee and Tonya Lewis Lee; *When Sophie Gets Angry, Really, Really Angry*, by Molly Bang; *I Ain't Gonna Paint No More*, by Karen Beaumont; *Lily's Purple Plastic Purse*, by Kevin Henke; *Quentin Fenton Herter III*, by Amy MacDonald; *The Grouchy Ladybug*, by Eric Carle; and *It's Hard to be Five: Learning How to Work My Control Panel*, by Jamie Lee Curtis and Laura Cornell.

Play games that encourage self-regulation. Is it any wonder that so many children's games provide opportunities for children to practice stopping or controlling an action? Play "Statues" and encourage children to stop moving completely when the music stops. "Simon Says" requires children to think before they act. In the game "Mother, May I?" children must ask for and receive permission before they move.

Using Positive Guidance Strategies

Positive guidance means encouraging appropriate behavior and minimizing unwanted behavior. You can act in two ways: 1) to prevent or minimize problem behaviors, and 2) to teach children which behaviors are appropriate and which are not. Both kinds of adult action help young children learn to manage their feelings and monitor their own behavior.

Children's behaviors are affected by the way the environment is structured, the amount and types of materials, and the daily schedule and routines. These factors are discussed in Chapter 2, "Organizing Your Home and Your Day." You can minimize unwanted behaviors by adjusting daily routines to minimize noise, confusion, and waiting times. Here are some ways to set up your environment and schedule to help prevent unwanted behavior:

Set up an interesting, safe space that children may explore freely without your constantly having to say, "No." Make the environment as free of frustration as possible. Offer toys, games, and puzzles that gently challenge the changing abilities of the children in your care. Always make available some familiar materials that the children have played with successfully.

Establish and maintain a consistent daily schedule. Having a predictable day allows children to know what to expect next and provides the sense of order upon which they depend.

Build cleanup time into the daily schedule. Being able to participate in cleanup without being prompted is a sign of self-regulation.

Allow enough time for children to run and play outdoors. Look at your daily schedule to make sure that children have outdoor play time in the morning and afternoon. If necessary, adjust your schedule to allow more time.

Provide unstructured time for pretend play every day. Researchers have found that one of the best ways for children to develop self-regulation skills is through daily dramatic play. Encourage children to use imaginary props and allow them to play for at least an hour a day.

Anticipate children's physical needs. Serve lunch before children get too hungry. Help children take naps before they become overly tired. Give them a chance to play outdoors when they are ready for active play.

You can also minimize problematic behaviors and encourage acceptable behaviors by the ways you interact with children. Think about the situation from the children's perspective before intervening. For example, be aware that what looks like one child's grabbing a toy from another child may be a game of "taking away and giving back." Here are some additional guidelines:

Remember that children may not be able to use speech to communicate their needs. Learn to read their nonverbal cues, such as gestures. As they grow older, help them use speech by telling them what they might say and encouraging them to practice saying it.

Use simple, clear language to communicate acceptable behaviors. For example, explain, "You may use the crayons on the paper, but not on the wall." Let your facial expression and tone of voice emphasize your message.

Acknowledge children's positive behavior by describing their actions when they show self-control. For example, say, "You let Jorge finish the puzzle before you tried doing it."

Be specific. Avoid giving empty praise. Instead of telling a child, "Good job," encourage him by explaining exactly what he did and why it is appropriate. For example, explain, "You put your dirty dishes in the sink. Now I'll be able to wash them quickly. When everyone helps clean up, it makes lunchtime more pleasant for all of us."

Tell children what they may do, rather than what they may not do. For example, say, "If you want to listen to music, please put on the headphones. The children near you are trying to look at books, so they need the room to be quiet."

Acknowledge children's feelings and help children express them appropriately. For example, explain, "I know that you are angry. That's okay, but people must not hit each other. When you feel angry, say 'I'm mad.' Then I will help you."

Share your feelings about particular behaviors. For example, explain, "When you hit other children, I feel worried."

Use the word *no* sparingly. Save this for dangerous situations so it will be effective.

Model appropriate behavior by being kind and respectful at all times. For example, ask, "Will you please help me carry these extra scarves outside? That way, if anyone gets cold, no one will have to go back indoors to get one. Thank you very much."

Learn what comforts each child. Be sensitive to cultural differences. Offer hugs and cuddles to children who are comfortable with them. If you or particular children are uncomfortable with cuddling, find other ways to express your caring. You might comfort a child by getting down on his or her level, by making eye contact, by singing, or by simply sitting near a child without actually touching. Some children look forward to a "high five" or bumping fists. Be aware that families express affection in different ways, and that, just because a particular way is different, it can be as warm and nurturing as another way.

Use your sense of humor. You can use humor to deflect tension, energize a child, and win his cooperation. For example, you might ask, "Will you please help me pick up these puzzle pieces? A tornado must have come through here while we were in the bathroom."

When you take a positive approach to guiding children's behavior, you help children learn self-control, solve problems on their own, and treat others with kindness and respect.

Your Teaching Practice

Take time to review the positive guidance strategies used within your program and the social–emotional *Intentional Teaching Cards*™ included related to guiding children's behavior.. What strategies do you already use that have proven successful with some children? Are there any listed that are new or that you don't often use? Select one of the strategies to focus on this week and use it several times in a variety of situations with different children. Take time to write down a few notes to reflect on how it is working. Were there times when the strategy was more successful than others? Do some children respond to it more positively? Why do you think the children responded that way? Share your successes and challenges with a parent or colleague.

Developing Rules

Rules and limits help both caregivers and children agree on what behavior is acceptable. You can involve children in setting general rules. When children help set the limits, they are more likely to understand, remember, and follow them. Allowing children to become involved in creating and determining rules can be a powerful way to encourage them to share responsibility and become part of your family child care community. After helping establish rules, children are more likely to understand and follow them. You can lead children throughout the rule-making process by first discussing the importance of rules and then helping them verbalize their own ideas. Preschool and school-age children should understand the concept of staying safe, and safety is the most important topic to address when discussing and making rules. Younger children, however, need clear, age-appropriate limits and an adult close by at all times to communicate which behaviors are acceptable and which are not.

Prior to meeting with children about rules, consider which behaviors are the most important to you. Remember that rules should be worded positively. It may be helpful to think about categories before thinking about specific rules. Consider these categories:

- maintaining physical safety
- respecting the rights of others
- not hurting others' feelings
- caring for the family child care home and materials

Using the categories as guidelines, you might then develop four simple rules like these:

- Be safe.
- Help each other.
- Be kind to others.
- Keep our home neat.

The "big rule–little rule" strategy found on *Intentional Teaching Card* SE15, "Big Rule, Little Rule," can help children remember and apply the general rules in a particular situation. To guide a child's behavior, state one of your four main rules (the big rule) and pair it with a very specific behavior that you want to encourage (the little rule). Here are some examples:

- Be safe. Keep your bottom in the chair when you are sitting.
- Be kind to others. Sit on the floor so everyone can see the book.

To begin the process of setting rules, talk with children about the consequences of their behavior. For example, ask, "What might happen if someone squirts water on the floor?" Children can point out that someone might fall. Responding to this, you might tell them that there is a need for a rule to "Keep water where it belongs. Keep it in the sink, in a tray, or in a tub."

Post the rules where you and the children can see them. Remind children about the rules and review them regularly. As children develop, they can handle more choices, more activities, and more responsibilities. In response, you will need to review and revise the rules in your home. It is also all right to individualize rules and limits to meet a child's needs. "If you do not want to join us in reading a book, you may do puzzles or draw a picture." When a rule does not prove effective, ask children if they know what the problem might be. You may be surprised by how they think about and try to problem-solve when they are part of a community that respects and listens to their ideas.

Teaching Social Problem-Solving Skills

Conflicts and disagreements are a normal part of life in family child care, so it is helpful to encourage preschool and school-age children to solve problems on their own. Children will need social problem-solving skills throughout their lives. By teaching children problem-solving skills, you let them know that you think that they are able to solve problems and that you expect them to take responsibility for doing so. It also helps keep conflicts from getting worse. Take the opportunity to teach problem-solving skills each time a conflict comes up.

Handling Problems Among a Few Children

1. Help the children calm down.

2. Identify the problem.

3. Help the children generate possible solutions.

4. Review the solutions and help the children choose one.

5. Check back.

Young children typically fight over actions or things. You will hear them say, "Mine," "He took my book," or "She pushed me." If possible, try to step in before a conflict escalates. As soon as you hear voices getting louder, move closer to the children involved. Once a conflict happens, the following steps can be taken to resolve it:

Help the children calm down. When children become upset, the first step is to defuse the situation. You might suggest a cooling-off time or describe what you think the children are feeling so that they know they have been heard and that you consider their concerns valid: "I noticed that you are upset and having a hard time waiting for your turn. It can be very hard to wait. It makes you feel frustrated. Let's take some time to calm down. Take a few deep breaths."

There are techniques that can be used to help some of your children calm down. It is a good idea to review your social–emotional *Intentional Teaching Cards*™ regularly so that you have a range of strategies in mind when needed. For example, taking deep breathes, counting slowly, and using positive self-talk: "Be calm. I can handle this." You can teach these techniques during group time when no one is upset or angry and children are likely to be more receptive. When stressful situations arise, you can remind children to use the techniques you talked about during group time.

Another approach is to establish a calm-down place in your home where children can relax or take a break. A calm-down place can be a positive alternative to acting out or losing control during a conflict. This designated space is not the same as a time-out chair in a corner. Rather, a calming space can be a cozy seat by a window, in your family child care library, or a listening or computer area. This area should contain comfortable furniture, like a rocking chair, beanbag chair, couch, soft rug, or pillows. Just flopping onto a beanbag chair, curling up with a book, staring at tropical fish, or listening to a favorite song can be calming.

In the beginning, you may have to guide the children you feel will benefit from going to a calming space. The main goal for children is to recognize when they have strong feelings and acknowledge when they need a break in a calm and quiet space. This way, children can become increasingly responsible for their own personal feelings and behavior.

Identify the problem. Most childhood disagreements and conflicts originate from confusion or misunderstandings. These situations can often be addressed and discussed when children have calmed down. Give every child the opportunity to speak and share their side. The goal is to have all the children who are involved in the conflict listen to one another. Like adults, children listen when they feel heard and understood:

"We need to hear what both of you have to say. Tell us what happened, Tyrone. When you are finished, then it will be Keisha's turn to talk...Did you hear what Tyrone said, Keisha?... Do you need to hear it again?...Do you have something you would like to say to him?"

Remaining calm and neutral is very important, even when you might have a strong opinion. Evaluate the situation by listening and paying attention to what the children have to say. Repeat what the children say so they have a chance to correct any misunderstandings:

"I hear you saying that. . ."

"You're saying. . ."

"You're feeling. . ."

Have children restate what they heard. A hug or pat on the back might reassure some children but not all. Open-ended questions encourage children to give their explanation or views on the situation: "What do you think happened? What made Keisha upset?"

It might be helpful to identify a special space or table for conversations like these. Children will then know where to go to work out their problems.

Generate solutions. After the children have identified their problem, encourage them to think about some possible solutions. You can begin this process by asking questions: "What can we do to solve our problem? Do you have any ideas? Would you like to share?"

If the same conflict happened recently or you talked about a similar situation during group time or after a read-aloud, you can encourage the children to remember the solutions they came up with then: "Remember when. . . Think about what you did then and see if that helps you solve your problem now."

If children do not remember, you may have to propose some ideas or ask questions to help children come up with solutions:

"What do you think would happen if. . .?"

"What do you think about. . .?"

"Would it help if we. . .?"

The goal is for children to come up with as many solutions as possible. One suggestion for encouraging many solutions is to give neutral responses to children's ideas by saying, "That's one idea. What's another?" This can help you avoid making premature judgments.

Review solutions and choose one. Remind the children of their ideas and ask their opinion on what idea would be most effective. Begin by listing the children's ideas. Then ask, "What solution do you think would work best? Do you think this solution would be fair to all of you?"

The goal is to choose a solution that the children who are involved can live with and for all children to feel that their needs are being met.

Check back. When a solution has been decided upon, check with each child to see how it worked for them. If the solution has proven ineffective, the children will probably reach out to you. Explain that they are experimenting to find the best solution, just as scientists do. At a group meeting you might invite them to share what happened and talk about their decision.

Responding to Challenging Behavior

While positive guidance sets a tone for managing children's behavior, it does not always prevent challenging behavior. This is especially true if you have toddlers or young preschool children in your program who have a developmental need to test limits—and your patience! They want to be independent, but they still haven't mastered the skills they need to do things on their own. This is a normal part of development, and your role is to support their skill development. The way that you respond to children can send a message to everyone in the program. It is important to be aware of the things you say when dealing with challenging behaviors. Imagine how children would feel when hearing statements like these day after day.

"Stop! Didn't I tell you not to do that?"

"I don't care what happened, you are both sitting out."

"You know better than that! You should know the rules."

"Why can't you all get along?"

"Instead of going outside, you need to sit in the time-out chair and think about what you just did!"

Statements like those make everyone tense and do little to help children change their behavior. Most likely they reflect an adult's frustration at being unable to establish control in the group. The better alternative is to have a repertoire of strategies for dealing with challenging behaviors.

Common Challenging Behaviors

Testing limits, physical aggression, biting, temper tantrums, and bullying are the most common challenging behaviors experienced by child care providers. Many of them struggle with these behaviors on a regular basis. Unfortunately, some children have personal experiences with violence or neglect, and their behavior is often reflective of those types of experiences.

The most important message for the children to understand is that your family child care environment is a safe place. Step in immediately when witnessing behavior that could injure someone. Be aware that challenging behavior is an opportunity to for you to set and explain limits to clarify the behaviors you find acceptable and the ones you do not.

Here are some suggestions on how to deal with challenging behaviors in a firm and positive way:

Testing limits is one of the ways children discover how much power they have and the kind of authority with which they are dealing. Some children test limits repeatedly and need adults who understand why they do it.

Physical aggression includes such behavior as hitting, scratching, and kicking. This type of behavior must be stopped immediately. The aggressor and the victim need to be addressed directly. Intervene by placing yourself at the aggressive child's level. Clearly explain the rules forbidding aggressive behaviors. "Tamika, stop now! You may not hurt others." Attempt to involve the aggressor in comforting the child who was hurt. This is a technique that can help the aggressor make connections between their actions and pain the victim is experiencing: "Please get a tissue right away so Jorge can wipe the tears off his face."

If an aggressive child loses control of her actions, you may need to hold her until she can calm down. If another adult is available, ask her to attend to the hurt child. Children often feel scared and sometimes embarrassed when they lose control; holding them can help the child feel safe because you have taken charge of the situation. A few minutes may be required for the child to calm down. Then you will have the opportunity to talk about what happened: "Do you want to talk about what made you feel so angry? I could see that you were upset." Remind the child that you care and want to listen to her feelings. Give an adequate amount of time for the child to recover prior to discussing alternative ways to handle anger and frustration.

Biting is common in groups of young children. It is always upsetting and can be frightening for children, families, and providers alike. Like other forms of aggression, it must be stopped immediately. State the rule you have about not biting and being kind to others. Involve the child who did the biting in comforting the one who was bitten, and talk about what caused the problem.

Refuse the idea that biting a child back teaches a child what it feels like to be bitten. That strategy only reinforces aggression. Instead, think of a way to redirect the child's energy and attention positively. When a child has great difficulty controlling the urge to bite, it may help to provide something that may be bitten (e.g., a clean washcloth) until the child learns to control this behavior.

If a child bites often, talk with family members to find out whether the child bites at home. Purposefully observe the child to see if you can determine what might be the cause of the problem. Create an action plan that can help prevent the behavior, for example, by intervening before the child reaches the biting frustration level. Observe, anticipate, and give alternatives to redirect biters before they reach their target!

Temper tantrums are a way that children express their frustration or anger by crying, screaming, and kicking. Tantrums occur when children have strong feelings that they cannot express through words. It is important to react quickly when a child is having a tantrum to protect the child as well as the people who are close by. Children may calm down when you hold their arms and legs down firmly, while others want you near them to hear your calm voice. Once a child relaxes, you can talk about what happened and what the child can do differently in the future:

"I could tell you were really mad. Your face looked like this (*demonstrate*) and you were moving your arms and legs like this. Your whole body was letting me know that you felt upset. You wanted a turn to paint a picture on the easel. Next time, try telling Nathan, 'I want to paint a picture on the easel when you are done.'"

Tantrums can often be avoided by offering an engaging, intentional, and developmentally appropriate program. Children who are tired, hungry, or easily frustrated are more likely to have tantrums than those who are well-rested, fed nutritious meals and snacks before they are too hungry, and provided with engaging, age-appropriate materials and activities. Watch children closely to determine when and why a tantrum occurs. Try to learn and recognize the warning signs a child exhibits when they are getting tired and frustrated. When you notice one of the warning signs, direct the child to a soothing activity such as water play, painting, or listening to music.

Bullying is a way some children exert control over others. Bullies are often the most insecure children. Bullies sometimes pick on particular children. They know which children will not stand up for themselves, so they disrupt the more timid children's play, grab their toys, and push them around. Bullying must be stopped and redirected. The longer children get their way by bullying others, the harder it is to change that behavior. Children who are victimized time after time can become targets of other types of aggression and suffer from low self-esteem.

You can stop incidents of bullying by teaching victims to be more assertive when an incident occurs or at a more neutral time such as with other children at group meeting. For example, you might introduce a story about bullying or other types of aggressive behaviors and invite the children to practice ways to respond. Model for the children specific language to use and encourage them to practice what they can say if someone does something mean to them: "I'm still playing with this," "Stop pushing me," or "Stop calling me that!"

Here is an example of how you can respond to challenging behaviors.

Nathan grabs the marker that Rosa is coloring with and begins to use it on his paper. You notice that Rosa is sitting still with tears beginning to come down her face. Rosa has a hard time defending herself, so you get Nathan's attention and say, "Hold on a minute. What happened here? Rosa, you were coloring with that marker. Tell Nathan, 'No. I'm using that marker. You cannot use it right now.'" Then you continue to support Rosa with verbalizing her feelings, "You try to say it now." When Rosa chooses not to respond, you say, "I know you can do it. Let's say it together first."

When children lose control, you can help them compose themselves by modeling calm behavior. Keep in mind that you cannot help children develop self-control if you are out of control, yourself. Screaming at children, isolating them with a time-out system, taking away privileges, and making them feel incompetent rarely produce positive results and often increase and prolong unwanted behaviors. **Physical punishment is never, ever acceptable.** Use positive guidance strategies to avoid power struggles.

Talk about unwanted behaviors at neutral times. Help children practice strategies for stopping their own unwanted behavior and reacting to the unwanted behavior of other children. While "time out" is a punitive rather than positive guidance strategy, you can redirect a child by helping her take a deep breath, move away from the situation, and find something calming to do, such as playing at the water table. Remember that no single approach works for every child or every situation and that it takes time for children to learn how to regulate their own behavior. The positive guidance strategies you use will help most children learn these skills over time.

Determining the Causes of Challenging Behavior

Challenging behaviors can often be cries for help. Children who exhibit aggressive or unacceptable behaviors may not know how to appropriately express their feelings in constructive ways. Focus your attention on what the children in your care need rather than what they are doing. Try to imagine what a child might say if he could:

"I don't feel well." Illness, allergies, lack of sleep, poor nutrition, or hunger can be causes of children's challenging behaviors. If there are signs of a physical problem, speak with the child's family and consider having the child evaluated by a health professional.

"I don't know what I'm supposed to do." Throughout the day, providers give children brief instructions: "Go wash your hands," "Clean up," and "Use the brush properly." When a child does not listen or comply, the provider might assume that the child is not following instructions on purpose. However, many young children may not understand what the provider is telling them to do. Instructions that include words such as *properly* have no meaning for the child, and she is not likely to ask what a strange word like that means. Children need the provider to help show them what they need to do and how to do it, for example, how to hold a brush with your hands so the paint doesn't drip down the page or onto clothing.

"Notice me!" Children need to feel important and valued. When they do not receive enough positive attention, they may seek out negative attention. These children have learned that, when they act inappropriately, adults notice them and give them attention. Once children are successful in getting the attention they desire by misbehaving, they are likely to continue these unacceptable behaviors unless the cycle is broken.

"I'm bored." Even in the most engaging and interesting environments, children may become bored because they struggle with finding new ways to use and play with materials and engage with other children. When selecting materials and planning activities, make an extra effort to consider children's unique characteristics and interests to help keep them actively engaged.

"I want to make my own choices." Some children have very few opportunities to make their own decisions or to have control over their lives. When children are offered choices, such as which materials to use in an activity, with whom to play, and alternative ways to express their feelings, children begin to feel more powerful and develop self-regulation.

"I'm scared." Often, the children who have aggressive behaviors toward others and who challenge adults are afraid. To overcome fear, the children want to have control and feel powerful. To help these children, find out what their fears are and what is causing them. Create a plan that will address children's fears and reassure them that they are safe.

Helping Children Regain Control

When children lose control, you can help them compose themselves by modeling calm behavior. This approach is not always easy because you need to manage your own frustration. Being human, you may get angry when a child's behavior is particularly challenging.

Keep in mind that you cannot help children develop self-control if you are out of control, yourself. Screaming at children, isolating them when they are out of control, and making them feel incompetent rarely produce positive results. These approaches only fuel the fire. Once you are in a power struggle with a child, you have lost the battle. Instead, keep the ultimate goal in mind: to help children develop self-control, not just to behave acceptably when adults are present because they fear the consequences of behaving otherwise.

It often helps to reframe the situation and talk yourself into a more positive way of responding. For example, suppose that a child is running around the room, screaming at the top of her lungs, turning over chairs, and throwing things. The interpretation you choose will affect the way you respond. You could think to yourself, "That's just what I would expect from her. I've had it! I'm going to show her who's boss." Instead you could think, "She is testing me. She needs my help. I need to be patient and consistent." The second choice can help you remain calm so you can respond constructively.

There are several steps to take in responding to challenging behaviors and helping a child regain control:

Intervene to stop dangerous behavior. Your job is to keep everyone safe. You cannot reason with a child who is out of control.

Establish a positive relationship with the child. A child who knows you care will be much more likely to respond to the help you offer.

Obtain more information by observing. Systematic observations over time reveal a great deal of valuable information about what triggers challenging behavior and which of the child's needs are not being met.

Develop a plan. When a child's behavior is particularly challenging, meet with those who share responsibility for the child. In this way you are likely to come up with a plan that will be implemented consistently by all involved.

Implement the plan and evaluate its effect. The first plan may take time, and it might not be the best one. If it is not working, develop a new plan.

When you are dealing with challenging behaviors of any kind, remember that reasons underlie all behavior. Children whose behavior is challenging may not feel safe or connected to others. They may lack the foundation of trust necessary to experiment with constructive activities. They need adults who care about them, form positive relationships with them, and build their trust. They need opportunities to express their fears and anger appropriately through creative art, dramatic play, storytelling, and talking with caring adults. They need you to remain calm and to be helpful. Only then will they be ready to learn.

Addressing Ongoing Behavioral Problems

What should you do if a child in your family child care program behaves in challenging ways repeatedly and does not seem to respond to your positive guidance strategies? The unwanted behaviors prevent the child from fully participating in and benefitting from the program. The behaviors are challenging both to the other children in the program and to you. You will have to figure out when they occur and what might be causing them. With that information, you and the child's family can develop a plan of action.

Keep in mind that a reason underlies all challenging behaviors. Challenging behaviors are often cries for help. Children who behave in challenging ways again and again may not know how to express their feelings in other ways.

To deal with challenging behaviors, make and carry out an ongoing prevention and intervention plan. Here are some steps you can take:

1. **Observe carefully to identify when the behavior occurs.** Every time there is an incident, write down the time of day that the behavior occurred, who was involved, and what preceded the unwanted behavior. Use objective, descriptive terms that do not label or judge the child. For example, write, "S was washing a doll in the water table. L went over to S and bit S on the arm. S screamed. L took the doll S was holding and began to play with it." Be sure to date your note.
2. **Talk with the child's family.** The child's family may know about events at home or in the neighborhood that may be upsetting their child. With the family's input and permission, it is sometimes appropriate to seek help from an outside expert. Talking with families and specialists about challenging behaviors enables you to collaborate with them in providing the best care for the child at your program and at home.
3. **Review and analyze the information to determine patterns and the causes of the behavior.** Systematic observations over time reveal a great deal of valuable information about when and why the child engages in the behavior. Note such things as the time of day; what else is going on at the time; and other factors, such as whether the child came late or is not feeling well. This information can often help you prevent unwanted behavior. For instance, if you notice that Nathan often hits Keisha when he is frustrated because she cannot understand his speech, you can restate what he is trying to say to Keisha. If Jorge has tantrums at around 11:00 a.m., you can think about whether he is hungry, tired at that time, or needs some time away from the group. Depending upon what you think is causing his recurring tantrums, you can give him an early lunch or an early nap, or spend some one-on-one time with him.
4. **Develop and implement a plan.** Together, you and the family can develop a consistent plan for responding to the behavior and teaching the child better ways to express strong feelings. It is very important to tell the child that he or she is still cared about and loved, even if the behavior is unacceptable. Most children want to learn how to behave in acceptable ways because they want you to like them and they do not want to disappoint their families.
5. **Assess progress.** Maintain regular contact with the family so that you can evaluate how well your plan is working and make any necessary adjustments. Change takes time, and it takes some children longer than others. If a challenging behavior continues for a long time, you might—with the family's input and permission—want to consult with an outside expert. You do not have to handle particularly challenging behaviors on your own.

Guiding children's behavior may sometimes appear to be occupying a great deal of your time. Remember that, as you help children learn to regulate their behavior, you build a solid foundation for their positive interactions with others and for their academic learning.

Teaching Intentionally and Responsively

Your intentional interactions with children promote meaningful learning during everyday experiences. While it is important to set up the environment, provide interesting materials, and have an appropriate schedule, your interactions with children support their learning in even more important ways. The questions you ask and the other strategies you use to extend learning are critical. Like all early childhood teachers, providers teach with intention. They are purposeful. They make learning meaningful to children, and they use specific strategies to guide children's learning. *The Creative Curriculum® for Family Child Care, Volume 3: Objectives for Development & Learning, Birth Through Third Grade* provides guidance, and specific information about the content areas is offered in Chapter 3, "What Children Learn." Family child care providers make learning purposeful by knowing what children should be learning. Providers make learning meaningful to children by helping them build on what they already know, promoting children's problem-solving skills, offering tools and materials, and encouraging children to interact with others.

Because all children have unique learning styles and needs, providers need to consider where and when to teach, that is, to determine the best environment or context for the different types of learning. Child-initiated learning in experience areas during choice time is sometimes the most beneficial. Specific skills may require large- or small-group instruction and others can be supported or reinforced during daily routines and transitions. A concept or skill introduced in small- or large-group can be applied and practiced during child-initiated experiences.

Helping children learn and apply new concepts, develop important skills, and gain knowledge about the world is one of your major responsibilities as a family child care provider. You help children become enthusiastic and active learners when you use these strategies:

Set up the environment so that it promotes safe exploration.

Encourage children to make predictions, experiment, and draw conclusions.

Encourage children to try new things.

Expect children to make mistakes and learn from them.

Allow children time to learn and practice new skills.

Build on children's interests.

Take children's individual temperaments and learning styles into account.

Listen to what children have to say and respond appropriately.

Ask children questions that stretch their thinking.

Learning Through Play

Young children learn through play. As they engage in pretend play, create block structures, work with puzzles and other toys, listen to music, look at books and retell stories, play outside, experiment with natural materials like sand and water, prepare snacks, and work on the computer, they learn about the world, explore concepts, and gain knowledge and skills. When children take the initiative as they play, they choose where to play, share ideas about roles and scenarios, and try them. However, this does not mean that providers do nothing but watch. You have an important role in facilitating children's play.

You set the stage for children's learning by selecting materials that engage children and stretch their thinking. You provide guidance when children need help, ask questions to support children's thinking, and encourage them to approach learning actively. In a choice-time period, a child might choose to work on a puzzle, build a block tower, look through a familiar book and retell the story, or play a game with a friend. When children are free to follow their interests in an environment that supports and extends their exploration, they progress in all developmental areas.

Children play throughout the day during routines and experiences. Here are some examples of what children are learning:

- Jeremy (8 months) pulls himself up and leans against the coffee table so that he is standing. He reaches for the snow globe that is on table. He picks it up, shakes the globe, and laughs as he watches the snow. He is developing motor skills and learning about cause and effect.
- Tamika (19 months) and Jorge (2 ½ years) are sitting with you on the couch as you read *Click, Clack, Moo: Cows That Type* together. Jorge complains that he cannot see the pictures. You move Tamika over slightly and reposition the book, and Tamika accepts the new arrangement. She is cooperating in a group situation.
- Jorge (2 ½ years) punches a hole in a ball of play dough and pretends to eat it. You ask him, "Did you enjoy that, Jorge?" "*Si*", he responds, "I like *donas*." He is learning to express his thoughts in two languages.
- Nathan (3 years) strings colorful wooden beads on a knotted string. He holds the beaded string around his neck and says "Exess." "Necklace," you confirm enthusiastically. "You made a necklace with red, blue, and green beads." Nathan is refining fine motor skills and learning to speak.
- Rosa (4 years) is dressed up as a doctor and pretending to give Nathan a shot. She tells him. "It's okay. *No te duele*." She is learning to work through her fears by taking on the role of a doctor and controlling the situation. She is beginning to form sentences in English and continuing to use her Spanish skills.
- Keisha (4 ½ years) is at the kitchen table, using a recipe card to make nachos as you supervise. Keisha is learning to be independent, master self-help skills, follow directions, and begin to read.
- Tyrone (8 years) is sitting at a picnic table outside, looking through the book *Birds of North America* and writing down the names of birds he has seen in the neighborhood. He is studying the characteristics of living things, reading, and writing.

Using a Range of Teaching Strategies

As providers work with children, they use a variety of teaching strategies individually and in combination in order to help children progress. The purpose of these provider–child interactions is to scaffold children's learning. Scaffolding involves determining the level and type of support that will help a child become more competent.

Providers use these five teaching strategies to guide children's learning:

1. **Acknowledge and describe.** To validate what children are doing and to make them more aware of their thought processes and actions, tell them what you notice:
   - "You are playing with an interesting group of animals. We would expect to see all of them on a farm, except for one animal. Which animal would you not expect to find on a farm?"
   - "I see that you are mixing yellow and blue paint. I wonder what new color you will create."
   - "When you clicked the computer mouse, the dog in the picture started to run."

This strategy can be used to help children build their vocabularies.

- "I heard you say that the glass of milk feels cold. You described the temperature of the glass."

Acknowledge initiative and independence from adults and cooperation with other children.

- "You started to clean up when you heard the bell ring, and I noticed that the blocks were put on the shelf."
- "You and Jorge worked together to put away the markers. It gets done a lot faster that way."

2. **Coach.** This strategy involves scaffolding children's learning by encouraging them to attend, engage, and persist in the learning process to succeed beyond what they can do on their own.
   - "That puzzle piece just doesn't seem to fit. I wonder what would happen if you turned it. Can you find another piece that has the same color? Do you think it's the boy's arm? Where would an arm go?"
   - "Cutting with scissors is hard. Let's see if I can help you by putting my hand on top of yours. We can try cutting together."

This strategy involves helping children use specific techniques when competing a task or activity.

- "If you place your finger on each counter, say the number, and move it to the side, you can keep track of how many counters there are altogether."

Coaching helps nurture the imagination and encourages flexible thinking and helpful peer relationships.

- "You found a way to cut that heavy paper. Will you show Rosa how you used the scissors to do that?"

3. Extend children's thinking with open-ended questions, prompts, and conversations.

Questioning extends learning and gives providers insight into what a child is thinking while engaged in an activity. There are two types of questions: closed and open. A closed question has one answer. It can be answered with a yes or no response or with one or two words. Providers usually already know the right answer. Here are some examples of closed questions:

What is this called?

What shape is this?

What color is this?

How many are there?

Closed questions are easy to ask children, and the answers provide insight into what a specific child already knows. Closed questions are appropriate when structured to encourage English language learners to respond using the English language. Open-ended questions give providers more insight because children are thinking more about the question before responding. These questions typically require more than a one- or two-word response, and the answer will vary with each child. Open-ended questions encourage children to think critically. If you ask a child, "When you mixed the red and blue paint what happened? Why do you think that happened?" you will gain more insight than if you were to ask, "What color did the two paints make when you mixed them?" Here are some open-ended questions that you can ask to extend your children's thinking.

To encourage children to verbalize their ideas: "Why do you think the little boy in the story was afraid to sleep over at his friend's house?" (*Intentional Teaching Card* SE35, "You & Me Time")

To encourage observation: "What do you see? Feel? Smell? Taste? What did you notice?" (*Intentional Teaching Card* M06, "Making Butter")

To encourage predictions: "What will happen if you keep adding blocks to your tower?" (*Intentional Teaching Card* M26, "Ramp Experiments")

To encourage thinking about similarities and differences: "How are these containers the same? What do you notice that is different about them?" (*Intentional Teaching Card* M21, "Missing Lids")

To encourage children to apply knowledge to solve a problem: What can you do to keep paint from dripping on the floor? (*Intentional Teaching Card* SE28, "How Can We Help?")

To encourage evaluation: "Nicholas, you chose to paint a tree. Why did you choose to paint a tree today?" (*Intentional Teaching Card* SE23, "Making Choices")

To encourage children to think and talk about feelings: ""I saw that you got a chance to go on the swings today. How did that make you feel?" (*Intentional Teaching Card* SE21, "Talk About Feelings")

Open-ended questions that invite children to make observations and predictions and apply what they know are effective for building children's understanding. These types of questions challenge the way children think and encourage children to infer and make generalizations that help support them in differentiating important information from irrelevant information, which leads to more meaningful learning.

4. **Demonstrate effective learning behaviors.** Providers can use this strategy to talk about what they are doing and why they are doing it. They model a skill or behavior for children to imitate.

Providers model to assist memory:

- "I need to make a list of all the materials that we will need to make play dough so I can remember what to use when I make it."

They model ways to learn and use skills:

- "The word on this box starts with the letter *B*. Brandon's name starts with the letter *B*. It makes the /b/ sound."

They model ways to sequence and organize activities:

- "The first thing we have to do before we have our snack is wash our hands. Then we find a seat at the table."

Modeling teaches social skills that you want children to learn. For example, when you show respect to children, families, and everyone else who enters your program, you show children what it means to be respectful.

- "Can you please excuse me for a minute? I need to answer Ms. Jenny's question. I'll be right back to help you."

5. **Give information to expand children's knowledge base and let them know what is expected of them.** Provide facts, model language, and help children find answers to their questions. You want to help children make discoveries on their own, and sometimes the most effective approach is to provide information or resources to satisfy children's curiosity and help them further their learning and development. For example, children who are in the beginning stages of learning how to recognize numerals and the letters of the alphabet need to hear the names of the symbols.
   - "Yes, Nathan, that letter on the box is the letter *A*. It is a big, or uppercase *A*."

These teaching strategies are used throughout the day as you guide learning during daily routines and experiences, during transitions, and when you gather a small group of children for a planned activity.

Supporting Learning Through Small- and Large-Group Instruction

Children learn many things through play and their interactions with others in experience areas, However, some skills and concepts require more deliberate teaching. Intentional instruction requires a provider to think about how to teach a concept or skill, what materials are needed, and if the activity is best taught to small or large groups or to an individual child. For example, suppose that you want children to begin using art materials. Because you cannot assume that all children know how to use various types of art materials, you cannot let them explore these materials without specific instruction on how to use and take care of them. You therefore show children how to use each of the materials in small groups, and you discuss the rules that must be followed in the art area. With clear instructions, children learn how to put on a smock and paint at an easel.

Learning the letters of the alphabet is another example for which small- and large-group instruction is appropriate. While children play with alphabet puzzles and explore magnetic letters, they need someone to tell them the names and sounds of the letters. Display the alphabet at children's eye level in the room and use large-group time to discuss the letters. You can also teach the names and sounds of letters during small-group time while children use magnetic letters to spell words and their names.

Small-Group Times

Throughout the day, you plan and conduct a variety of small-group activities. These activities are intentional and focus on specific learning objectives. Each child may be at a different level within your small group. Your knowledge of each child's development regarding the various objectives will support you in determining how to organize and conduct each activity. *Volume 3: Objectives for Development & Learning* provides you with the developmental progression for each objective. This information provides guidance on how to individualize activities for specific children. *Intentional Teaching Cards*™ also show you how to adapt activities to meet individual children's needs.

The following example shows how you might guide learning during a small-group activity. It is the beginning of the year, and you are choosing materials that invite exploration and provide opportunities to observe your children's math skills.

A Small-Group Activity

During choice time, you invite two children to join you on the carpet for a small-group activity. You bring a collection of buttons and ask each child to take a few to look at and explore. You have a few buttons in front of you. As you begin using the buttons, you observe how each child is using the buttons and listen carefully to what they say. You say, "Keisha, you put all the black buttons, white buttons, and blue buttons together. I am going to look at the colors I have and put them together."

Keisha points out, "You have a lot of white buttons and only a little bit of black buttons."

You respond, "Yes, Keisha, I have more white buttons than black buttons."

Nathan organizes his buttons into a long line and begins counting them. He counts to 5 correctly, but gets confused about which buttons he has already counted. You ask, "Can I help you count your buttons? One, two, three. . ."

You move each button to the side as you count together.

You make an announcement to the group that in a few minutes they will clean up. Then you make clean-up time a game. "Find all the buttons that are blue and put them into the basket."

Nathan says, "I help. Black buttons."

Keisha takes a turn. "Find all the small buttons and put them in the bucket."

The children take turns until the buttons are all put away. While the children are finishing cleaning up, you write notes about your observations of the children who participated in the small-group activity.

This small-group activity was successful in many ways because:

- All children had materials to use.
- Use of materials was correctly modeled.
- The activity was short (10–15 minutes).
- Children played at their own developmental levels.
- Observations were taken on how the children explored and used the materials, and different challenges were offered.
- The children shared ideas and problem-solving strategies. They learned new ways to use materials by watching and listening to each other.
- Skills that related to several objectives were addressed throughout the activity: counting, classifying, and problem solving.

Small-group activities should be intentional and focus on specific skills. When preparing for small group activities, refer to *Intentional Teaching Cards*™ for guidance. Each card focuses on specific objectives and gives you step-by-step instructions for implementation that allow you to adapt the activities for children at different developmental levels.

Large-Group Times

At different times of the day, you may have all the children come together as a large group. The beginning and end of day meetings are an example. Large-group times can also be the times of day when the group listens to a story, participates in a music and movement activity, or discusses a topic the children are studying. Meetings that involve all children enable them to learn from one another and feel a sense of community.

In the following example of a large-group meeting, you want to teach the children how to use and care for materials. You know that the children need guidance prior to using the materials independently.

Introducing Materials to the Program

You decide to introduce magnifying glasses during large-group time. You structure the meeting in a way that gives the children time to explore the materials freely. You introduce a collection of magnifying glasses at the meeting and encourage the children to play with several of them.

You: *What do you notice about the magnifying glasses?*

Tyrone: *I can see through them!*

You: *Tyrone noticed that when you put the magnifying glass up to your eye, you can see through it.*

Keisha *The top is shaped like a circle.*

You: *Keisha noticed that a part of the magnifying glass is in the shape of a circle.*

Rosa: *Mine is verde.*

You: *Rosa noticed that her magnifying glass has the color green on it.*

Tamika: *(Holds the magnifying glass on her hand.) Oh!*

You: *That's right, Tamika. If you hold the magnifying glass close to an object, it magnifies or makes it look bigger. That's a good thing to know.*

You then invite the children to think of ways to use the magnifying glasses, and you observe and make suggestions on how to use them. After the children have shared what they discovered, you conclude the discussion.

You: *When you are playing, you may use toys in many ways. We just learned that magnifying glasses can be used in different ways. The magnifying glasses will be here for you to use every day. During choice time, the discovery area is one of the areas you may choose, and you may use the magnifying glasses to look at whatever you'd like. When you are done using the magnifying glasses, there is a special place for them to go on the shelf. Who knows where the magnifying glasses go? Can you show us, Tyrone? When we put the magnifying glasses in the right place, it makes it easier for others to find them when they want to us them.*

There may be times when a large-group meeting takes place spontaneously because you see an opportunity to have a teachable moment. For example, imagine you and the children have just returned from a walk around the neighborhood. You decide to bring the children together because there is an opportunity for intentional teaching.

A Teachable Moment

You:	*When we went on our walk, we saw a lot of things. Let's make a list together so we can remember what we saw. Let's start. What did you see?*
Jorge:	*Pretends to push and says, "Rrrr..."*
You:	*That's right, Jorge. That machine making that noise is called a lawn mower.*
Keisha:	*And a ladder on the side of a house.*
Nathan:	*Bug!*

You write the words *lawn mower, ladder,* and *ladybug* on chart paper and ask everyone to say each word with you as a group as you point.

Keisha:	*Hey, those words all start the same.*
You:	*That's right: lawn mower, ladder, ladybug. (Draws a line under each* l*.) They all start with the letter* l.

If you plan on teaching a skill or concept directly, you must consider whether it is best to work with children in a small group, in a large group, or individually.

Including All Children

All children can thrive in your program. Some providers think they have to do something dramatically different to accommodate advanced learners, children with disabilities, or children who are dual-language learners. This is not usually the case. As you develop relationships with children and use a variety of instructional strategies, you will be able to judge how children respond and which strategies work best in which situations.

Teaching Children Who Are Advanced Learners

A provider's role is to offer all children appropriately challenging and stimulating experiences. Advanced learners are often eager to explore a topic more in depth and show interest with high levels of enthusiasm and intensity. Here are some suggestions for supporting the needs of advanced learners:

Provide materials that are interesting and challenging. Plan and create a stimulating home environment that promotes children's curiosity, independent exploration, and experimentation.

Pay attention to what advanced learners are interested in. When a child shows interest in a topic, such as trucks or airplanes, help him explore it by providing pictures, books, and other resources. Ask open-ended questions about the child's interests that encourage him to dig deeper into a topic.

Have realistic expectations. Always keep in mind that being advanced in one area of development does not mean that a child is advanced in all areas. A child who is advanced in language might not be advanced in terms of physical, social–emotional, or mathematical skills. It is important to individualize your approach to meet each child's unique set of skills.

If a child is reading, provide books that are at or slightly below her reading level for independent reading. For instruction, select books above her reading level. When selecting books, it is important to find books that are appealing to a child of that age. The content of books for young children may not appeal to older children and vice versa, so choose your program books thoughtfully.

Teaching Children With Disabilities

Children with disabilities need to be included and successful. Your general knowledge about child development and your specific knowledge about the children in your care can be applied to your work with children who have diagnosed disabilities or other special needs. As you support each child's development and learning, you must look beyond the specific diagnosis to see how the disability affects the particular child. You must not generalize about a child on the basis of his diagnosis. Here are some guidelines:

See the child as a child first. Learn about each child's strengths and interests first, and then consider the child's special needs. Use language that shows your understanding of this. For example, speak about a child with autism, rather than an autistic child. The difference is significant. It reflects your philosophy about children with disabilities.

Learn about the effects of a specific disability to decide what, if any, adjustments you need to make. Here are some examples.

- A child with a visual impairment relies more heavily on her senses of hearing and touch for communication. When offered choices, it will be helpful for her to touch each item and hear about the choices.
- A child with a hearing impairment relies heavily on his sense of sight for communication. It may be useful for you to learn sign language and to use cards with pictures of routines, experiences, and materials so that you can communicate with him.
- A child with a brain injury may need more time to think about what you are saying and more time to transition from one activity to another. Slowing your conversations and actions may help engage this child.
- A child with physical limitations needs you to free the environment of barriers that would restrict his or her mobility. When you help her move, she will feel respected if you explain what you are doing and why.

Work closely with the child's family. The family members of a child with a disability are your greatest sources of support and information. Ask them to share what they know about their child's interests and how the child's disability affects what he can do. Invite them to share tips and strategies they use at home, especially those that have been taught to them by a special educator.

Work with a specialist. Depending on the child's age, a child with a diagnosed disability will have either an Individualized Family Service Plan (for children birth to age 3) or an Individualized Education Program (ages 3–21). (See Chapter 1, "Knowing How Children Develop and Learn.") Many objectives on these plans will be the similar to those you have for all children, so many of the strategies you use as you care for the child with disabilities will fit easily into your regular plans and daily schedule. For other objectives, you might need to add special toys and adaptive equipment, or you might need to change strategies (such as blinking the lights to catch the attention of a deaf child). These adaptations and strategies should be included in the child's plan. As with all children, observe continually with the objectives for development and learning in mind and adapt equipment, materials, and teaching strategies as necessary.

With the family's permission, work with the child's specialist(s) to develop strategies that will work in your program. Be sure to share information with the specialist about the daily routines and experiences in your program and talk to the specialist about ways that all children can participate in activities suggested for the child with disabilities. Encourage the specialist to find opportunities to support the child's development and learning in the family child care environment.

Encourage, but do not force, appropriate independence. Some children need extra support to develop skills and self-confidence. Help children with disabilities play with other children. Remember that sometimes children with disabilities do not initiate play as often as other children. They may need more support and opportunities to practice entering social play.

Use peer buddies as teaching models. This technique not only facilitates interaction, but it also builds the peer-mentoring capabilities of children who have strengths in particular developmental areas.

Supporting Dual-Language Learners

Some children in your program may be learning more than one language at the same time or learning another language sequentially. In our example, Jorge (2 ½ years) is learning both English and Spanish at the same time. Rosa (4 years) already speaks Spanish and is learning to speak English now that she is in a family child care program. You can support children who are dual-language learners by using these strategies:

Learn some words in the children's home languages and, if possible, label materials and storage places in those languages as well as in English. Seeing and hearing their home languages will help children feel welcome and safe in an environment where people speak a different language.

Use concrete objects and gestures to communicate with children while they are nonverbal. Keep in mind that they are actively learning, observing, and making sense of what is going on around them. Help them feel included in your program.

Use objects and hands-on experiences to help children understand language and make the transition from nonverbal communication to using a few words. Focus on the child's intent, and extend or repeat what the child says.

Encourage children who are dual-language learners and children whose home language is English to play together. Children can engage in dramatic play, catch and throw balls with each other, move to music, and dig and bury objects in sand even if they speak different languages.

Encourage nonverbal communication. Remember that children understand more than they are able to say. Let children show you how much they understand by following directions that call for an action (e.g., standing up, sitting down, turning around, running, walking, or jumping). Ask questions to which children can respond by pointing to, picking up, showing, or giving something. Use pictures, props, and other visual cues to help children understand.

Offer encouragement and, as children feel more confident, support conversations in English. Avoid correcting the child's grammar, but model correct language as you speak and read aloud. Do not be concerned if the child mixes languages, even in the same sentence.

Build your relationship with each child. Play with children. Have fun together. Be patient. Give children time to express themselves, and be careful not to rush them.

Provide books in the children's home languages if possible. If you do not understand the language, scan illustrations and lengths of the texts to see if they look appropriate.

Incorporate pictures and familiar objects that will help the children feel comfortable in your program. For example, if appropriate for the children in your group, add a tortilla press for dramatic play and use one in the kitchen. Offer familiar music and dances. Include dress-up clothes from children's home cultures as appropriate.

Involve families by encouraging them to continue speaking their primary languages when they visit your program. Invite them to record books on tape or to help make signs and books for the program in their home languages.

Keep in mind that your attitude is very important. If you value and support multilingualism, all children will benefit, not only those whose home languages are other than English.

Assessing Children's Learning

Assessment is an ongoing process of observing children that enables providers to gather information about individual children to plan instruction and ensure that every child is progressing. Assessment is most beneficial when it is used alongside the curricular objectives. In *Volume 3: Objectives for Development & Learning,* you will find detailed information about the 38 objectives. The colored bands allow you to see which objectives are developmentally appropriate for the children in your care. While observing, be mindful of the objectives to help you observe with purpose in the context of everyday routines and experiences. Purposeful observations help you assess each child's level of development and provide guidance when considering next steps. As you learn about each child's needs, interests, and strengths, you can use the strategies and information included in *The Creative Curriculum®* to build responsive relationships and offer developmentally appropriate experiences to the children in your care.

The objectives for development and learning are the same as the objectives in the *GOLD®* assessment system within *MyTeachingStrategies™*. *GOLD®* includes the guidance and forms you need for ongoing assessment as you implement *The Creative Curriculum®*. If you use a different assessment system, be sure that it is compatible with these objectives. Whatever system you use, there are four steps in the ongoing assessment cycle: (1) observing and collecting facts; (2) analyzing and responding; (3) evaluating; and (4) summarizing, planning, and communicating.

Step 1. Observing and Collecting Facts

Best practices in early childhood education require providers to observe each child across all areas of development and to use their observations to inform their practice. The information they collect helps them decide how to set up the physical environment and structure the day, how to plan for individual children on the basis of each child's interests and skills, and how to interact spontaneously with children throughout the day. The objectives for development and learning guide your observations by helping you think about what to look for. See the Introduction, Chapters 1 and 3, and the Appendix of *Volume 1: The Foundation*. You use the information from your observations in your ongoing planning, as described in Chapter 2, "Organizing Your Home and Your Day." You also share information with families to help each other build a more complete understanding of how their children are developing and learning. See Chapter 5, "Building Partnerships With Families."

Children develop and learn best in programs that respond to their individual skills and interests. Observing children is one of the best ways to get the information you need. Observation tells you about children's skills and interests as well as how they handle frustrations, get involved in group play, and cope with separation. Children change over time, so observation is an ongoing process.

Observation is the act of watching and listening to a child. You observe children every day. For example, you notice Jeremy using his thumb and forefinger to eat breakfast cereal. You see that Nathan's blowing on his warm cereal has helped him learn to make the sound of the letter *f* and that Tyrone likes to spend a few minutes with his sister, Tamika, when he arrives in the afternoon.

You observe children for a variety of reasons:

- to determine each child's interests, strengths, and needs: "Nathan uses the tongs nearly every day to sort buttons."
- to meet individual needs: "Tyrone has completed every jigsaw puzzle we have. I need to offer him more challenging puzzles."
- to document progress: "The recording I made of Rosa's conversation documents how many English words she learned in the last month."
- to determine the cause of a challenging behavior: "According to my notes, it appears that Tamika has started hitting other children when they are playing with something she wants."
- to report children's progress to families: "As you know, I've been encouraging Jorge to sleep during nap time. My notes from the last two weeks indicate that there was only one day when he didn't go right to sleep."

Setting Up a System

Setting up a system is a great way to organize and keep track of daily observations. Being organized with observations will help ensure that you have documentation for each child's development and learning and stored samples of work. If you are using *GOLD*®, the system for organizing and storing observations notes and digital samples of children's work is already set up for you to use. You can store information in the Child Assessment Portfolio. Documentation can be added into children's online portfolios or uploaded using the *GOLD® Documentation* app. If you are currently using an alternative assessment system, you can create a portfolio for each child. Documentation and samples of work can be stored in folders or large envelopes, accordion files, magazine holders, or hanging files.

Observations are a quick and easy way to learn important information about what each child knows and where they are developmentally. It is best practice to take documentation during or after an observation. Jotting down quick notes right away can prevent forgetting the events that took place during an observation. If needed, refer to your notes and add more detail. Here are some helpful ways for you to record your observations.

- Use sticky notes or a notecard to write what you observe throughout the day. Prior to starting your day, place three or four notes on a clipboard that include the names of the children that you plan to observe. Keep a few extras for additional or spontaneous observations.
- Keep notecards or sticky notes that are easily accessible around your home.
- Use a voice recorder or a digital pen to take notes when using an online assessment system that includes this feature.
- Develop a system using short hand or brief phrases that will help you recall what happened during an observation.

Documenting Your Observations

Observations that are objective and factual are the most accurate and useful when assessing a child. When your documentation includes words such as *stubborn*, *manipulative*, *selfish*, *upset*, or *shy*, it reveals your impressions, interpretations, or assumptions rather than the facts about what the child said or did. Words that are judgmental do not tell an accurate story.

Interpretations, impressions, or assumptions include

- intentions (*want to*),
- labels (*shy, active, stubborn*),
- negatives (*didn't, can't, won't*), and
- evaluations and judgments (*great job, awesome, sloppy*).

Observations that are objective include only the facts of what you saw and heard. Factual observations include

- descriptions of a creation,
- descriptions of a facial expression,
- descriptions of an action,
- descriptions of a gesture, and
- quotations of language.

Compare the following two examples of observation notes about a child in the block area.

Example 1

Jorge is being destructive today. He knocked down another child's building on purpose. He checks to see if I can see him and laughs at the other child.

Example 1 is not an objective note. It uses a label (destructive) and makes judgments ("He knocked down…on purpose"). The provider speculated about Jorge's intentions ("checks to see if I can see him. . . laughs at the other child").

Example 2

Jorge is building in with blocks. He uses his hand and knocks another child's building over. He looks at me and then at the child and begins to giggle.

Example 2 is an objective note. It includes only the facts of what Jorge did ("building with blocks"), what happened ("He uses his hand and knocks another child's building over"), and his reaction ("He looks at me and then at the child and begins to giggle"). Accurate notes include only the facts about what a child did and said, and they are recorded in the order of occurrence.

Writing objective notes takes practice. The more aware you are of what objective notes include, the more skilled you will become at writing them.

Here are two examples of objective observation notes.

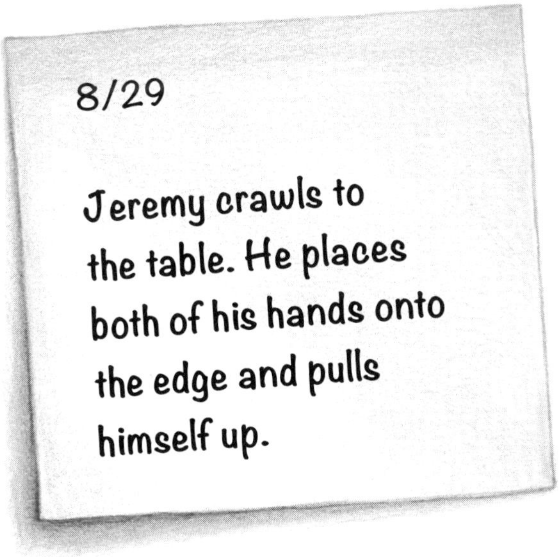

8/29

Jeremy crawls to the table. He places both of his hands onto the edge and pulls himself up.

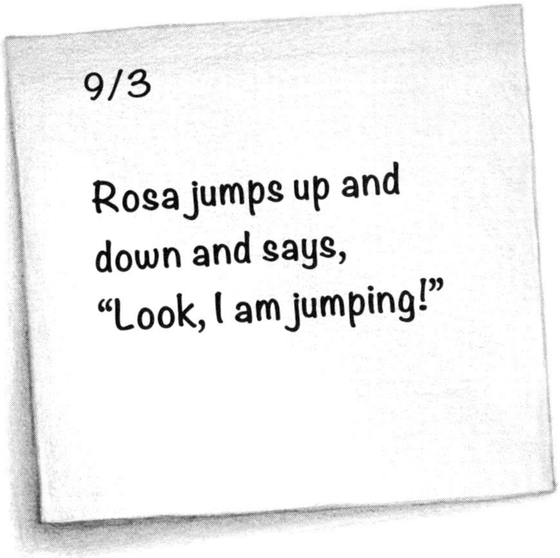

9/3

Rosa jumps up and down and says, "Look, I am jumping!"

Other Forms of Documentation

Documentation can be done in different ways. A variety of documentation provides additional information to providers on how a child is developing. Here are some examples:

Children's work samples—Select samples over time that are similar and focus on a specific skill (e.g., at the beginning, middle, and end of the year). Collect drawings, writing samples, stories the child dictated and illustrated, and computer or digital print-outs.

Photographs—Take pictures of a child's work, such as a block structure, artwork, and a pattern or other design made with table blocks. Be sure to label and date each photo and write a brief description of what the child did and said.

Checklists, participation lists, frequency counts—Systematically record things such as which experience area a child prefers, the letters or numbers a child recognizes, the completion of an activity, physical skills, and so on.

Audio and video clips— Be selective about what you film or tape. Try to record activities without bothering the child or keeping her from completing the activity.

When you are collecting documentation for a child's portfolio, include observation notes that explain what the child was doing and attach the notes to the back of the samples. Always remember to date any documentation to keep track of a child's progress over time.

Observing With the Curricular Objectives in Mind

The objectives for children's development and learning presented in chapters 1 and 3 of this volume and described in detail in *Volume 3: Objectives for Development & Learning* give guidance for making your daily observations systematic and meaningful. When you are familiar with the objectives and indicators for the children in your care, your observation notes will be objective and factual. When observations are based on specific objectives, they provide insight and important information that help track and evaluate a child's progress over time. For example, instead of recording, "Counts blocks when placing them in the bucket," a more valuable note would be, "Counts 13 blocks accurately when placing them in the bucket."

A small-group activity will often give information about multiple objectives. For example, if the children are asked to create a block pattern using 10 blocks, you can note which children can count the blocks (Objective 20), note the children who use the blocks to create and extend a pattern (Objective 23), note who listened to and followed directions (Objective 8), and record the number of exchanges that take place during a conversation (Objective 10). Keep sticky notes or a notepad nearby to document what you see and hear immediately. *Volume 3: Objectives for Development & Learning* includes a chart of the 38 objectives for development and learning. Refer to the chart when planning and completing your documentation.

You do not have to write an observation note about every child, every day. However, do try to select a few children to observe each day and write three or four brief notes about them. For some objectives, it is sufficient to see a child use a skill once or twice (e.g., a physical skill). You may record such accomplishments on a checklist; an observation note is not usually necessary. Other objectives require more evidence and documentation. No set number of observation notes or amount of other documentation is required for each objective. Use common sense to determine what is needed.

Step 2. Analyzing and Responding

The information that you gain from conducting an observation gives you guidance on how to respond to and support the children in your care. Knowing the skills that each of your children have in relation to the objectives tells you whether a child can follow multiple step directions, how a child solves problems, and how well they interact with their peers. Information like this can help you decide which activities and experiences will meet the needs and interests of every child.

This step in the assessment cycle involves organizing your documentation and making judgments about what the collected information tells you about a child's progress in relation to the objectives. As you observe children or review your notes, ask yourself, "What does this behavior mean?" At the end of the day, or when you have time, organize your notes and reflect on what you are learning. At other times, you can respond immediately.

To analyze documentation, refer to and review notes and samples of work to determine what objectives apply. Write the objective number on your notes and samples of work. It is important to keep in mind that one observation can relate to several different objectives. Ask yourself, "What does this observation tell me about the child's development and learning?

The observation note about Tamika is clearly related to Objective 7, "Demonstrates fine-motor strength and coordination." You would write *7* on the note and place it on the appropriate page in Tamika's Child Assessment Portfolio or enter it online. The observation note also gives information about Tamika's social–emotional development, particularly about Objective 1, "Regulates own emotions and behaviors," and Objective 11, "Demonstrates positive approaches to learning." You may want to make a copy of the note to put on the pages for those objectives. If you are using the online system, simply select multiple related objectives after entering the documentation.

Tamika 9/8

T looks at the scissors and picks them up. T uses her hands to make the blades go back and forth onto a piece of paper. T can't get the paper to cut. She frowns and drops scissors on table. She looks at Nathan, who is tearing paper. Picks up her paper and tears it with her hands.

Jorge 10/30

Walks over to the Art area and pulls out the clay. He turns around and looks at me. I shake my head, "No." Then J puts the clay away and picks out a puzzle.

The observation note about Jorge also provides information about at least three objectives. It gives you information about Objective 4, "Demonstrates traveling skills"; Objective 1, "Regulates own emotions and behaviors"; and Objective 8, "Listens to and understands increasingly complex language."

If you use *GOLD*®, you can easily evaluate each child's progress by selecting the objectives and dimensions while adding in your observations. You can also refer to the teaching sequence on *Intentional Teaching Cards*™ to respond appropriately to the needs of each child.

Throughout the day, you continually observe, reflect, and respond to each child. You observe what you see and hear children doing, reflect on what happened, and respond using what you learned to plan experiences that will extend children's learning. In each of the *Volume 2* chapters on routines and experiences, you will find charts with examples of how to observe, reflect, and respond to children throughout the day, keeping the objectives in mind.

Step 3. Evaluating

Evaluating children's progress means deciding which indicator of an objective best describes where the child is at developmentally. When you begin to analyze and evaluate the collected documentation, you will be able to determine each child's level of development in relation to each objective. You can organize your observation notes as well as the information in children's portfolios by regularly asking yourself, "What does this mean?" If you use *GOLD*®, you can evaluate each child's progress while entering documentation and while finalizing your checkpoint ratings. Refer to the chart of objectives to decide which objectives apply and note the numbers right on the note or on the back of the work sample. For example, suppose you have a writing sample and an observation note about Keisha.

Keisha 10/27

Draws some lines and curves and says, "I am writing a story about my dog Patches." (#7, #9, #19)

This work sample and observation written about Keisha covers more than one objective.

Her experience involved physical development (Objective 7, "Demonstrates fine-motor strength and coordination"); literacy (Objective 19, "Demonstrates writing skills"); and language (Objective 9, "Uses language to express thoughts and needs"). You can use this observation note to evaluate Keisha's development and learning on various dimensions of these three objectives.

Volume 3: Objectives for Development & Learning includes developmental progressions for each objective, allowing you to evaluate and determine Keisha's level for each objective. Let's look at Objective 19. When looking at this note, and other observations about Keisha, you can see that Keisha makes mock letters or letter-like forms. That is the indicator for level 6. She writes segments of letters (lines and curves) but does not orient letter segments correctly.

Objective 19 Demonstrates writing skills

a. Writes name

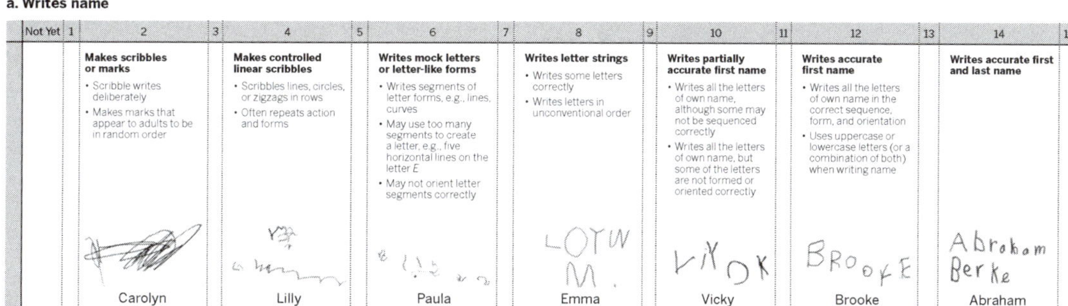

Not Yet	1	2	3	4	5	6	7	8	9	10	11	12	13	14	15
		Makes scribbles or marks • Scribble writes deliberately • Makes marks that appear to adults to be in random order		**Makes controlled linear scribbles** • Scribbles lines, circles, or zigzags in rows • Often repeats action and forms		**Writes mock letters or letter-like forms** • Writes segments of letter forms, e.g., lines, curves • May use too many segments to create a letter, e.g., five horizontal lines on the letter *E* • May not orient letter segments correctly		**Writes letter strings** • Writes some letters correctly • Writes letters in unconventional order		**Writes partially accurate first name** • Writes all the letters of own name, although some may not be sequenced correctly • Writes all the letters of own name, but some of the letters are not formed or oriented correctly		**Writes accurate first name** • Writes all the letters of own name in the correct sequence, form, and orientation • Uses uppercase or lowercase letters (or a combination of both) when writing name		**Writes accurate first and last name**	
		Carolyn		Lilly		Paula		Emma		Vicky		Brooke		Abraham	

You can make determinations about the other objectives using the documentation you have collected for Keisha.

Step 4: Summarizing, Planning, and Communicating

The final step in the assessment cycle involves summarizing your findings for every child, developing appropriate plans to support individual children and the group, and communicating what you have learned to families. Collecting assessment helps you with planning routines, transitions, and activities and how to change or adapt the environment to meet children's needs.

Summary Form

Some assessment systems suggest that you compile and summarize children's development and learning at least three times a year. *GOLD*® includes forms specifically designed to summarize information you have collected. Providers who use a different assessment system also need to summarize the information they have collected throughout the year to prepare reports.

The objectives for development and learning include widely held expectations for children birth through third grade; this gives you the ability to assess all children, those developing according to expectations and those who are advanced, have a developmental delay, have a disability, or lack experience in an area. It is important to understand that every child in your program will not progress to the highest level for each objective. Over time, you can expect to see evidence that every child is making progress.

Planning for Individual Children

The amount of information you collected on each child is only meaningful if you use it to inform your teaching practice. Documentation can help you plan for individual children and for your entire group. Here are some examples of decisions you might make based on assessment information:

- Nathan understands that text is meaningful and can be read (Objective 17, "Demonstrates knowledge of print and its uses"). He is beginning to notice print in his environment. To support him in learning more about print concepts, I will read books he is interested in and call his attention to the way I read the words from left to right and start from the top of the page to the bottom.
- Rosa is beginning to initiate brief conversations (Objective 10, "Uses appropriate conversational and other communication skills"). She seems quite enthusiastic when talking about her pet lizard during large-group time. I can build on her interest in lizards to help promote her language and literacy development. I will read books about lizards to her and encourage her to talk about what she knows about lizards.

Planning for the Group

Assessment can also provide information that will assist you in planning for the group. If you review the progress that your children are making as a group, you may find that focusing on specific objectives can benefit everyone. Take the time to plan when and where to teach particular skills. You will focus on some skills during small- and large-group settings. For an example, let's take a look at Objective 15, "Demonstrates phonological awareness, phonics skills, and word recognition." Imagine you have a group of five children aged 3–5 years. Suppose there are

- two children who join in rhyming songs,
- one child who fills in the missing rhyming word, and
- one child who can decide whether two words rhyme.

When you reflect on this information, you determine that most of the children are developing the skill of noticing and discriminating rhymes. You decide to make Objective 15 a group focus and try these strategies:

- Provide recordings of poems and chants with repetition and rhyming words. Encourage children to listen to them independently.
- Gather a small group of children who are at a beginning level of understanding rhyme. Invite them to participate in doing fingerplays and singing simple songs.
- Play rhyming games during transitions.
- Read aloud books that contain rhyme and repetition (e.g., *Chicka Chicka Boom Boom* or any Dr. Seuss book). Omit some of the words that rhyme as you read and encourage children to guess which words to fill in.

Based on your findings of how children are developing and learning, you can identify the ones that would benefit from more focused instruction and practice. This information will assist you when planning individual support and small-group activities and will help you decide on the appropriate ways to respond when unplanned teaching opportunities arise.

Communicating

It is important to share the progress your program's children have made with others. Families are very interested in hearing how their children are doing and could have valuable information to share.

A great time to communicate a child's progress over time is during a conference with families. It is important to schedule conferences about three times a year. It is important to prepare for conferences and include a form that summarizes the information you want to share with families. The "Family Conference Form" that is part of the *GOLD*® assessment system serves that purpose. Prior to your conference, review the observation notes, samples of the child's work, and the child's levels of development for the various objectives. Determine what information and evidence is going to be the most important to the child's family in the areas of development. Take the time to write down a child's strengths and give examples of what the child can do in each area. Make sure to identify a few learning goals you want to work on. In Chapter 5, "Building Partnerships With Families," we provide more information on how to prepare for and conduct family conferences.

If you are using *GOLD*®, the process of creating a report is simplified for you. Data collected on each objective can be aggregated and disaggregated to generate a range of individual and group reports.

The Creative Curriculum® for Family Child Care

Family Conference Form

Child's Name: Tamika Date: May 4, 2017

Social–Emotional Development	Physical Development
Tamika joins our daily circle when we are singing, doing fingerplays, or reading simple books. Sometimes she walks away for a minute, but she usually comes back and joins the group again.	Tamika walks like a toddler. She places her feet apart widely and holds her arms out for balance. She can do simple fingerplays.
Language Development and Literacy	**Cognitive Development**
Tamika makes simple requests, such as asking us to sing and to read books again. She shows that she understands a lot of verbs when she follows simple directions like "Lie down on your cot" or "Please get your coat." When we reread familiar stories, she is beginning to fill in the word if I omit one from a refrain.	Tamika names many common objects, such as *ball, bottle, car,* and *dog.* She responds to simple directions and requests. When she uses our toy phone she shows that she understands that a toy can stand for something else. Tamika shows her curiosity by gesturing and asking simple questions.

Mathematics, Science, Social Studies, and the Arts
Tamika is learning about math and science. She likes to fill boxes and buckets with toys, but she sometimes finds that they're too big. She puts a napkin on each plate when we set the table. She asks, "More?" when she wants more play dough or more food at lunch. She likes to help feed our fish.

Summary

As a family child care provider, you may have the pleasure of guiding a child's development and learning from the time he enters your program as a baby until he leaves your program as an older school-age child. You will watch and help him as he learns to walk, talk, read, solve problems, practice self-help skills, and regulate his own behavior. Yours is joyful and satisfying work!

This chapter focused on the many roles you play as a family child care provider. The secure relationships you develop with children give them a strong foundation for learning. You help them learn to get along with other children. You guide their behavior, support them as they learn through play, and guide their progress in all areas of development. The next chapter, "Building Partnerships With Families," focuses on another important role for family child care providers. It explains how to develop relationships with families, provide continuity between the child's home and your family child care home, and use a partnership approach to resolve differences.

5

Building Partnerships With Families

Building Partnerships With Families

Family child care providers are in a unique position to build strong, positive relationships with families. You have only a small number of families at any particular time, you see family members every day, and your relationship can continue for many years. This gives you a tremendous advantage because children benefit when their families and providers have positive relationships built with good communication, mutual respect, trust, and a commitment to providing the best care and education for the children.

In many ways, you are *sharing the care* with families. The issues you must discuss and agree upon with families are rooted in strong beliefs and ideas about practices. The partnership you create together is essential to the way children experience child care and how much they develop and learn during the years they spend with you.

This chapter explains the fifth component of *The Creative Curriculum® for Family Child Care*. It offers practical ideas for working with families to develop partnerships based on trust and mutual respect. It has five sections:

Initial Contacts and Enrollment discusses the questions a family might ask; the information that families need from you; and the process of enrolling a child, including developing an individual care plan.

Getting to Know Families explores differences among families and the influence of culture upon child-rearing practices.

Communicating With Families shows how mutual trust is built through daily interactions with families, suggests some more formal ways of communicating, and explains how to conduct conferences with families.

Partnering for Children's Learning suggests a variety of ways families can participate in your program and describes resources that you can use to help them support children's learning at home.

Responding to Challenging Situations addresses ways to respond to families under stress and presents strategies for supporting the families of children with disabilities and the families of children who are dual-language learners. It also describes a partnership approach to resolving differences with families.

Initial Contacts and Enrollment

When a family initially contacts you about child care, they often have number of concerns. These are some of them:

Will my child...

- be safe and free from harm?
- receive a lot of attention?
- feel comfortable and happy in this family child care home?
- receive warm, loving, and responsive care?
- still love me best?
- have interesting things to see and to do?
- learn to get along with other children?
- hear lots of language?
- be ready for school?

These questions reflect the uncertainties and fears that many families experience when they seek care for their children. Everything you do to assure families that your program will respond constructively to their concerns will encourage the trust and confidence essential to partnerships.

Determining Whether Your Program Is the Right Fit

Your program may or may not be the right one for a child and family. This is a decision that both you and the family will have to make. Families will have questions for you, and you will need information from each family. Together, you will determine whether your program is the right fit for everyone.

A family may call at any time to inquire about your program, but you do not want to take time away from the children to talk on the phone. Use voicemail so you do not miss an important call if you are busy when it comes. Include a message about when you are available to talk and ask the caller to leave a phone number so that you can contact the family at another time.

When you speak with a family, take notes about important information such as the following:

- family members' names, addresses, and phone numbers
- child's name and age
- hours of care required
- when care would begin

Families will need information from you as well. Be prepared to share the following information:

- your hours of operation
- the location of your family child care home
- your experience and qualifications
- the number and ages of the children in your program
- your fees
- names and phone numbers of references

If you and the family determine that enrollment is a good idea, set up a time for the family to visit when you will have time to talk. It is important for you to get to know one another and for you to meet the child. Some topics you might cover in this initial meeting with the family include the following:

- your philosophy and your use of a comprehensive curriculum to guide your planning for children of different ages
- your daily schedule and the kinds of experiences you offer children
- your approach to guiding children's behavior
- how you handle mealtimes, toilet learning, and naps
- suggestions for easing hellos and good-byes

Use this initial contact with a family to determine whether your program is a good fit for the child. This may be the beginning of a long relationship. You need to feel comfortable with the family, and the family needs to feel comfortable with you. Pay attention to your own feelings and intuition before accepting a family.

Enrolling the Child and Family

Many providers have an enrollment form to gather basic information about each child and family. They record such information as the names of family members, the child's age, the names and ages of siblings, contact information, the child's health history, experiences with care away from home, and any special needs. Your licensing agency might provide registration forms for you to copy or adapt.

Family child care is a business. You should share clear, written policies and procedures with families so everyone knows what to expect. Provide information about the following:

- the hours during which you provide child care
- the meals and snacks you provide and what you expect families to contribute
- holidays and vacations when child care will not be provided
- your fees and payment schedule (including late fees)
- the need for written authorization if you are to give a child medicine
- your policy about what to do if their child is sick
- the names and ages of your own children who interact with the children attending your program, and the names of any other adults who may help care for the children

Information to be discussed and clarified with each family includes the following:

- the hours their child will attend and the need to notify you of any changes
- who will bring and pick up the child each day, including contact information and a list of individuals to whom you are authorized to release the child
- what you will do if a child gets sick, including which family member you will call first
- the name and phone number of the child's doctor or clinic (to consult in an emergency)
- any allergies the child may have and what should be done in the case of an allergic reaction

In addition to sharing basic information, signing an agreement about terms, and providing written policies, an informal conversation will enable you begin to learn more about each child and family. Here are some important open-ended questions to ask the family over time:

- What would you most like me to know about your child?
- How is your child comforted best?
- What does your child most enjoy doing?
- What does your child find particularly challenging or frustrating?
- What are your hopes and dreams for your child?
- What do you want your child to learn in my program?
- Are there any special traditions, celebrations, stories, or songs that are especially important to your family and your child?
- Are there any special concerns I should know about in order to care for your child well?

As you talk with each family, find out what language(s) the child hears and speaks at home. Ask which family member speaks which languages. Find out if the child knows any English. Especially if the child is a dual-language learner who is just beginning to learn English, ask the family to teach you some important words in their home language. Your use of these words will help ease the child's entry into your program.

During these initial meetings, begin to share information about your daily schedule, routines, experiences, and other aspects of your curriculum. Remember that these initial meetings can take place over time. You do not have to ask all of these questions at once. You can continue to learn more about the family as you develop your partnership.

Developing an Individual Care Plan

When a child attends your program, you will be sharing the child's care with the family. The more you know about the child's daily routines and habits at home, the better you will be able to provide care that is consistent with the way the family cares for their child. The "Family and Child Information Form" enables you to obtain detailed information about how the child is cared for at home. For example, you might learn that an infant is a fitful sleeper who likes to be rocked to sleep, is startled by loud noises, and is soothed by singing. This information will be invaluable to you as you try to comfort the child. The form is included in the appendix of this volume. It includes questions about arrival and departure times, breast-feeding or bottle-feeding, food preferences and allergies, diapering needs, and sleeping habits. There are also questions about school-age children.

Once you have completed the form with the family, use the information to develop the child's Individual Care Plan (ICP). As you can see in the example below, an ICP summarizes the information you obtained from a family about how best to care for their child. The plan is developed *with* the family when the child enters your program. A form for writing an ICP is also included in the appendix of this volume.

Developing an individual care plan with the child's family lets them know that you intend to share the care of their child. It also sends the message that you recognize families as experts on their children and that you want to benefit from their knowledge. Because young children develop and change so quickly, you will need to update the plan regularly.

After enrolling the child and developing a plan for the child's care, the next step is to ease the child into your program. Some children adjust easily and seem to fit right in. Others resist the transition and cling to their family members. Ask family members to try to arrange their schedules so they can stay for a while during the first few days to help their child feel comfortable and begin to trust you.

The Creative Curriculum® for Family Child Care

Individual Care Plan

Child: Jeremy Soloman Date of Birth: 8/29/16 Family Member(s): Karen Soloman Date: 3/16/17

Arrival	**Eating**
Mom will bring Jeremy at around 7:30 a.m.	Jeremy is nursing. Mom will bring expressed milk for him. She will usually breastfeed him at the program before she leaves for work and again when she picks him up in the afternoon. He is eating infant cereal, strained vegetables, and fruit. Mom thinks she will be adding more foods now and will coordinate with me. She also wants to start introducing a sippy cup and would like us to use one here as well.

Diapering	**Dressing**
Jeremy needs his diaper changed about 30–45 minutes after eating. He likes to be actively involved and enjoys playing with his fingers and toes during diapering.	Jeremy has a couple of extra sets of clothing in his cubby. Mom is not too worried if he spills something on his clothes. She wants him to wear his shirt when he goes outside in the summer and a hat and mittens in the winter. She'll attach his mittens to his winter jacket so they don't get lost.

Sleeping	**Departure**
Jeremy takes two naps, one from 10:00–11:30 and another from 2:30–3:30. Mom likes to rock him gently in the rocking chair and sing a lullaby to help him sleep. She puts him in his crib just before he dozes off. He is a bit slow to wake up and needs a little time before he's ready to play.	Mom will pick Jeremy up at around 5:45. She'll call if she's going to be late, but she doesn't expect that to happen very often.

Making Families Feel Welcome

Taking the time to get to know families will help you welcome them to your program. Families who feel welcome will continue bringing their children and are more likely to become involved. A nurturing and warm environment along with an introduction to the program can make families feel that they belong and that you value their role in their children's development and learning. Over time, you will build trust by consistently communicating and reaching out to all family members.

Creating a Welcoming Environment

When a family is entering your program for the first time, you want them to feel welcome and that there is a place for them and their child. Take time to assess your home environment to determine what messages are being conveyed to families. Does the environment feel welcoming? Does your home have a place for families to sit and engage with their child? Do you greet families as they enter? Questions like this help you improve your environment to make it more welcoming and family-friendly.

Assess your home environment continually to determine whether your environment conveys the messages that you intend. Remember that the environment plays a significant role in making families feel comfortable and confident having their child enrolled in your program. Always express to families that their ideas, help, and contributions are always welcome.

Ways to Make Families Feel Welcome

Make the **entranceway** to your home inviting, neat, and attractive. Include items such as plants, displays of children's work, and photographs.

Provide **places for family members** to place their purses, coats, and other personal belongings during their visit.

Provide a **mail or message box** for each family. Place daily notes, paperwork, and any materials needed to go home to families in this box. Consider color coding mailboxes according to families' home languages to help you sort the information being shared.

Place an **adult-sized rocking chair** in a quiet area in your home.

Display **up-to-date information** about program activities, meetings, and events taking place within the community.

Make an attractive display of **photographs** of the children in your program and their families. Place it at the children's eye level.

Offer **resources** featuring various topics that family members can read and check out.

Display a collection of **books and photographs** that respect the diversity of your program.

Have a daily **sign-in sheet** for families to check in their child. Provide an additional sheet for children to sign in and practice writing their names.

At the beginning of the year, invite families to come into your home for an open house. During the open house, you can briefly describe your program, share important information, answer questions, and distribute family resources. Take the time to go over the daily schedule and explain the experience areas located around your home, and the purpose of choice time. Invite family members to walk around and look at the displays and experience areas that are offered to their children. Comment on what families are doing and explain what the children learn when in those specific areas.

There are others ways you can share how and what children are learning with families. Create an attractive display or book that features photos of children engaging in meaningful activities and play throughout the day. Display photos with children's work samples and a brief description of what the children were doing, saying, and learning.

Building Trust

Establishing mutual trust helps families feel more welcome in your program. Trust between providers and families takes time, and is created by positive and respectful interactions. When a family first enters your home, they may feel uneasy and unsure of how they will be treated. Conveying positive messages will help with building trust with families. Here are some additional suggestions:

Conveying Positive Messages to Families

Positive Messages	What Providers Can Do
You are always welcome.	Greet each family member by their preferred name and share something positive that you have noticed about the child, family, or your program.
You are invited to contribute to the program.	Find ways to discover each family's special skills and interests and invite them to contribute.
You are competent.	Acknowledge any information or insights family members share about their children. Let them know how valuable these conversations are to you as a caregiver.
You should be informed of what's happening in the program.	Provide families with journals or daily notes to share the events of the day. Use jargon-free language and translate the information if necessary.

Conveying Positive Messages to Families

We both play a role in caring for your child.	Complete the "Individual Care Plan—Family Information Form" with the family of each infant in your program and update it regularly. Communicate with family members daily about their child. Use daily forms to share information about each child's day and talk about their child's day in person or via phone or email.
You understand what is happening in the program.	Explain the process of how children learn through play. Especially if your program is not what families initially expected, assure them that research confirms and supports that the children in your program learn the skills needed for their age.

All families have expectations for what their children should be learning while in your care. It is important to find out what their expectations are and provide them with the information and reasoning behind the learning experiences you offer. Responding to families in a positive and respectful manner will help them trust you enough to engage in conversations that help support the learning and care of their child.

Getting to Know Families

Just as you get to know each child and use what you learn to build a relationship, you begin building partnerships with families by getting to know the most important people in each child's life. Learning about the unique characteristics, strengths, and issues important to each family will help you find ways to build the necessary trust and respect. Begin by recognizing the many ways families differ and how a family's culture shapes the way a child responds, interacts, and thinks.

Appreciating Differences

Every family is different. The traditional family—two parents and their children—is not as common as it once was. Many children are growing up with one parent. Some are being reared by grandparents or other relatives. Other children live with two mothers or two fathers. To appreciate differences among the families you serve, start by keeping an open mind about what constitutes a "family." Always remember that, to children, their families are the most important people in the world.

Each family brings a wide range of life experiences that shape who they are and how they relate to others. The level of education that family members have achieved, socioeconomic status, health issues, and length of time in this country also account for differences among families. Some are new parents and are very young themselves. Others are caring for elderly or ill family members as well as their own children. Some are facing challenging circumstances such as unemployment; substance abuse; low literacy skills; unstable or unsafe housing; depression; or lack of access to a phone, computer, or transportation. Others are experiencing long separations from loved ones who are away for military service or in prison. You may have families who came to this country recently, who do not know the language well, and who are trying to understand how to fit in. They may expect to be here permanently or plan to return to their country of origin.

Most family members in your program will be working. Some may have demanding jobs with major responsibilities. Others may be working more than one job just to put food on the table and meet their family's basic needs. You may also have family members who are attending school or a training program. Families may be struggling to balance the demands of work or school responsibilities with home responsibilities, finding little time for themselves or their child. Your sensitivity to these different life circumstances influences how families relate to you, and it can help you build the partnerships that are essential to providing high-quality care. Sometimes just being a responsive listener and reassuring families can go a long way.

Understanding the Influence of Culture

Culture involves the customary beliefs, values, and practices people learn from their families and communities, either through example (watching what others do) or through explicit instruction (being told what is expected). Culture affects how people communicate and interact with others, and it shapes their expectations of how others will respond. Because every culture has its own set of rules and expectations, different cultures interpret what people do and say differently. Culture has a very strong influence on child-rearing practices, beliefs, and goals.

It is common to associate "culture" with ethnic and religious groups. In fact, there are many different cultural groups. Families who are in the military, for example, have a distinct culture. Because they move around so much, their friends in the military become their extended families and provide support to one another when spouses are deployed. The fact that a family member is far away and often in danger has an influence on child-rearing practices and family relationships. Another example is the culture shared by people who are deaf. Many use a common language, American Sign Language, as their primary way of communicating with one another. In the hearing community, it is sometimes considered socially unacceptable for people to stare intently at one another. In the Deaf community, watching each other closely is critical to communication.

Try to learn as much as possible about the cultures of the families in your program, keeping in mind that every family is different. Try not to generalize about any group's characteristics. Consider the many factors that influence the practices and values of an individual family, including the family's country of origin, its social class there and here, the family members' educational background, and whether extended family members live in the home. Rather than making assumptions about cultural influences, it is better to keep an open mind and consider the values behind each family's beliefs and practices. For example, in some families only men speak about matters that relate to the family. In others, it is not polite to make direct eye contact, which might make is difficult for you to assess how well you are communicating. You have to be comfortable with the idea that you may have different relationships with different families and that you might communicate a little differently with each. Nevertheless, all of your relationships can be equally positive.

Listed below are a variety of questions to help you learn more about each family. Use your judgment about what questions to ask of each family and when. Keep in mind that not all families are comfortable with responding to direct questions. You can learn a lot by observing how family members interact with their child. Be selective about the kinds of questions you ask each family.

- Who are the people in the child's immediate family?
- Who are the decision makers in the family? Are decisions made by one person or several people?
- Do all family members live in the same household?
- How often has the family moved?
- Who is the primary caregiver for the family's young children?
- How are children's names chosen?
- How does the family balance children's independence with doing things for them?
- When should toilet learning begin, and how should it be handled?
- What, when, and how are children fed?
- How is discipline handled?
- Do family members have different and distinct roles in rearing children?
- Are boys and girls treated differently?
- Is it acceptable for children to be noisy and to get dirty?
- How do adults respond to children's questions?
- How do people interact with one another? Do they look each other in the eye? Are they taught to pause and think carefully about a response before giving it? Do they touch each other as they communicate?
- How do families show respect for elders? For children?

Communicating With Families

Partnerships depend upon ongoing and open communication. Families want to know all the details about their children's experiences during the day, everything from what and how much they ate to what and with whom they played and how they reacted to events. You need important information from families as well. Because you see families every day, you have many opportunities to exchange information. Several times during the year, you might also want to have family conferences.

Making the Most of Daily Exchanges

Daily exchanges are the primary way to communicate with family members and keep everyone informed about what is happening at home and at the program. Respectful and sincere interactions show children that the most important people in their lives—their families and you—are connected and like each other.

Here are some suggestions for daily exchanges with families:

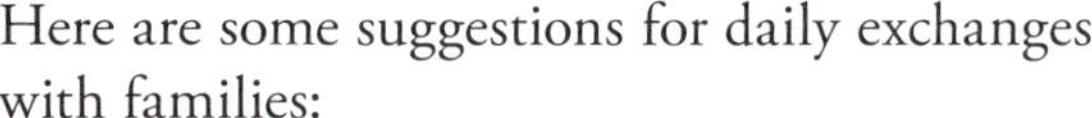

Greet each child and family personally. Use their names. Observe indications of how they are feeling and say something specific about the child, the family, or your plans for the day.

Share information about something the child has accomplished or about an event that involves the child. News can be shared in the morning, but the end of the day is often a good time to talk with families about what their child has done and to explain its significance. You might say, "Rosa worked very hard to finish a new puzzle today. Let me show it to you. She didn't give up until she figured it out. Her ability to stay with a task until it's finished is important to her learning."

Solicit their insights and advice about their child. You might prompt, "I see that Nathan doesn't want to say good-bye to you today. Can you think of any particular reason?"

Give support to families when needed. For example, you might respond, "Thank you for letting me know about his grandmother's illness. I'll give him extra attention today, and we'll talk about her."

Be a good listener. Active listening skills convey that families' concerns and ideas are taken seriously. You might tell a family member, "I understand how upset you are about the biting incident. I can assure you that I am taking steps to prevent more biting."

Make sure you understand what is being said. If there is uncertainty about a family member's statement, clarify your understanding: "Tell me whether I understand what you are saying. I think I heard you say..."

In communicating with families, try to be specific and factual. Vague or subjective comments can leave family members uncertain about what you mean or make them defensive. Notice the difference between the subjective and objective comments in the two examples below. Think about how the family member might feel in each case.

Subjective Comments	Family Member's Thoughts
When Jeremy's mother comes to get him at the end of the day, you tell her, "Jeremy was very crabby today! I had the hardest time trying to comfort him."	"What did he do? How did you try to comfort him? Why didn't you call me? He's not crabby at home. I'm not sure you know how to take care of my baby. Maybe something is wrong with him or with me as a parent."

Objective Comments	Family Member's Thoughts
At nap time, you call Jeremy's mother to discuss his fussiness. You tell her, "Jeremy cried when he drank his bottle this morning. I tried holding him the way you showed me, but it didn't help. Do you have any suggestions for me?" When Jeremy's mother arrives at the end of the day, you tell her, "Jeremy was still a bit fussy when he ate this afternoon. He was pulling on his ear, so I wonder if he has an infection. Maybe he is still just adjusting to me, though. What do you think?"	"I wonder what's wrong. I appreciate being asked for my advice and ideas. I know his family child care provider is doing all she can to take care of him." "Perhaps he is not used to being in family child care yet, but maybe he is getting sick. If this continues, I'll take him to the clinic for a checkup. I feel good about leaving Jeremy with this provider. I know she will call me if she has any concerns."

Subjective Comments	Family Member's Thoughts
When Nathan's father comes to pick him up at the end of the day, you tell him, "Nathan was such a good boy today. He just makes my day."	"I wonder what he did. Nathan is a real challenge at home. He won't clean up his room or cooperate when we ask him to do things. If he is good here but challenging at home, are we doing something wrong?"

Objective Comments	Family Member's Thoughts
When Nathan's father comes to pick him up, you tell him, "Today, Nathan really helped me. While I was putting lunch on the table, Nathan sat with Tamika and Jorge and showed them the pictures in his favorite book. Then he went with them to wash hands."	"My son is able to cooperate and relate well to other children. I guess the bedtime stories we read to him every night have made a difference, even if I have to read the same stories over and over! I feel good about the way he is developing and learning."

The examples above show how being specific and factual in your daily communications with families gives them helpful information. Families know that you are really taking an interest in their children and that you genuinely care about their well-being. In addition to informal oral exchanges, there are brief written forms of communication. Here are a few ideas:

Daily communication form—Create a form with space for families to record information about their child when they arrive at the program each day. Request information that is basic to the child's daily care and explain that it helps you meet each child's current needs more effectively. You may need to encourage family members to take the time to complete this form when they bring their child. Request any information that you find helpful, such as when the child last ate, when her diaper was last changed, her general mood that day, how well she slept last night, when she will be picked up, and who will be picking her up.

A family resource area—If you have space in a corner or on a wall to display family resources or announcements, that is an efficient way to share information with families.

Email—Sending e-mail is a quick way to stay in touch and to share specific information. Find out from families if they would like to communicate in this way.

A Web site—Many center-based programs have a Web site where program news is posted as well as articles of interest and photos of program events. Why not create a Web site for your program? You may have a family member who can help you set one up and even assist in keeping it up-to-date. An older school-age child might be learning to do this in school.

Journals—A simple journal for each family is a place for each of you to write entries and share information. The journal can travel with the child and family from their home to yours and back.

Holding Conferences With Families

A formal conference with each family should be held at least twice a year and more often if needed. Conferences are a time to sit together, uninterrupted, and talk as partners about caring for their child. They are opportunities to share information, observations, and questions. You can solve problems together when necessary and celebrate new milestones and accomplishments. If a child has a diagnosed disability, you can express your interest in participating in the meetings of the team of people who develop goals for the Individualized Family Service Plan (for a child under age 3) or the Individualized Education Program (for children age 3 and older). Preparation and the many positive interactions you have already had with the family help ensure a successful conference.

Here are steps to take as you prepare for a family conference:

- Arrange a time that is convenient for you and the family, and find out whom they would like to include in the conference.
- Let the family know what to expect. When you set up the conference, explain that conferences are a time to focus entirely on their child.
- Find out what the family is interested in learning about and whether there are any special issues they want to discuss.
- Review your observation notes and samples of the child's work that you want to share. This will help the family understand more about their child's experiences and accomplishments at the program.
- Be prepared to share what the child is learning. The information in Chapter 3, "What Children Are Learning," will help you explain the significance of what each child is able to do.
- If language differences might be a barrier, arrange for someone to interpret. Many families know someone who can serve as an interpreter. If a family does not, try to make other arrangements. (It is not usually a good idea to ask a child to interpret.)

Start the conference by sharing your observation of something new, interesting, or delightful that their child has done or said. Invite family members to share what they have noticed about their child's development and learning and what their child talks about.

In the appendix, you will find a "Family Conference Form" to use as a record of the conference. Under the appropriate heading on the form, highlight the child's new discoveries and skills. Offer specific examples from your observation notes.

Throughout your discussion, encourage families to share their observations, questions, challenges, and joys. Explain that this is time to exchange information and that combining what each of you knows will give all of you the clearest possible understanding of their child. In addition to recording your own ideas, ask families for their ideas when you discuss the other sections of the form: "Favorite Activities and Special Interests" and "Family Comments and Special Circumstances." Family conferences are also good times to update the "Individual Care Plan" form you complete for each child.

Talk about each other's expectations for the child's development and learning. Together, complete the "Next Steps at Family Child Care and at Home" section of the "Family Conference Form." This will become your blueprint for working with the child. Keep it where you will have ready access to it, so you can remind yourself of areas you want to focus on during the next few months. At the next conference, the form can serve as a starting point for your discussion.

Sharing Concerns With Families

It is very possible that you will have children in your program who have special needs. Many of these children and families will already be receiving early intervention or special education services for a developmental delay or another diagnosed condition. Other children may have special needs that have not yet been identified. Sometimes a family child care provider is the first to detect that a child is not developing typically and that there may be a problem. You may be able to help the family find specialists to determine whether there is a particular problem and to obtain the necessary services.

These conversations are challenging for families because they are often getting new and concerning information about their child or are having their own concerns validated. You can best support a family by being well-prepared with documentation of your observations, research, and community resources.

Here are some steps to help you prepare for sharing concerns with families:

- Schedule a conference at a time that is convenient for you and the family.
- Gather pieces of documentation that relate to your concern.
- Research community resources that are available to support the family, such as early intervention services, support groups, and family resource centers. Print information or bring brochures to offer the family.
- Be ready to offer some strategies that you would like to implement to better support the child and family.

When sharing information with families, highlight things that the child is able to do. For example, if you have a concern about a 3-year-old who is not yet using words to communicate you could say, "Have you noticed how Nathan points and grunts to let you know what he would like? I am glad that he is able to make choices and tell me what he needs, but I would like to help Nathan start using words or signs in place of the pointing."

Encourage families to share their own observations about their child's development using questions such as:

- How does your child communicate with you at home?
- How does your child move and play compared to other children his age that you see at the park?
- What is an activity that keeps your child's attention?
- Have you noticed how your child favors looking to the right?
- When you place your child in a sitting position, what does she do?

Partnering for Children's Learning

Families have been teaching their children since birth, so they are already your partners in supporting their children's learning. By inviting them to participate in your program and by sharing resources, you can gain valuable support and strengthen their confidence in their parenting skills.

Inviting Families to Participate

When you invite families to visit and to participate in the program as much as possible, you send a very positive message that you view the relationship as a real partnership. An open-door policy says that you are confident about your program and the way you care for their children. You want families to know that they are always welcome and that their involvement—no matter how extensive or limited—enhances the program and their children's experience.

Almost every family has something to offer your program and can make a meaningful contribution. The more possibilities they are offered, the more likely you are to involve every family. Here are some possible ways by which families can participate:

- gathering materials, such as old magazines, fabric scraps, collections (for example, bottle caps, buttons, keys, or shells), dress-up clothes, and toys
- helping with special projects, such as building a sandbox, making doll clothes, or constructing an easel
- participating in celebrations, such as birthday or holiday parties or celebrating children's learning at the end of a study
- accompanying you and the children on a field trip
- joining you and the children for a meal
- helping with an activity such as cooking, reading to children, or putting together a photo album
- sharing a special skill with the children

Keep in mind that parents are not the only family members who might want to participate in your program. Grandparents, for example, might have more free time to share than parents and may have a great deal of patience with young children. They might enjoy an opportunity to feed an infant, read to a child, play games and sing with the children, help a child settle for a nap, teach preschool and school-age children a skill such as knitting, or help with a woodworking project. Make a special effort to include a father or another significant male who is a steady influence in the child's life: the mother's partner or husband, an uncle, an older sibling, a grandfather, another relative, or a family friend. Find out which adults are important in a child's life. Learn about their interests, jobs, hobbies, and what they would like to share with the children. They may be able to make a positive contribution that will benefit everyone.

Supporting Children's Learning at Home

Children are learning all the time, when they are with you and when they are with their families. As a professional family child care provider who has taken the time to learn and use a comprehensive curriculum to guide your program planning, you have knowledge and experience in supporting children's positive development and learning. Sharing aspects of your curriculum and other resources with families can be a very effective way to ensure that children are getting the best preparation for success in school and in life. *The Creative Curriculum® for Family Child Care* includes two resources for sharing ideas. They are 1) the letters to families about routines and experiences and 2) the set of selected *LearningGames®*.

Letters to families—You will find letters to families in *Volume 2: Routines and Experiences.* Each sample letter explains why a particular routine or experience is an important part of your program, how you support children's learning and development in your family child care program, and how you hope to work together with families. You may adapt the letters or use them as they are. Sharing them periodically during the year or at a family conference will help families understand what you are doing every day to help children learn through routines and meaningful play experiences.

LearningGames®—The 200 *LearningGames®* activities that are part of this curriculum are a resource to use and share with individual families at appropriate times. The ideas in most of these games will already be familiar to you, and, if you use them in your family child care home, families will receive the message that these are important interactions that professionals and *families* can have with children. Each activity helps teach families how everyday interactions and simple games support their children's positive relationships and important learning. Several games are listed at the end of each of the five chapters on routines and the 11 chapters on experiences in *Volume 2*. Games are included for each age-group from birth to age 5, along with suggestions for sharing them with families. These games involve interactions that you have with the children in your care, so families will see you demonstrating them. Each game also lists a children's book that is related to the game.

You may find that families react differently to the *LearningGames®*. Some may love the idea of posting a game on their refrigerator for a week or two and learning something new to do with their child. Others may be less interested, although these families may change their minds when they see you using these simple, research-validated games in your program; see how interested their children are in playing the games; and notice other families' enthusiasm for the games. Be sensitive to each family's needs and interests. Base your selection of *LearningGames®* for each family on your knowledge of their child's strengths, needs, and interests. Each *Intentional Teaching Card™* recommends *LearningGames®* that are related to the same objective as the activity on the card. After completing the *Intentional Teaching Card™*, share the *LearningGames®* with the families to continue the children's learning at home.

Responding to Challenging Situations

Despite all of the positive steps you take to build a partnership with each family, you will encounter challenging situations. Some families are struggling with meeting basic needs, and the ongoing stress makes it difficult for them to be available to their children. You may have children who are learning more than one language and children with disabilities. These families need your understanding and support. Even in the best relationships, misunderstandings and conflicts emerge. Challenging situations must be handled carefully and positively in order to maintain a partnership with every family.

Supporting Families Who Are Under Stress

Families experience different kinds of stress, and they may have difficulty coping. Ongoing and unrelenting stress can come from many sources:

- living in a violent community
- limited financial resources
- seeking employment or job training without knowing whether they will be able to continue bringing their child to the program
- long commutes to a job
- limited transportation
- a job that does not allow flexibility in work hours to accommodate family needs
- a family member with a physical disability, physical or mental illness, cognitive delays, or low literacy skills
- domestic and/or substance abuse
- adapting to a new culture and/or language
- substandard, overcrowded housing or living in a shelter
- barriers to health care

Families that are under stress from these or other life situations do not always have the emotional energy or physical resources to nurture their children. Sometimes they have trouble meeting their children's most basic needs. They may not be able to solve problems, communicate positively with their children, or give them the attention and affirmation they need. Their discipline may be inconsistent, overly punitive, or nonexistent. For many children in these circumstances, life is unpredictable and dangerous. They may seem angry, withdrawn, or fearful when they come to your program.

The stress a family is experiencing can affect the way they relate to you. Because you see families every day and get to know them well, you will probably be able to recognize when a family is under stress. In many cases, because they trust you, they may tell you about problems they are having. Try to be as supportive as you can. Avoid adding to the stress by being overly critical, such as when a parent forgets to bring boots for her child despite several reminders. Also be mindful of a family member's stress when you need to discuss a problem you are having with a child. Sometimes it is wise to wait for a better time. Seek ways to reassure families about the positive things they are doing.

Most communities have social and legal service agencies that offer resources and guidance to families in need. Find out what exists in your area. Perhaps you can put together some information for families to share as needed. This might include:

- an up-to-date list of community agencies and hotlines for referrals
- brochures and resources for families to borrow
- a list of support groups that deal with family issues

Raising a child is one of the most important jobs in the world, yet there is very little training for this critical role. Family members who were fortunate enough to have caring, nurturing experiences when they were children have a solid foundation for becoming supportive family members themselves. Those who had less constructive experiences still want the best for their children and are doing what they think is right. Although some families do things that bother you, hold to the belief that most are doing the best they can. Learn as much as you can about the strengths and needs of each family so that you have realistic expectations and can individualize your approach to your partnership. Your way of working with one family will not necessarily be the same as with another.

Supporting the Families of Children With Disabilities

Approximately 1 in 6 children is reported to have a developmental disability. This means that there is a good chance that some of the children in your care have a diagnosed condition such as attention deficit hyperactivity disorder (ADHD), an intellectual disability, cerebral palsy, autism, seizures, speech concerns such as stuttering or stammering, moderate to profound hearing loss, blindness, learning disorders, and/or other developmental delays (Boyle et al., 2011).

Every child is unique, and even children who have the same diagnosis will differ in their needs and preferences. Some children may begin care with an Individualized Family Service Plan (IFSP) or Individualized Education Plan (IEP) already in place, while others may be just starting their journey through the early intervention or special education process. Regardless of the situation, families will need additional support to address their child's unique situation.

While the needs and level of support will vary with each child and family, here are some ways you can support families and children with disabilities:

Ask families to share information about their child's diagnosis. Families are experts on their children and can provide a wealth of information about their child's unique needs and interests. Schedule a conference with the family to learn more about the child's diagnosis and how you can best support him while he is in your care. Come to the meeting prepared with questions about any special accommodations that may be needed to help the child function in the program alongside her peers.

Familiarize yourself with your community's early intervention and special education processes. Contact your local early intervention or school special education services and request information about the processes families go through to receive services. Often times, there are information sessions that you can attend to ask questions and learn about how each system works. Knowing this information will help you be a valuable resource to families who are using these services and help you better understand how to support the family.

Request a copy of the child's IFSP or IEP. IFSPs and IEPs are full of valuable information that will help you better understand the child's individual needs. When you are reviewing these documents, pay special attention to what the family's goals are for their child. A child may have a speech delay, but the family's main concern may be about how the speech delay is impacting their child's ability to socialize and make friends. Knowing the families' goals will help you choose and plan for activities that best support the child in those areas.

IFSPs and IEPs also list the services a child is receiving, such as occupational therapy, speech therapy, or physical therapy, along with their service providers. These providers make up the team that is supporting the child. Let the family know that you would like to be part of this team and work with the other providers to provide continuity of care for their child.

Work with the family to schedule some of the child's therapy appointments in your home. Many times, children who are receiving private therapy or therapy through an IFSP see the practitioner in the child's natural environment, which is usually in their home. However, it may be possible for some therapy appointments to take place while the child is in your family child care home. Seeing the child in the family child care environment can benefit the therapist because he is able to learn how a child interacts with other adults and children and see how that child's diagnosis impacts her day in child care.

While these appointments are taking place, it is important to continue the typical daily routine for all of the children in your care. It may be helpful to have an assistant caregiver during these appointments so you can observe any strategies the therapist uses to support the child and ask questions as needed.

Learn what strategies other providers are doing to support the child's development. Ask families about what strategies other providers are using to support their child and find ways to implement them in your family child care program. For example, if you are working with a child who is working on her fine-motor skills, knowing that she loves peeling stickers off paper and making collages with her occupational therapist helps inform your planning and allows you to incorporate similar activities into your daily experiences.

Learn about special tools or technology the child uses. Many times, children with disabilities use special equipment, such as orthotics on their feet or legs, light boxes, communication boards, or special programs on tablets. Work with families to familiarize yourself with the devices so that you can confidently use them when the child is in your care.

Incorporate activities to support the child's development into your daily experiences with all children. Children thrive when they are able to participate in the same activities and experiences as their peers. When planning for children with disabilities, think of ways to provide activities that address their unique needs that all children can participate in. For example, while creating sticker collages will help a child who has concerns with her fine-motor skills strengthen her fingers, it can also be an enjoyable activity for all children.

Intentional Teaching Cards™ are specifically written so that they can be individualized and used with all children during large-group, small-group, and one-on-one experiences. Refer to the "Including All Children" section on the right-hand side of the card for ways to support all children during these activities.

Supporting the Families of Children Who Are Dual-Language Learners

Dual-language learners comprise nearly 25 percent of the school-age population in the United States today. As explained in Chapter 1, "Knowing How Children Develop and Learn," a dual-language learner is a child who is learning more than one language. The child and family both need your understanding and support.

Families of dual-language learners have a variety of expectations. Some want their children to learn English as quickly as possible. Others have concerns about the potential loss of children's ability to communicate in their home language. Families may think that they have to choose between their home languages and English. Fortunately, this is not the case. Maintaining and developing children's home languages actually helps them acquire English. Children who have larger vocabularies and language skills in their home languages are able to learn English more quickly because language skills in their home languages are the foundation for learning another language.

As a family child care provider, you play an important role in supporting families to encourage their children's optimal language development. Reassure families that children can learn English without losing their home languages. Here are some ways you can support the families of children who are dual-language learners:

Encourage families to continue to speak their home languages with their children. Help families understand how important it is to talk, sing, and play with their children in their home languages. Suggest resources, such as the local library where they can check out books in their home languages to read to their child. If family members do not have strong reading skills, encourage them to "talk" the books by discussing the pictures with their child and making up their own stories. Many cultures have strong oral storytelling traditions. Encourage families to share stories with their children about their countries of origin and their own childhoods.

Children benefit by maintaining their home languages while learning English. One of the most important benefits is the ability to communicate with family members who do not speak English. Language is a vital part of culture and family history. If children lose the ability to communicate in their home language, they may also lose the ability to communicate with family members and other members of their cultural group. Giving children the gift of being bilingual is one that will benefit them throughout their lives.

Bring the families' languages into your home. Play songs in children's home languages. Invite families to record songs, read books, and tell stories on audio recordings that can be played during the day in your program. Children will not only hear their home languages, but they will also hear the familiar voices of their family members. That may comfort them and ease their transition into the group.

Share information about dual-language learning. Let families know that most children who are learning English after already having a foundation in their home languages go through a nonverbal stage in which they do not speak in either language. During this period, the children still communicate with gestures, vocalizations, and body language. This is typical and no cause for concern. Continuing to offer opportunities to hear, use, and play with both languages is the best way to support children during this stage.

Communicate with families in their preferred languages when possible. When communicating with families who speak a home language other than English, find out their preferred language for communicating with you. Provide written communications in the family's preferred language to help them understand program news and events and catch details they may have missed in face-to-face exchanges.

If you and a family do not share a common language, arrange for the services of an interpreter for family meetings and conferences. It is best to avoid asking a child or an older sibling to interpret. Some families do not consider that to be a child's responsibility. Furthermore, you and the family might use language that the child is not able to interpret accurately. You might also want to discuss concerns about which you do not want the child to become anxious. A bilingual parent from another family might be willing to interpret, but be sure to follow confidentiality guidelines. Another great source for interpreters could be local community centers, religious communities, and social service agencies that work with families from diverse language backgrounds.

Help families understand what you are saying when you speak with them in English. When you do speak English with families, a few simple strategies can help you communicate your message. Use pictures, objects, gestures, and other body language to provide context and visual cues. Speak slowly and clearly. Be careful to avoid idiomatic phrases with meanings that may be hard for families to understand, such as "He slept like a log" or "You're pulling my leg." Pause and give families plenty of time to respond. Many adults who are learning a new language need time to interpret information they hear in the new language into the home language, formulate a response, and then interpret it from the home language back into the new language. This process requires patience.

Support families as their child transitions to school. Enrolling a child in school can be stressful, especially for families who do not understand and speak much English. Families may need assistance with filling out forms, understanding school requirements, and communicating with school personnel. Help connect families with resources that can support them in this transition. Let families know that all children, regardless of language background or immigration status, are entitled to attend public school and receive some form of language support services.

Resolving Differences: A Partnership Approach

If you work with families who share your values and beliefs and have similar life experiences and personal characteristics, you are more likely to interpret what they say and do in similar ways. If you work with families who are very different from you—and if you know little about their beliefs and practices—miscommunication and misunderstandings can easily take place. Understanding and respecting practices that are different from your own help you to build positive relationships with all families.

When the adults in their lives share a consistent approach, children are more likely to feel safe and secure in your program. This does not mean that you have to agree about everything. There will probably be times when you and a family will have different points of view about caring for their child. Always ask yourself this question: How can we work out our differences in a positive way?

Here are examples of how misunderstandings can occur because your views about a situation differ from that of a family member. Following each example, a resolution that respects the partnership is suggested.

Situation	Your View	The Family's View
After careful observations over time, you are concerned that a toddler's language is delayed. You suggest an evaluation by a speech specialist. The family members fail to make an appointment with a specialist.	If a problem exists, it should be identified as early as possible. Families should want to get all the help they can get for their child.	My child is fine. There's nothing wrong.

Partnership View: There may be a number of reasons why families might resist having their child evaluated by a specialist for a possible problem. It is not unusual for families to be reluctant to accept that there is a problem the first time you talk about it. (See the section of this chapter on "Sharing Concerns with Families.") If you suspect that this is the reason for their not following your advice, be patient for a while. Suggest that you all observe more carefully for a few weeks and keep in touch about what you learn. Try to find out about community resources the family could consult and provide that information to them.

Situation	Your View	The Family's View
A family requests that you continue their practice of toileting their 12-month-old child. They explain how they are aware of when their child is about to urinate or defecate, and they simply take him to the toilet in time.	"Catching" a child in time to bring him to the potty is not toilet learning. Children let us know when they have the muscle control and awareness to use the toilet. That is the most appropriate time to begin the process of toilet learning.	It is important for us to train our children to use the toilet at this age. We did it with our other children, and it works just fine. It saves the cost of disposable diapers and is better for the environment.

Partnership View: Toilet learning is a topic that you and families are likely to have strong feelings about and perhaps different approaches. It is helpful to discuss the family's approach to toilet learning when they are first considering enrolling their child in your program. You should also explain the steps that you typically use when helping children learn to use the toilet. This may prevent some problems. When toileting practices differ, it is important to listen to the family's perspective and find some aspect of their approach to affirm. You can explain, "As you can imagine, it's more challenging with a group of children. I will do my best to watch for the signs you mentioned and take him to the potty." This approach conveys your appreciation of the family's preference without making a commitment that you cannot fulfill.

Situation	Your View	The Family's View
When you first meet a toddler's grandfather, he tells you that he does not understand why you do not spank his grandson for hitting other children.	You teach children to be gentle with others by modeling gentleness and guiding their behavior in positive ways. You stop children when they hit others and help them learn to verbalize their thoughts and feelings instead of hitting.	The grandfather believes in using a strong-handed approach to rearing children. His philosophy is "Spare the rod, spoil the child." It worked for him with his children. He's concerned about his grandson's "bad" behavior.

Partnership View: When a family member whom you do not know well comes to discuss a concern, it is helpful to begin by first taking a few minutes to get to know the person better before attempting to address the issue. Explain that you understand the family's concerns. You might tell this grandfather, "It sounds as though it's very important to you that your grandson learn how to get along with others. Is that right?" Then take the time to discuss your program's approach to promoting positive behavior. Share the social–emotional objectives of the curriculum and talk about how you help children develop self-regulation skills and other positive behaviors.

Summary

When you develop partnerships with children's families, everyone benefits. Children feel more secure and comfortable when their families and child care provider share their knowledge respectfully and interact positively. They are more likely to experience consistency in the care they receive when families are invited to share what they want for and know about their children. Families feel more secure about leaving their children in the care of someone who takes the time to build relationships with them. They gain confidence in their parenting skills when you invite families to participate in the program and when you share resources that support their children's learning at home. You acquire valuable support and information from families that enable you to get to know each child better and provide more individualized care. Your partnerships enable children to relate positively with others, control their behavior, and have the skills and motivation to learn.

Appendix

Child Planning Form

Week of: ______________________

<table>
<tr><td>Child:
Current information:

Plans:</td><td>Child:
Current information:

Plans:</td></tr>
<tr><td>Child:
Current information:

Plans:</td><td>Child:
Current information:

Plans:</td></tr>
</table>

Group Planning Form

Week of: ______________________

Changes to the Environment:

Changes to Routines and Schedule:

Family Involvement:

Group Planning Form, continued

Week of: ____________________

Events and Play Experiences

	Monday	Tuesday	Wednesday	Thursday	Friday
Morning meeting					
Choice time					
Outdoor time					
Read-aloud time					
Special activities					

Ideas for next week:

Family Conference Form

Child's Name: ______________________________ Date : ______________

Social–Emotional Development	Physical Development
Language Development and Literacy	**Cognitive Development**

Mathematics, Science, Social Studies, and the Arts

Favorite Activities and Special Interests

Family Comments and Special Circumstances

Next Steps at Family Child Care and at Home

Provider's Signature: ______________________________ Date : ______________

Family Signature(s): ______________________________ Date : ______________

Family & Child Information Form

Child: ______________________ Date of Birth: ________ Family Member(s): _________________ Date : ________

About Your Family

Tell me about your family.

What language(s) do you speak at home?

What are some activities your family enjoys doing together?

Is this your child's first early childhood program experience?

What is the best way for our program to exchange information with you about your child?

Favorite Activities and Special Interests

What are some of your child's favorite activities?

With whom does your child play? How do they play together? What do they play together?

What is your child most interested in right now? How can you tell?

Does your child have favorite toys? How does your child play with them?

What books does your child like to read? Does your child read alone or with you?

What songs does your child know and like to sing?

Family & Child Information Form, continued

School

If your child is in school, please answer the following questions:

In what grade is your child?

What is the name of your child's teacher?

What are your child's favorite subjects?

Will your child have homework? If so, do you want your child to do homework at my family child care home or at your home?

If homework should be done at family child care, how should I help?

Does your child prefer to do homework right away, or to relax or do other activities first?

Arrival/Departure

What time will you usually arrive?

What will help you and your child say good-bye to each other in the morning?

What time will you usually come to pick up your child?

What will help you and your child say hello to each other at the end of the day?

Family & Child Information Form, continued

Mealtime

Describe your child's mealtimes and how your child eats or is fed.

What are some of your child's favorite foods? What foods does your child dislike?

Is your child sensitive or allergic to any foods? If so, what are they?

Are there any foods that you don't want your child to eat?

Nap Time/Resting

Does your child nap during the day? If so, what helps your child fall asleep?

How long does your child usually sleep?

When does your child usually sleep?

If your child does not nap during the day, does your child have a rest time?
What activities does your child usually do during this rest time?

Family & Child Information Form, continued

Other Routines

Does your child use the toilet? If so, are there any special instructions for toileting?
How does your child let you know that he or she needs to use the toilet?

If not, how often do you change your child's diaper? When does your child usually need a diaper change?

Is there anything special that we should know about dressing and undressing your child?

How much help does your child need with toothbrushing?

Additional Information

What else would you like us to know about your child and family?

Individual Care Plan

Child: ______________________ Date of Birth: ________ Family Member(s): _________________ Date : ________

Arrival	**Eating**

Diapering	**Dressing**

Sleeping	**Departure**

References

August, D., & Shananhan, T. (2006). *Developing literacy in second-language learners: Report of the National Literacy Panel on language-minority children and youth.* Mahwah, NJ: Lawrence Erlbaum Associates.

August, D., & Shanahan, T. (2010). Response to a review and update on *Developing literacy in second-language learners: Report of the National Literacy Panel on Language Minority Children and Youth. Journal of Literacy Research, 42*(3), 341–348.

Bailey, B. A. (2003). *There's got to be a better way: Discipline that works!* (Rev. ed.). Oviedo, FL: Loving Guidance.

Bialystok, E. (1997). Effects of bilingualism and biliteracy on children's emerging concepts of print. *Developmental Psychology, 33*(3), 429–440.

Boyle, C. A., Boulet, S., Schieve, L. A., Cohen, R. A., Blumberg, S. J., Yeargin-Allsopp, M., …Kogan, M. D. (2011). Trends in the Prevalence of Developmental Disabilities in US Children, 1997-2008. *Pediatrics,127*(6), 1034-1042. doi:10.1542/peds.2010-2989d

Bronson, M. B. (2000). *Self-regulation in early childhood.* New York, NY: Guilford Press.

Cable News Network. (2008, August 13). *Minorities expected to be majority in 2050.* Retrieved from http://www.cnn.com/2008/US/08/13/census.minorities/index.html

Campbell, F., Conti, G., Heckman, J. J., Moon, S. H., Pinto, R., Pungello, E., Pan, Y. (2014). Early childhood investments substantially boost adult health. *Science, 343*(6178), 1478-1485.

Campbell, F. A., Ramey, C. T., Pungello, E., Sparling, J., & Miller-Johnson, S. (2002). Early childhood education: Young adult outcomes from the Abecedarian Project. *Applied Developmental Science, 6*(1), 42–57.

Chang, F., Crawford, G., Early, D., Bryant, C., Howes, M., Burchinal, O., Barbarin, R., … Pianta, R. (2007). Spanish speaking children's social and language development in pre-kindergarten classrooms. *Journal of Early Education and Development*, 18(2), 243–69.

Chess, S., & Thomas, A. (1996). *Temperament: Theory and practice.* New York, NY: Bruner/Mazel.

Division for Early Childhood. (2007). *Promoting positive outcomes for children with disabilities: Recommendations for curriculum, assessment, and program evaluation.* Missoula, MT: Author.

Durgunoglu, A.Y., & Öney, B. (2000). Literacy development in two languages: Cognitive and sociocultural dimensions of cross-language transfer. In U.S. Department of Education, Office of Bilingual Education and Minority Language Affairs (Eds.), A research symposium on high standards in reading for students from diverse language groups: Research, practice & policy (pp. 78-99). Washington, DC: U.S. Department of Education

Geist, E. (2003). Infants and toddlers exploring mathematics. *Young Children, 58*(1), 10-13.

Genesee, F. (n.d.). Bilingual acquisition. *Earlychildhood NEWS*. Retrieved from http://www.earlychildhoodnews.com/earlychildhood/article_view.aspx?ArticleId=38

Hanson, K. (1992). *Teaching mathematics effectively and equitably to females*. New York, NY: ERIC Clearinghouse on Urban Education Institute for Urban and Minority Education. (ERIC Document Reproduction Service No. ED348465)

Hart, B., & Risley, T. R. (1995). *Meaningful differences in the everyday experience of young American children*. Baltimore, MD: Brookes Publishing.

Helm, J. H., & Katz, L. (2001). *Young investigators: The project approach in the early years*. New York, NY: Teachers College Press.

Howes, C., Burchinal, M., Pianta, R., Bryant, D., Early, D., Clifford, R., & Barbarin, O. (2008). Ready to learn? Children's pre-academic achievements in pre-kindergarten programs. *Early Childhood Research Quarterly, 23*(3), 27-50.

Jablon, J. R., Dombro, A. L., & Dichtelmiller, M. L. (2007). *The power of observation: Birth to age 8* (2nd ed.). Washington, DC: Teaching Strategies, Inc. and National Association for the Education of Young Children.

Koda, K. & Zehler, A. (Eds.). (2008). *Learning to read across languages: Cross-lingüistic relationships in first- and second-language literacy development*. New York, NY: Routledge.

Mather, M. (2009). *Reports on America: Children in immigrant families chart new path*. Washington, DC: Population Reference Bureau

National Association for Family Child Care. (2013). Quality standards for NAFCC accreditation (4th ed.). *National Association for Family Child Care*. Retrieved from https://www.nafcc.org/file/35a7fee9-1ccf-4557-89d4-973daf84a052

National Council of Teachers of Mathematics. (2000). *Principles and standards for school mathematics*. Reston, VA: Author.

National Institute of Child Health and Human Development. (2007). *Report of the National Reading Panel: Teaching children to read: An evidence-based assessment of the scientific research literature on reading and its implications for reading instruction*. Washington, DC: Author.

National Research Council, & Institute of Medicine. (2000). *From neurons to neighborhoods: The science of early childhood development*. (J. P. Shonkoff & D. A. Phillips, Eds.). Washington, DC: National Academy Press.

National Survey of Early Care & Education Team. (2015). *Fact sheet: Who is providing home-based early care and education*? Washington, DC: U.S. Department of Health and Human Services, Office of Planning, Research, and Evaluation. Retrieved from https://www.acf.hhs.gov/opre/research/project/national-survey-of-early-care-and-education-nsece-2010-2014

Palermo, F., Hanish, L. D., Martin, C. L., Fabes, R. A., & Reiser, M. (2007). Preschoolers' academic readiness: What role does the teacher-child relationship play? *Early Childhood Research Quarterly, 22*(4), 407-422.

Peisner-Feinberg, E. S., Burchinal, M. R., Clifford, R. M., Culkin, M. L., Howes, C., Kagan, S. L...Zelazo, J. (1999). *The children of the cost, quality, and outcomes study go to school: Technical report.* Chapel Hill: University of North Carolina at Chapel Hill, Frank Porter Graham Child Development Center.

Riley, D., San Juan, R. R., Klinkner, J., & Ramminger, A. (2008). *Social and emotional development: Connecting science and practice in early childhood settings.* St. Paul, MN: Redleaf Press.

Rothbart, M. K., Ahadi, S. A., & Evans, D. E. (2000). Temperament and personality: Origins and outcome. *Journal of Personality and Social Psychology, 78*(1), 122-135.

Schickedanz, J. (1999). *Much more than the ABCs: The early stages of reading and writing.* Washington, DC: National Association for the Education of Young Children.

Slaby, R. G., Roedell, W. C., Arezzo, D., & Hendrix, K. (1995). *Early violence prevention: Tools for teachers of young children.* Washington, DC: National Association for the Education of Young Children.

Snow, C.E. (1997, November 1). The myths around being bilingual. *NABE News, 29*, 36.

Snow, C. E., Burns, M. S., & Griffin, P. (Eds.). (1998). *Preventing reading difficulties in young children.* Washington, DC: National Academy Press.

Sparling, J., Lewis, I., Ramey, C. T., Wasik, B. H., Bryant, D. M., & LaVange, L. M. (1991). Partners: A curriculum to help premature, low-birth-weight infants get off to a good start. *Topics in Early Childhood Special Education, 11*(1), 36–55.

Tabors, P. O. (2008). *One child, two languages: A guide for early childhood educators of children learning English as a second language* (2nd ed.). Baltimore, MD: Paul H. Brookes.

Tansey, S. (2009). Playing fair—gender equity in child care. *Putting Children First, 31*, 14-16.

U.S. Department of Education, Office of Special Education and Rehabilitative Services, Office of Special Education Programs. (2009). *28th annual report to Congress on the implementation of the Individuals with Disabilities Education Act, 2006, vol. 1.* Retrieved from http://www.ed.gov/about/reports/annual/osep/2006/parts-b-c/index.html

Weitzman, E., & Greenberg, J. (2002). *Learning language and loving it* (2nd ed.). Toronto: The Hanen Centre.

Yoshikawa, H., Weiland, C., Brooks-Gunn, J., et al. (2013). *Investing in our future: The evidence base on preschool education.* Society for Research in Child Development and Foundation for Child Development.